SUPERMAN IN MYTH AND FOLKLORE

SUPE

RMAN

IN MYTH AND FOLKLORE

DANIEL PERETTI

UNIVERSITY PRESS OF MISSISSIPPI • JACKSON

www.upress.state.ms.us

Designed by Peter D. Halverson

The University Press of Mississippi is a member of the
Association of American University Presses.

First printing 2017

∞

Library of Congress Cataloging-in-Publication Data

Names: Peretti, Daniel, author.
Title: Superman in myth and folklore / Daniel Peretti.
Description: Jackson : University Press of Mississippi, 2017. | Includes biblio-
graphical references and index. |
Identifiers: LCCN 2017018496 (print) | LCCN 2017019568 (ebook) | ISBN
9781496814593 (epub single) | ISBN 9781496814609 (epub institutional) |
ISBN 9781496814616 (pdf single) | ISBN 9781496814623 (pdf institutional) |
ISBN 9781496814586 (hardback)
Subjects: LCSH: Superman (Fictitious character) | Superheroes in literature.
| Superheroes in art. | Heroes in mass media. | BISAC: SOCIAL SCIENCE /
Folklore & Mythology. | SOCIAL SCIENCE / Popular Culture. | LITERARY
CRITICISM / Comics & Graphic Novels.
Classification: LCC PN6728.S9 (ebook) | LCC PN6728.S9 P44 2017 (print) |
DDC 741.5/973—dc23
LC record available at https://lccn.loc.gov/2017018496

British Library Cataloging-in-Publication Data available

SUPERMAN's story is about fathers and sons,
but I dedicate this book to two Peretti mothers:
Patricia Joyce and Mandy, who made me who I am.

The real tragedy of life is that the most valuable ideas are, from the point of view of reality, worthless.

—HANS VAIHINGER, *The Philosophy of "As If"*

CONTENTS

PREFACE: WHY SUPERMAN?

I WANTED TO WRITE A BOOK ABOUT MYTHOLOGY IN AMERICA. TO THAT END, I could have chosen any of a number of subjects, such as the experiences of the first colonists, the men and women on the frontier, or the way old world religion and mythology has been transformed in a new context. My doctoral work focused on American versions of the Greek story of Prometheus, so I could have continued that project. But Prometheus, no matter how frequently his story is told in the United States, is an imported figure. I wanted to study something with roots planted in American soil. While studying Prometheus, I thought it would be a good idea to look over the sorts of things that Americans refer to when they use the word *myth*. To my surprise, a lot of the time they were referring to Superman—or to other comic book superheroes. That's when I remembered some jokes I'd heard about Superman. I did a bit of digging on the internet, and learned of the Superman Celebration in Illinois.

I soon discovered that there was simply too much material. Superman's presence saturated popular culture shortly after initial publication, and things haven't slowed down. The number of experts, devoted fans, and people with compelling interpretations is just too high to study in full. Thus, this book counts among its flaws an inability to cover the entire spectrum of Superman's significance. In organizing this book, I chose to emphasize the themes that I encountered during interviews and in the literature, organized in a way that shows the breadth of affinities people feel with the character. I saw the emphasis on community in Superman stories, so I wrote about the Superman Celebration as an example of how community can cohere—if only for a weekend—around a fictional character. I noticed how frequently the concept of Superman's morality came up and organized the chapter on humor around that idea. I collected a lot of data early on in this project, but it soon became obvious that I had to justify my choice of subject matter. The volume of data available about Superman wasn't enough to exclude other superheroes.

Then, in December of 2009, I was invited to give a short talk about Superman at Jackson Creek Middle School in Bloomington, Indiana. The school organized a week during which students got to learn about various topics other than their everyday school subjects. These included a class on superheroes, and I was asked to talk for half of that class. I was paired with a Spider-Man fan. I arrived and set up my short slide show. Then the woman who was going to talk about Spider-Man arrived. Having been told about my project, she approached me with a question: "You're studying Superman? Why aren't you using Spider-Man?"

"I don't know." I said. "I don't think Spider-Man works for my book."

"But Spider-Man's better . . ." There followed a list of reasons why Spider-Man is a better character.

All I could say was, "I'm not writing about Superman because I like him better than Spider-Man." I continued, "I probably have a hundred Spider-Man comics from when I was a kid. Spider-Man's great. He just doesn't work for this project."

"But why?"

I didn't have an answer. That bothered me. I knew that I should have one—even though the research for this book was in its early stages—and that I probably wouldn't be able to get very much further without figuring it out. As I talked to those middle-schoolers, whose questions were insightful and interested, it picked at the back of my mind. I talked mostly about Superman jokes I had collected, and about how the chevron on his chest had changed over time. My fellow speaker had toys. She showed them actual comic books, stuff she'd gotten from other countries, and all sorts of pop culture ephemera. She demonstrated to me that, as far as popular culture is concerned, the characters are prominent to an approximately equal degree. At the end of our presentations, she asked the same question.

"I still don't understand why Spider-Man's not right for your book."

I hadn't come to any conclusions during my talk, but suddenly the answer was right there in front of me. There is a difference, and our presentations had made that fact clear.

"Have you heard any Spider-Man jokes?" I asked.

"No."

"That's why Spider-Man doesn't work," I said.

It's not simply that Superman was the first superhero. It's not that his stories are more compelling than those of Spider-Man or Batman; in some ways, Superman's stories are less compelling to many readers. It's not that other superheroes are less meaningful to people. The lack of Spider-Man jokes (though not the absence of them; other superheroes show up in jokes with increasing frequency) points us to the widespread resonance of Superman. The character means something specific to the larger culture, and that meaning has caused people to internalize him and use him as part of their everyday expressions—in other words, Superman's transition from popular culture to folklore signals his importance to American culture in general.

I would like to take the opportunity to make clear what kind of book this is not. It's not an analysis of Superman comics, movies, television shows, or video games. You will find no in-depth discussion of Superman's history, or analysis of what he does in the movies or comic books. This book is also not an example of fan studies. That area of research, like comic book studies, is a burgeoning field, tangential to folklore. I call this book *Superman in Myth and Folklore* because I want to distinguish my subject from other media—in other words, this is not a book about Superman in the movies, television, or comics. It's a book about people and what they do with a story they love. Also, I just like the way the title sounds.

This book grew from a desire to study what people do with stories that are important to them. I'm a folklorist by training, and I have strived to study Superman as an example of folklore. There are certain holes in my research (I interviewed no children, for example) that could not be avoided. For this project, it's impossible to do the sort of ethnographic fieldwork that many folklorists strive to do. There is no single, real-world community held together and informed by Superman. My methods were not ideal, but they fit the project. I developed them as I went along, rather than following any particular agenda. As a result, this is just one possible book that can be written about Superman using the folkloristic method. I read as much as possible on the subject, and I endeavored to interview people about these sorts of stories. My fieldwork method involved face-to-face conversation and continued correspondence. I also traveled to comic book conventions and to the Superman Celebration in Illinois. I would have liked to attend more of these events, but that wasn't possible. Everyone I met, in person and online, was remarkably helpful, and I would like to thank them.

Those to whom I am most indebted are named throughout this book, but it is worth expressing my gratitude to them up front: Scott Bayles, Jodi Chromey, Sean Dulaney, Josh Elder, Kristina Johnson, Bob Lyzenga, Michelle Lyzenga, Brian Morris, Cookie Morris, Karla Ogle, Jeff Ray, Chris Roberson, Mark Waid, and Josh Walgenbach. I owe a great debt to Angie Shelton, the rest of the Metropolis, Illinois, Chamber of Commerce, and the Superman Celebration Committee for making me feel welcome. There were many more people who talked about Superman with me, and I regret that there isn't room in this book to share all their stories: Ashley Bayles, Andrew Chandler,

Charlee Chartrand, Nick Cole, Lisa Gower, Jim Hambrick, Trevor Hawkins, Steve Henderson, Gena Henderson, Jamie Kelley, Ronda Kelley, Danny Kelley, Heather Kelley, Steven Kirk, Stephanie Perrin, Alex Rae, John Rinaldi, Alex Rinaldi, Matt Traughber of Vintage Phoenix Comics and Collectibles, and Mike Werner of Mike's Comics and Games.

Many people listened to my ideas about this project, provided insight into early drafts of this book, or referred me to resources. I want to thank Peter Bibler, Liz Burbach, Cassie Chambliss, Rhonda Dass, Christopher DuVernay, John Fenn, Lisa Gabbert, Shawn Galdeen, Henry Glassie, Diane Goldstein, Anthony Guest-Scott, Matt Guschwan, William Hansen, Robert Glenn Howard, Michael Judd, Jessica Judd, Sean Kleefeld, Andy Kolovos, Mikel Koven, Dustin Long, Moira Marsh, Paul McGarity, Bill Meeks, Toni Perrine, Aileen Scales, Greg Schrempp, Robert Segal, Pravina Shukla, and Craig Gill.

I must also thank my family: My parents Julio and Joyce helped me out in so many ways, from reading drafts to taking care of my kids on occasions when I was doing research. My sister Julie was supportive and gave me some Superman collectibles to use as visual aids. My sons Jacob, Calvin, and Roland have endured many hours when I wasn't able to play with them because I was doing work.

Above all, I thank my wife, Mandy.

SUPERMAN IN MYTH AND FOLKLORE

- 1 -

SUPERMAN AND THE
FOLKLORISTIC PERSPECTIVE

IT'S LIKE SOMETHING OUT OF A TALL TALE. HOW FAST COULD HE RUN? FASTER than a speeding bullet. How high could he jump? He could leap tall buildings in a single bound. It's also like something out of heroic myth. Born in amazing circumstances, he is abandoned to the elements, only to be saved and brought up in humble surroundings in a far off land. He discovers that he has miraculous powers, which he uses to protect his adopted home. There are folktale elements: childless parents wishing for a baby, a magical transformation turns an apparently ordinary human being into a fantastical Prince Charming who can rescue any damsel in distress. It's a science fiction story of alien contact. It's a fantasy story of a being with great powers that defy the laws of physics. There's romance, mystery, action, and adventure. Superman has it all.

Superman began in popular culture, but readers embraced the character to the extent that he has become part of folklore. This transition from popular culture to folk culture, from mass media to folklore, signals the importance of the character on the level of the individual and on the level of the larger American populace. Superman's story has become one with which people work through the vital issues of their lives. It dramatizes questions of identity, morality, and politics. This book will focus on how Superman has become a part of folklore, and how the study of folklore—folkloristics—can contribute to an understanding of the character's place in people's lives. Folklorists have long been interested in genres: folktale, myth, legend, folk speech, proverb, riddle, folk song, joke, and a score of others. By examining the ways that Superman has entered several of these genres,[1] this book will look for the meanings of the character as he exists outside the official texts (though sometimes within those texts as well).

Superman has become part of a number of folkloric genres, such as jokes, tattoos, festivals, and costuming. Ben Saunders writes that from the very beginning, Superman "had a different kind of intellectual currency from his fellow comic book characters; he stood for things in a way they could not" (2011: 18). Superman is unique.

WHO IS SUPERMAN?

Superman is the name given to a cluster of fictional characters with a relatively stable core set of traits, including his alien origin and journey to Earth, his distinctive costume and insignia, his Midwestern upbringing, and his home in a large city where he uses his superhuman abilities for the protection and betterment of humanity. The cluster that is Superman[2] extends beyond the fictional stories to annex both the actors who portray him and his creators. He is an example (by most accounts, the first instance) of a superhero. Superman first appeared in comic books in 1938, and is often credited with contributing to the success of that art form and of the superhero genre.[3] His presence soon spread into licensed merchandise and other entertainment media until, by the beginning of the twenty-first century, he had appeared in radio, film, television, video games, novels, short stories, and the internet. Superman usually dresses in a blue, yellow, and red skintight suit accented with a cape and a stylized S on his chest. He wears this in part to differentiate himself from his secret identity, Clark Kent, who dresses in normal, modern American attire and usually works as a journalist. His birth name is Kal-El, the structure of which is typical of people's names on his home planet, Krypton. This planet exploded when he was an infant. His father, knowing of the impending doom but unable to stop it or to save himself, sent the infant to Earth in a rocket, where his physical resemblance to human beings allowed him to fit in. Differences in environment and physiology give Superman extraordinary abilities.[4]

I asked the writer and Superman fan Brian Morris how he would describe Superman to someone who had never heard of the character. Brian, who answered in an e-mail, began by noting that it is probably not necessary since everybody's heard of Superman. He continued, "Anyway, I'd describe Superman to someone, in brief, as a costumed adventurer with unimaginable powers of strength, speed, and flight who uses those abilities to help others in need. If I had to go into detail—and indulge my sense of drama—the best description was the classic from the radio and TV shows:[5] 'Faster than a speeding bullet! More powerful than a locomotive! Able to leap tall buildings in a single bound! Superman! Strange visitor from another planet who came to Earth with powers and abilities far beyond those of mortal men.

Superman, who can change the course of mighty rivers, bend steel in his bare hands, and who disguised as Clark Kent, mild-mannered reporter for a great metropolitan newspaper, fights a never-ending battle for Truth, Justice, and the American Way'...No matter how the character changes when it moves to a new medium or even when the comic books change writers or editors, he's still the infant survivor of the dead planet Krypton who was raised in humble circumstances to become the world's mightiest hero who does what's right because it's the right thing to do. He's so powerful, he can withstand even the various alterations to his backstory." [6]

Brian's note about change is important. Most of the characteristics covered—everything from the spelling of his given name to the location where he lands on Earth to the nature and explanation of his powers—have been altered over time. This has caused Tom DeHaven to contemplate just exactly what is essential to Superman: "Exploding planet. Rocket ship to earth. Secret identity. Original costume. Lois Lane. What about Lex Luthor? Essential? No, not really, none of the bad guys are. So. Anything else? Then just this, the basic-basic, saved for last: he can fly, and perform marvelous feats of strength, which he chooses to do because it brings him great satisfaction" (2010: 205–206).[7] Peter Coogan's (2006) book-length academic analysis of the superhero genre's history and development takes into account its literary and critical aspects. He traces its origin to Superman's initial appearance in the first issue *Action Comics*, created by Jerry Siegel and Joe Shuster, but proceeds to work backward to find precursors ranging from ancient myth to early twentieth-century fiction. In his final two chapters, Coogan looks closely at some criticisms of the genre that read superhero stories as problematic portrayals of the oppression of late capitalism. Coogan disagrees, finding that the scholars' analyses do not match that of the majority of readers.

Over the years, the stories of Superman have developed an extensive supporting cast, including the character's friends, family, and opponents. Prominent among these are his biological parents Jor-El and Lara, his adoptive parents Jonathan and Martha Kent, his foil Lois Lane, his archenemy Lex Luthor, and his friend Jimmy Olsen. His primary concern has always been protecting people, though the types of events that require his intervention have evolved from social injustice and organized crime to megalomaniacs, natural disasters, and alien invasions. He has become integrated into the continuity of a larger fictional cosmos including other superheroes (Reynolds 1992). Superman's stories are owned by Time-Warner, published by DC Entertainment as comic books and produced by Warner Brothers as films and television shows. Licensed merchandise is too extensive to chronicle, and includes costumes, pajamas and other clothing, lunchboxes, collectible figures, jewelry, and statues. Countless amateurs proficient in using media have made fan films focusing on the character, written their own stories about him and his world, and generally engaged in all of the activities that fan studies has focused on since the 1990s.[8] Despite the fact that a corporation owns the character, the public feels a general sense of ownership as well, to the extent that rumors of a new Superman film being put into production inevitably result in fans discussing how it should be made, who should star in it, and what the story should be. This notion of public ownership, of the sustained interest in the character's development, gives rise to his presence in folklore and his evolution into myth.

An example will help illustrate the extent to which some fans have made Superman a part of their lives. Superman became the subject of national news in 2013 when DC Comics revealed that they were getting ready for publication a Superman story written by novelist Orson Scott Card. Card's stance against and writings about homosexuality led some readers and comic shop owners to boycott the story long before it would have been released. The argument presented by those boycotting the story was that Card's viewpoint was in direct opposition to any opinion Superman would hold on the subject. Autumn Sandeen sums up the issue: "Superman may not live in the real world, but I'd like to think that if he were a real being he would be on the side of justice for LGBT community members. With Orson Scott Card writing issue one of a new Superman series, I'm less sure that Superman would, if asked, support marriage equality" (Sandeen 2013). The story was eventually pulled from publication when its artist, Chris Sprouse, left the project. The series in which the story would have appeared was published without it. In the words of Graeme McMillan, "The now non-homophobic *Adventures of Superman* no. 1 will be launched digitally on April 29" (McMillan 2013). In the outcry and its result—at this writing, the story in question has not been published—the relationship between the public and the corporation responsible for publishing Superman stories is revealed to be complicated. At heart, the Card story, regardless of its actual content, diverged from the morality that readers see at the heart of Superman because of its writer's views. In other words, Superman's values matter, as do the values of those who tell his stories, because Superman signifies something beyond his status as an intellectual property owned by a corporation.

THE FOLKLORISTIC PERSPECTIVE

Any superhero can be analyzed from the standpoint of a variety of academic disciplines. I approach Superman through the lens of folkloristics because this discipline can offer a valuable perspective through the use of fieldwork and attention to the character's situated context. Thus, a few words need to be said about the folkloristic perspective on culture. Folkloristics began as curiosity about various products of human expression, particularly those in oral tradition, with the intention to preserve them in fixed media. The folkloristic method approaches the dynamics of human interaction as people communicate to each other, expressing ideas and solving problems through a number of genres, such as legend, folk tale, proverb, and myth.[9] Folklore emerges and can be collected as people interact, so we have to pay attention to both content and context, the latter of which includes the attitude of the performers and audience. The best folkloristic studies take into account the human element: the real, motivated, interested, biased, and creative individuals behind the folklore. Attention to the individual is one great advance of performance studies, which is, as Pravina Shukla puts it, "a paradigm that emphasizes the individual in the social moment of creativity. Creation is understood by attending at once to individuals and their circumstances, looping standards and acts of desire with the forces of consumption and social response. The contrast is with studies that focus on a lone genius floating free of the world, and with studies that see everything as the result of superorganic powers at play. Our [that is, the folklorists'] commitment is to a believable dialectic of people and the world" (2010: 386). Several tensions inform the study of folklore, and we might characterize the first tension as existing between the individual and the group (Glassie 1982).

The study of folklore now begins, when it can, with performance—the manifestation of creativity and competence in human interaction (Bauman 1972).[10] Each performance is treated as an emergent event, the result of a process involving numerous potential requirements, leading to what is called a variant—named for the variation that necessarily results from the exigencies of unmediated and repeated performance.[11] The variant, which may become reified as a text when recorded, arises in a context that can be broken down into its social, cultural, psychological, environmental, historical, and dialectical components. What sets folkloristics apart is its attention to the creative, human element as it shapes any given variant, particularly in cultural and psychological contexts. Performance studies takes into account the moment of creation, as it manifests itself in an unmediated environment.

Some folklorists go so far as to classify folklore itself as a medium, akin to television or magazines or film (de Caro and Jordan 2004: 2–3). Viewed in this way, we can study Superman in folklore just as we study Superman in film or in comic books.

Folklorists have paid particular attention to the performance of folklore since Richard Bauman's book *Verbal Art as Performance* galvanized a trend in the early 1970s.[12] This is not to say that folklorists limit themselves to performance theory. Gregory Schrempp (1992), to give one example, incorporates a folkloristic attention to variants as he studies the cosmological implications of mythical narratives among the Greeks and Maori in pursuit of the modes of thought-designated myth and philosophy. Schrempp's focus broadens to culture in general, working with the mythical mode of thought inherent in other genres of folklore and literature (see also Schrempp 2012). The attention to folklore as a dynamic process has crystallized the folkloristic reliance on variation. The variant is understood as the result of the individual reacting to the tensions of the moment of performance. Variation can arise from time constraints, creative whims, economic factors, cultural ideas of appropriateness, and a myriad of other factors.[13] The important concept to understand is that variation arises not merely from the reworking of old texts, but from the imprinted pattern that exists in the mind of the performer, making itself manifest during the exigencies of performance. In the study of narrative, folklorists collect as many variants as possible, since in oral tradition no single version of a story can be considered definitive.

A common conception of folklore is that it is old—the survivals of yesteryear—and this is accurate enough as a popular definition. The folklorist, developing technical definitions, *is* interested in things that persist, but antiquity is not the focus; the focus is the persistent utility of the past in the present. The interest is in tradition (Glassie 1995). People value things that are new and fresh, to some extent, but "while novelty is exciting," writes Michael Owen Jones, "familiarity is comfortable. These two forces compel much of human behavior" (1989: 244). This is the second tension of folklore—between the new and the old.[14]

In pursuing the meanings of a performance, folklorists will often elicit what's known as oral literary criticism (Dundes 1966; Narayan 1995), which refers to the performer's and audience's own interpretations of and thoughts about the folklore in question. Folklorists also look for native categories, how performers and audiences classify things, as opposed to the analytical categories developed by scholars (Dundes 1962; Ben-Amos 1972). Much of my method has relied on applying this sort of oral criticism to Superman;

determining what the character and stories mean to people who read them and love them.

Superman—indeed, the form of comic books in general—has also been called folklore, or an extension of it (Inge 1990: 141 ff.; Peretti 2015), and exploring how and why is important. The character appears in cultural forms of folklore in the analytical or scholarly sense of the term, but there are plenty of examples of the character being called folklore by people who aren't folklorists. This usage of the term refers to the character's place in American culture, placing him on the same level as other folkloric characters such as Bigfoot, Paul Bunyan, and Davy Crockett. M. Thomas Inge writes that Superman "immediately captured the American imagination and became our first twentieth-century folk hero, a perfect mythological figure for an age of technology in which man was methodically to step beyond every limitation on his intellectual and physical abilities and master the universe" (Inge 1990: 141). Scholars have also used the term *folklore* to refer to the medium in which Superman originally appeared.

Ellen Rhoads (1973), in her structural analysis of *Little Orphan Annie* comics, begins with a survey of the idea that comics are a quintessential form of American folklore. She is not alone in characterizing comics as folklore. Rolf Brednich engages in a similar type of analysis, beginning with a common rhetorical move by which scholars equate comic books with earlier forms of art, such as those found on "Egyptian tombs, on Greek vases, Roman victory columns, and so forth," as a means of simultaneously demonstrating the validity of their study and establishing a link to other forms of scholarship (1976: 45). Brednich demonstrates the similarities between superhero comic books and oral folktales: "Like folktales, comics tend to project outwards, to materialize abilities in concrete pictures. The superheroes' costumes are visualized magic; their wearers are the folktale heroes of our time" (1976: 50). Brednich's analysis finds many similarities in the content and patterns of folktales and superhero comic books, though he does offer some account of the differences between the commercial comic book and oral tradition, notably, that of mechanism—standardized production, which omits a great deal of attention to the specific audience. Around the same time, Ronald Baker (1975) delved into specific folkloric motifs that can be found in superhero comic book stories, finding that Superman shares several characteristics with folktale heroes. Following up on Brednich's analysis, Alex Scobie looks at the extent to which comic books have a pseudo- or quasi-oral nature—they are occasionally read aloud or recorded and are produced by sometimes-anonymous artists. Many of these characteristics have changed greatly since Scobie's 1980 publication (notably, many comic book covers now include the names of the creators), but the notion of comic books being folkloresque in nature has remained.[15]

In a less academic venue, Denny O'Neil, who wrote Superman comics in the 1970s, sees comic book characters as folk heroes because of the way they develop over time: in different media, under the guidance of different editors, arising from the creativity of different writers, Superman has undergone what O'Neil calls a "maniacally accelerated version of the folk process" because of the need for new material to fill pages of books and minutes of airtime. "If you read random Superman stories in chronological order," writes O'Neil, "you get the sense of guys around a campfire trying to top each other with tall tales . . . like fairy tales and myths, the Superman stories were begun by one creator but embellished and altered by many. Because of the need to *produce*, to fill those pages, to meet those deadlines, get the stuff out there, what would have taken generations in the preindustrial era took only a few years. And as will folk tales, and particularly myths, the personality of the hero, as perceived by the public, was a residue left in the collective consciousness after audiences and readers were exposed to several different versions of the same character" (1987: 51–52). O'Neil is describing the Superman story as, essentially, one story with many variants, created by many artists over time. But whereas the same process in oral tradition would take a very long time, the production schedule for Superman stories condensed this process into a few years, the result of which is a concept of Superman that is not particular to any one version.[16]

More recently, Terrence Wandtke (2012) has explored the idea of the production of superhero comics—especially comics from the golden age (roughly, the 1930s and 1940s)—as a process that bears striking resemblance to the processes by which stories are told in oral tradition. Wandtke even uses the early Superman stories as an entry point into his larger discussion of superhero comics as an example of "new orality." Wandtke's argument is nuanced and compelling, drawing upon the works of scholars of oral composition such as Albert Lord, Milman Perry, and John Miles Foley, combining their insights into the comic book creation process with the more theoretical works of Walter Ong and Marshall McLuhan. Though he doesn't use the term *folklore* to describe the genesis of superhero comics, he's talking about the same processes that generate the performance of narrative folklore. For Wandtke, superhero comics represent a shift away from the aesthetics of literate culture, returning to something very much like oral culture (a characteristic of new media in general), which he also calls traditionality. Even though they are the product of mechanically reproduced printing, Wandtke argues that superhero comics are related to ancient oral epic in composition (2012: 29–52), in collective ownership (2012: 58), and in content. Although the topic of this book is related to Wandtke's subject, he discusses different material—namely, the creation of the content of the comics themselves. He wants to get at the psychology of the producers and readers of superhero comics, as well as related media in which superheroes appear. It is a compelling approach, generating real insight into the process of creating comic books.[17]

The continuing printed stories told about Superman less resemble folklore—or the folk process of oral tradition—and more resemble the midrashim of Jewish tradition, exegetical writings that expand on what is found in the Torah (Lewis 2002). If we consider that, after Jerry Siegel stopped writing stories and Joe Shuster stopped drawing them, Superman was wholly part of popular tradition, then the analogy is perfect: "It is as if a story had been told and the ones responsible for retelling it had been given the freedom to embellish it as they pleased, within the limitations of very precise and demanding rules," writes Howard Schwartz about the Torah (1998: 9); he could just as well have been describing the subsequent writers of Superman. Schwartz equates the writing of these sacred texts to oral tradition, though in doing so he is referring to the often radical ways the stories were revised—again, much like new Superman stories often revise elements of previous stories.[18]

The difference between comics and folklore is that comics are mass-produced and remain extant in the same form after creation. They are material culture, but not a folkloric version of material culture. They are mechanically reproduced, which goes a long way to eliminating variation. This distinction is important. The difference here is variation as the result of non-standardized production. When a comic book is created, the singular work of artists is mass-produced for public consumption. Copies of each issue of a Superman comic book are all the same, relatively speaking. Some changes creep in, such as when a comic is bound in a collection, or when recolored; the same is true of films, prints of which are virtually identical (and again, changes do occur, such as with the release of a "director's cut"; the same can be said for literature; see Wandtke 2012 for a discussion of variation in the revision of superhero comics; Aichele 1997 also examines the notion of variation between media). These changes may be meaningful, but they are the result of different processes than those that produce the variations in folklore. For popular culture, all a reader needs to do to experience the same thing again is to press a play button or to open the book again. Folklore must be recreated continually through creative processes. If you want to hear a story a second time, somebody has to tell it again; that telling is subject to all sorts of factors that may cause it to vary from one version to the next. The standards of mass-production separate popular culture from folklore.

That is not to say that the distinction is relevant to the people who are watching films, listening to stories, and generally participating in their culture. The folklorist John William Johnson, who developed the idea that the standardization of production is the key distinction between folklore and popular culture,[19] fully acknowledges that the distinction is a minor one; both convey important cultural expressions.[20] It's a good place to start the study of culture, but not a good place to finish. Some recent folkloristic scholarship has incorporated the analysis of literature, cinema, and general popular culture into ethnographic analysis (Glassie 2010, Shukla 2010). Nonetheless, it is important to see the difference, because the distinction between folklore and popular culture does reveal things about the contents of each and the expressions created in them.

Although Superman did not begin in a medium that could be considered folklore, his entry into folklore is important. The migration from a fixed medium such as comic books to the fluid processes of folklore has received much less attention than its opposite. Folklore in literature, film, and other arts has long been an interest of folklorists and of scholars outside the field (see, for example, Hoffman 1961, de Caro and Jordan 2004, and de Caro 2013, though there is a vast corpus of material about this).

Where does Superman fit in to all this? There are several answers to this question. First, I borrow Sandra Dolby's delineation of several components of the folkloristic perspective. She applies this perspective to American Studies, writing that it offers "1) an examination and celebration of microcosms, 2) an identification of antecedents that modulates the perception of determinism in human expression and worldview, and 3) a recognition and exploration of the role of tradition and innovation" (1996: 59). While she notes that these components are not exhaustive, they do provide a place from which to start. The study of folklore could thus look to oral tradition to find precursors to Superman in antecedents (Dolby's number 2)[21] or ways in which Superman has changed over the years yet held a constant core of coherence for (3).[22] There has been no attempt to explore the first of her points, the microcosms. To study Superman in microcosms (i.e., folk groups and individuals, the heart of human interaction) is to look at the way Superman has become part of people's lives. The superhero genre, as Jeffrey A. Brown writes, is "fundamentally intertwined with a subculture of devoted consumers to such an extent that consideration of fans is an essential element for understanding the cultural significance of the genre ... textual analysis alone cannot account for the various ways that dedicated fans use superheroes to establish a sense of community, express ideological identification with the characters, or how they use the genre to project a sense of their core personal identity" (Brown 2012: 280). That is the focus of this book.

We find a second answer to how Superman fits into folkloristics by considering native and analytical categories. Scholars determine analytical categories. The native category is the genre as it is known to the people who experience and perform it. The idea is easily illustrated—someone telling a narrative drawn from personal experience usually labels it a *story*, a native category; folklorists use the analytical label *personal experience narrative* for the same story. A person telling a story about an encounter with a ghost usually calls it a *story*; folklorists call it a *memorate*. Nomenclature and categorization get easier when looking at different languages; since there are often no specific translations for foreign terms, scholars often use the foreign word (Malinowski 1984; Basso 1996).[23]

Since one of the purposes of folkloristics is to contribute to the greater understanding of humanity, oral literary criticism and native categories are especially important. These are learned and recorded through fieldwork, the process of observing the behavior of and interviewing people who perform folklore. We can see the exchange of academic terms across disciplinary boundaries. For example, Richard Reynolds seems to have brought the increasingly common usage of myth[24] in reference to superheroes to academic attention with his book *Superheroes: A Modern Mythology* (1992). His study, while perhaps drawing its inspiration from the native usage of the terms *myth* and *mythology*, did not focus on individuals as understood through fieldwork. He arrived at his own idea of how the terms apply to superhero narratives, which will be examined in the concluding chapter.

FROM FIXED TO FLUID

The boundary between folklore and popular culture—and it's worth mentioning that popular culture here refers specifically to "cultural events which are transmitted by media and communicated in mass societal contexts" (Narváez and Laba 1984: 1)—has been of interest to scholars, but little has been written about popular culture becoming folklore. To some extent, I am conflating print literature and popular culture; for the purpose of this study, the mechanisms by which these two forms of expressive culture are transmitted are roughly equal—they both represent fixed sources from which people draw material for folkloric performance.[25] In the middle of the twentieth century, Richard Dorson observed the connection between the different forms of communication, noting, "If folk tales ascend into literature, so literary stories descend into popular tradition [he means folklore], when they suit the needs of oral narration and folk fancy" (1945: 212). For Dorson, those tales that migrate from media to oral tradition "must fit a preconceived pattern of American yarning. Where this process occurs, the original narrative can be described as the literary parent of a folktale, but the offspring must be accounted live folklore" (1945: 213). Dorson's descriptions of tales migrating from literature to oral tradition is based, to a large extent, in his attention to the dynamics of American culture, and he encourages scholars to recognize "that in the U.S. the electric currents of tradition flow through a grid of mechanical as well as human circuits" (1945: 215).

A bit of theory lurks in this passage: the notion that we can consider unmediated human behavior (which in this case refers to oral tradition and the processes of folklore) and literary products (and thus, by extension, all media) in a figurative sense to be like cogs in the mechanism of culture, contributing to the operation of the whole. The idea of "live folklore" reminds us that any given tradition requires human beings to propagate it. Yet this migration from popular culture to live folklore remains undertheorized, even when it gets the attention of scholars. The same year Dorson published the essay discussed above, Frances Lee Utley characterized a similar phenomenon occurring with sacred literature in "The Bible of the Folk." Utley's study focuses on "what the folk did to adorn a tale when the Bible refused to tell the whole story" (Utley 1946: 6), by which he means that because the Bible is so valuable to its adherents, they will explore its silences and work with the material to fit their own worldview and local circumstances. Scripture doesn't prevent a concomitant oral tradition from developing. Utley points to the story of the Adam's apple as an example: "Not only is this story a product of the folk, but it and others . . . are something more unusual, oral lore ultimately derived from a narrowly localized center and an identifiable written text" (1945: 1).[26] A scholar may, according to Utley, search for sources of folktales already in the Bible, collect and compare folktales to those in the Bible, or analyze the tales which have been derived from the Bible. It is an analogue to this third enterprise—which Utley describes as "an uncharted wilderness"—that I engage in throughout this book. I want to show the ways in which folklore derived from popular culture, in this case Superman stories, behaves.

Some scholars have taken up this sort of study. Louise Pound analyzes "'Monk' Lewis in Nebraska" (1945), and Albert Friedman examines gondoliers' songs in Venice (1967), providing data more so than analysis.[27] Some depth has been provided by scholars like Wolfram Eberhard, who examines three narrators in Taipei who told stories they had learned from novels. Eberhard's agenda keeps him focused on the past, which he hopes to illuminate by looking at the present, but he provides lots of useful observations, such as the fact that many in the audience were literate and simply preferred to hear these stories read aloud (1970: 3). The storytellers in these instances often read directly from the printed text, though others use them to refresh their memories before performing without any aids. Eberhard engages in a comparative analysis of printed text and performed text—a technique employed by other scholars as well (for example, Glassie 2006: 229–49)—and observes some differences: the compact language of the printed text becomes more colloquial in performance, "which means that he [the storyteller] added grammatical particles and loosened the sentence structure" (1970: 9); the language is often translated into a local dialect; the introduction of stereotypes, puns, and other local idioms; a general shortening of the text by leaving out some minor characters; the stressing of certain points through repetition; the heightening of traits in descriptions. "For instance," writes Eberhard, "the description of the color of the hero's face is omitted, because the audience today would not regard a black face as a good trait, while formerly, black faced heroes were well-known positive figures in the Chinese theatrical tradition" (1970: 9).

Eberhard does notice many differences in the live performance; some arise from the narrator's memory lapses, while others derive from the narrator's wish to make the story more compelling and interesting. He also notes that some narrators are more effective than others, in particular because of the distance between the performer and the printed text; those who perform without reference to the text during performance are considered better. Also of note is the observation that the storytellers portrayed themselves as having altered the text in performance to a much greater extent than Eberhard found when comparing them (1970: 26). Storytellers, in Eberhard's analysis, are agents of change in the ever-evolving process of narrative art, in which the printed material itself is not immune to suppression or supersession: "The longer a novel lives, going through the cycle of being told and perhaps rewritten and performed, the more people participate in its growth, the more it becomes a piece of real folk literature" (1970: 31).

Other fieldwork has revealed that the distinction between stories descending from oral tradition and from printed sources can be important to people. Hasan El-Shamy found that Egyptian storytellers have a separate term for the latter, *qiṣṣàh* (El-Shamy 1980: xliv), though some claim their stories come from books when in fact no printed source can be found. Furthermore, the stories derived from books "usually deal with religious and historical themes" (1980: xlviii). "Clearly," writes El-Shamy, "oral and written narratives belong to separate cognitive systems. Although the two systems do to some extent overlap and affect each other, the separation between the two systems is the dominant trend" (1980: l). They do intertwine, though. This sort of analysis might vary considerably from culture to culture, and even from folk group to folk group.

One way to analyze the way fixed (that is, mediated) and fluid (i.e., oral) narratives intertwine is to compare the text with performance, as Eberhard does. Several studies have done so. We can look to Sylvia Grider's examination of children's "media narraform," which she describes as "a new category of children's narratives which are basically re-tellings of mass media presentations about the supernatural, using traditional storytelling techniques" that are "symbiotic" in nature (1981: 125). The symbiosis results from the union of media content and the dynamics of oral storytelling. Grider delineates the characteristics of the performance of such content: an identification of the source, frequent backtracking to relate half-forgotten episodes, shallow character description, an interpretive element, and the presence of other types of oral narrative within the performance context. She devotes this study to children's storytelling, but notes that it is not exclusive to any age group. Grider observes that "folklorists have been concerned primarily with the influence tradition has exerted on the media, and not vice versa" (1981: 131). Her assessment of folkloristic attention still applies, at least broadly. Scholars tend to notice the similarities and differences between media and unmediated expression; according to Peter Narváez and Martin Laba, for example, both popular culture and folklore "demand creative enactment within a wide variety of conventionalized systems that engender and disseminate their own aesthetic and traditions" (1984: 1). Additionally, popular culture and folklore both "structure and provide repeatable expressive forms for individual and group experience in everyday life. In other words, they offer a means of rendering experience intelligible and graspable through recognizable forms that are both pleasing aesthetically and relevant in a social interactional sense" (Narváez and Laba 1984: 2).

Narváez and Laba edited a volume titled *Media Sense*. Therein, Laba expands on the perspective that folkloristics can bring to the broader study of expressive culture: By examining how people respond to popular culture and interpreting this expressive response, a scholar proceeds in a folkloristic manner. Attention to the social dimension of popular culture is a folkloristic enterprise. Laba points out the value of rituals of consumption and interaction that congeal around a television show, just to use one example: "Shared affinities for a popular culture form develop the form as an expressive vehicle, and in this way commodities produced commercially are reproduced in the social life of the reference group" (Laba 1984: 13). Furthermore, "the essential connection between folklore and popular culture is in the social sphere—the impulse to, and ways in which meaning is made by people in relation to the more or less determining material conditions of life in modern society. The social practice of folklore is a means by which individuals and groups ritualize, organize, and make sense of those forms of their day-to-day experience" (Laba 1984: 17).

Other articles in Narváez and Laba's volume attend to folklore in popular culture, with a couple of exceptions that note the presence of pop culture in oral performance, or even a blending of the two. Gerald L. Pocius explores a practice related to folklore that incorporates elements of popular culture: the way individuals and families use printed religious pictures in their homes. People will place homemade items alongside mass-produced candles, photographs, and other materials in shrines and altars within their residences (Pocius 1984). James Hornby's "Rumors of Maggie: Outlaw News In Folklore" looks at how Canadians have incorporated news stories into conversational jokes and opinions, often expressing ideas that the mass media wouldn't address (thus the "outlaw" descriptor, which refers to the status of these jokes and opinions as outside the dominant discourse, not as a description of the content of the stories). According to Hornby, a certain song became popular in Canadian oral tradition; this song ridiculed former Canadian Prime Minister Pierre Trudeau by including a caricature of his distinctive speaking voice. This song entered oral circulation to the extent that many people whom Hornby interviewed had only ever heard it performed in person (1984: 103). The aesthetic of the voice parody, in particular, made this a commonly performed song. Hornby writes that this song, in its oral circulation, was not created by the dynamics of a "folk process," but was "simply learned. Thus it is not a folk parody, but a folk use of a parody, as it was transmitted orally to a large extent" (1984: 106). Implicit in this statement is that the genesis of folklore—as it is traditionally understood—lies in the folk process of dynamic human interaction, not in a recording studio. Analogously, we would then characterize virtually every instance of Superman in folklore as a folk use, rather than folklore. This notion will be complicated throughout subsequent chapters of this book.

In truth, there has been little said about the presence of material derived from literature and popular culture in folklore. Even books devoted to the study of both—such as Bruce Rosenberg's *Folklore and Literature: Rival Siblings* (1991) and de Caro and Jordan's *Resituating Folklore* (2004)—focus almost entirely on the way a given technological medium incorporates content from folklore, not the other way around. Yet there is but a "fragile line" (Levine 1992: 1377) between the relatively fixed worlds of popular culture and folklore. In "The Folklore of Industrial Societies," Lawrence Levine quotes children who engage in play—a folkloric activity—based on radio shows; this certainly continues with children pretending to be characters from movies, books, television shows, and the like. Levine, writing at the advent of fan studies, seeks to expand the critical apparatus of scholars and to focus on audience members as well as artists; generally, he encourages the sort of attention to popular culture that folklorists today give to their subject matter through fieldwork (this has happened to a great extent in both folkloristics and other disciplines; see Koven 2007 for a survey of some of this work).

The study of folklore through fieldwork reveals that we should look for the relevance of Superman through the ways that people make use of him. Superman provides a cluster of motifs by virtue of many elements of his stories. These motifs have semantic resonance with the public in ways that manifest in other folklore genres. Examples include folk speech: terms such as *Brainiac, Bizarro,* and *kryptonite* have entered the popular lexicon from Superman stories; proverbial phrases, like "faster than a speeding bullet," enjoy wide distribution; as a nickname, *Superman* has often been applied to athletes, especially in basketball, and the phrase "our Superman" often describes someone whose work is invaluable; and there is also the folk metaphor of equating Clark Kent and Superman to a person who appears mild-mannered but does something spectacular or heroic. Superman's folkloric presence points to the fact that he holds meaning among members of the general public. While we might argue that his presence in popular culture has come largely from commercial exploitation, thus cementing his popularity through exposure, the same argument cannot be made for folklore. Superman's folkloric presence persists because it reflects something deep in the culture.[28] Superman resonates; this book explores how.

Contrasting Superman to elements of popular culture demonstrates the appropriateness of using him in a study such as this. Consider the television

show *Babylon 5*. Kurt Lancaster (2001) studies how fans of this show immerse themselves in the universe created by the show and ancillary products.
Lancaster writes of his purpose, "Using *Babylon 5* as a case study, I analyze
how one can participate in simulacra of science fiction through role-playing
games, war games, collectible card games, CD-ROMs, fan fiction, and online
fan Web pages" (2001: xxiv). These are all mass-produced and part of popular
culture. Fans do frequently create their own expressions using elements of the
show, especially costumes. A variety of different productions lend themselves
to this type of study—Lancaster gives the examples of *Star Wars*, *Star Trek*,
and Middle-Earth—finding the ways that people "poach" the texts (Jenkins
1992). One could also use Superman as a case study, as Camille Bacon-Smith's
does with *Star Trek* and science fiction fans (1992, 1999). My interests are
different from theirs; I'm more interested in the people—the creators, fans,
and those who simply find themselves involved in Superman-related activity.

HAVING ESTABLISHED A METHOD OF APPROACHING SUPERMAN, THE BALANCE
of this book will concern itself with the question of how Superman is important on the levels of the individual and the larger culture. Chapter 2 examines
three fans in an attempt to establish a baseline of possible affinities people
feel for Superman while describing some of the functions the character
serves. It looks at folklore genres such as life story and tattoo. From there,
Chapter 3 moves on to a preliminary exploration of the role Superman plays
in morality. It is an examination of how Superman has impacted the moral
decisions some people make, using several personal experience narratives. It
incorporates a discussion of the philosophy of "as if" to understand the use
of Superman. In Chapter 4, the Superman Celebration in Metropolis, Illinois,
takes center stage, but is viewed through the lenses of several of its attendees.
Because the Celebration is social in nature, it provides an opportunity to
see several different kinds of appreciation for the character as people come
together to make an imagined community real for a single weekend a year.
Chapter 5 takes as its subject matter the humor that has arisen regarding
Superman. Both jokes and cartoons that center on Superman show us some
of the ways that the character resonates on a larger cultural level. Issues of
body image, moral perfection, and psychological well-being come to the
foreground.

Chapter 6 centers on two men whose lives Superman has influenced in
profound and similar ways. These two men have contemplated morality,
religion, and how to raise their children using Superman as a focal point.
Finally, Chapter 7 brings the concept of myth to the foreground. I use several

theories of myth for a concluding discussion of the mythical nature of Superman at the beginning of the twenty-first century. In structuring the book in this manner, I've chosen to expand and contract; things begin on a personal level with Chapter 2, moving to broader perspectives in Chapters 3 and 4, then slowly contracting again to the individuals of Chapters 5 and 6, before expanding again in the conclusion.

IN HIS ESSAY ON SUPERMAN, TOM DEHAVEN WONDERS ABOUT THE CHARACTER's impact on people: "Every day, something Superman hit me in the face. But is Superman's ubiquity just that—ubiquity? Saturation marketing? Or is there more to it? You wear a Superman shirt *because* . . . ? A Superman wristwatch *because* . . . ? A Superman belt buckle? Associating ourselves, *accessorizing* ourselves, with Superman and Superman imagery does *what* for us, *to* us, exactly? Does it have any meaning? It must, I decided" (2010: 21, emphasis in original). What drives this behavior? What does Superman do for people that makes them lifelong fans, willing to seek out others who are equally devoted to the character in order to express their affinity for him? The remainder of this book seeks some answers to those questions through the methods of folkloristics. I can best introduce my perspective through the words of comics writer Mark Waid. An editor challenged him to write a new origin for Superman that delved into the question of why Superman does what he does. Waid was already a tremendous fan of the character, possessing an encyclopedic knowledge of his history. Nonetheless, Waid learned quite a lot in the process of examining Superman's motives. He sums it up this way: "Superman stands revealed to me as a tool through which I can examine the balance of selflessness and self-interest in my own life, which is every bit as valuable a lesson as the ones he taught me years ago. He really does fight a never-ending battle" (Waid 2005: 10).

Superman, for Waid and for others, has become "goods to think" (Lévi-Strauss 1962). He is a tool with which to negotiate one's way through difficulties, providing a framework for handling new situations, as well as a way for coming to terms with life as it unfolds.

- 2 -

THREE CASES

HAVING DESCRIBED THE FOLKLORISTIC METHODS AND PERSPECTIVES, IT'S time to demonstrate them. Sandra Dolby writes that folklorists, as scholars who explore the lives of human beings, must insist upon "the examination of real examples rather than quantitative samples" (1996: 60). In the spirit of examining real examples, I offer here three case studies of people for whom Superman has become particularly meaningful: Jodi Chromey, Jeff Ray, and Kristina Johnson. They differ in range and scope; Jodi is less driven by Superman than are Jeff and Kristina, for example. These are brief demonstrations of the results of fieldwork, intended to serve as hints of things to come in the rest of the book.

In these three cases, I first noticed that to ask a person about Superman is to elicit a life story.[1] Together, these three life stories represent points on a continuum of affinity with Superman. To imagine this as a continuum, consider that to the far ends are extremes that are not entirely imaginary. On the one end lies apathy toward Superman, on the other lies a state that approaches identification. The attitude that troubles this continuum is dislike, or contempt. It is not my intention to delve into the psychology of these affinities to any great extent beyond what is revealed in the process of interviews, which would be one way to approach contempt. Instead, I have chosen to focus on what I consider positive attitudes toward Superman; this applies to the book generally, but I do give some attention to the notion that Superman is not a worthwhile fictional character to read about or watch (see Chapters 3 and 5). For now, I begin by looking somewhere in the middle of the continuum.

JODI CHROMEY

Jodi Chromey has a tattoo of the Superman chevron[2] on her sternum. She's had it for a few years, but she doesn't consider herself a true fan of Superman. She doesn't read the comics or watch the movies regularly, and she didn't keep up with the television shows focused on the character, such as *Lois and Clark: The New Adventures of Superman* and *Smallville,* as they aired. Yet she does have extensive discussions with her nephew about whether Batman or Superman is the better hero. Her tattoo, when visible, ensures that people will talk with her about the character. She also has a cookie jar shaped like a Superman bust. It's the first thing she sees when she comes downstairs in the morning. Interestingly, it is this cookie jar that has informed her mental image of the character. I asked her what actor or artist's portrayal of the character was most prominent in her mind. She told me, "When I think of Superman, I think of my cookie jar."

This conception of the character, based on the limited body of stories she has read and images drawn from popular culture, is nebulous, flexible, and idiosyncratic. When I interviewed her over the telephone, Jodi didn't talk much about particular stories or about the specifics—such as issue numbers, artists, writers, and editorial influence—that fans tend to discuss.

The tattoo's location between her breasts marks it as an index of her sexuality. She writes about it with some frequency on her weblog, *I Will Dare*[3] (though the relationship of her sexuality and her tattoo did not come up during our interview). She has written about the public perception of the tattoo; other people get a glimpse of it when she's out in public and will either request to see it (eliciting some embarrassment on both ends of the request) or will talk about it without including her in the conversation, per-haps thinking that she can't hear. A friend points out that it is a potentially intimidating mark on her body in an intimate situation. And it becomes an icebreaker when she's approached by men who wish to get to know her.

It seems doubtful that the tattoo was intended to emphasize her sexual-ity; she certainly never said so. She told me that she chose it because of she feels an affinity for the character. According to Clinton R. Sanders, tattoos are preeminently social markings. The choice to get one and the image that is chosen reflect a person's definition of self (Sanders 2008: 41, 45; Kuwahara 2005: 5). Jodi is tall, well over six feet. Superman's stature and physically imposing nature is often commented upon. While her similarity in stature to Superman may possibly be the source of her affinity for the character, it is not the reason she describes. She got the tattoo because of Superman's existential plight—he is alone among beings who are like him. He is an alien who looks human but isn't. For Jodi, this is part of the appeal. She is the sole offspring of her parents, although she has three half-sisters. She is like them in many ways yet ultimately different. And she felt different growing up with them. She sees in Superman someone who has to battle this difference every day of his life. The differences don't disappear, but they cease to be a primary concern for him. She writes, of Superman's solitude, "I think that's why Superman has always appealed to me. He is the only one of his kind, he doesn't fit in. It's like the very definition of loneliness. As a 6'5" woman who is the only child of her biological parents' union, I can relate" (Chromey 2009a).

Feeling an affinity for a character does not necessarily entail tattooing that character's symbol on one's body. Nor does it dictate the tattoo's location. If we wish to continue the folkloric approach, we need to compare Jodi's tattoo with others. This is relatively easy, in a depersonalized manner. The internet provides a variety of images of people's tattoos, and a quick survey reveals that the variation is astounding. Most common, it seems, are tattoos of the chevron on a person's shoulder or bicep—we'll see an example of this later in this chapter during a conversation with Kristina Johnson. This is a logical location, since the chevron and the character represent strength above all, and the upper arm connotes strength as well. It is most commonly a location for men to get tattooed; women more commonly get tattoos on their breast or hip (Sanders 2008: 47–48).

Tattoo variation ranges from what's depicted to where it's depicted. It seems that all parts of the body have been adorned with Superman images. The images themselves are most often the chevron, but some depict the full figure of the character, or busts, or images of Superman with other heroes. One variation depicts the chevron as if it lies beneath the person's skin, visible because the skin itself appears torn away—a use of negative space that at once gives the illusion that the wearer cannot be injured while making apparent that there's more to the person that the surface would suggest. There are further variations as well. Many tattoos consist of the chevron flanked or surrounded or beneath a series of Kryptonian letters, a variant of the tribal tattooing style.

Even when we stick to an examination of the basic chevron, we find variation. The first thing to vary is the color. The chevron may be done in full color, red and yellow—as Jodi's is—or in black alone. It may be personalized (there are common additions of flames or blood, the latter to resemble the cover image of *Superman* issue 75, in which Superman dies).

The Superman chevron seems a very rigid image, but it has changed over time. The current image is a pentangle containing a red S on a yellow background, with a red border. Yet this is rather different from the chevron as it appeared in the character's early years. The first published drawing showed a rounded, almost-triangular shape, with semicircles cut out near the top. It resembles a stone-carved arrowhead, notched just right for a rope to affix it to a piece of wood. However, this was on the cover of *Action Comics* 1. Within, the chevron was an isosceles triangle, pointing downward. By 1940, the chevron had become a pentangle in some versions, though this was not a permanent change. The evolution of the *S*-chevron is of interest to fans, and has been chronicled in detail.[4] The shape of the chevron itself is of importance in some interpretations of the character, particularly in the Christian analysis of Stephen Skelton (2006), who sees in the original shape a symbol of the trinity. The shift toward the more stylized, five-sided chevron is possibly related to the fact that such a distinct symbol is easily trademarked.

Tattoos, being a modification of the body, are intensely personal.[5] They are also often put on display. There is a tension between showing them and not showing them—a transformation of the individual-collective tension discussed in Chapter 1. A person with tattoos must decide what stories to tell about the reasons for getting them, and with whom to share this information. Much of the scholarship on tattoos is about the process of getting them, the status of those who are tattooed, and the status of tattooing as art. There remains a lot of work to be done on how people communicate with others about their tattoos (see Fedorenko, Sherlock, and Stuhr 1999: 110–14 for some examples of this). Jodi was not reticent to discuss the matter with me, despite the fact that we'd never met in person. Yet reading through her website revealed much more information than I could possibly have gleaned from our brief interaction. I had never broached the subject of the gender and sexuality issues brought to the foreground by the tattoo's location. Yet she writes about it with some regularity. She's a writer, so to some extent it might be expected for her to express these issues more fully in writing, where the distance of mediated, written words can facilitate expression.

Jodi's tattoo (which is one of six on her body; the others do not relate to Superman or to her identity in any way that she expressed to me) is a standard Superman chevron. It is about an inch-and-a-half wide, easily covered, and reflects an idiosyncratic affinity with the character. Nonetheless, Jodi appreciates other aspects of Superman, particularly his morality and powers. The debate regarding Batman spills over into her writing as well. In reviewing *All-Star Superman*, she writes: "But my absolute favorite part, the part that gets to the true crux of why Superman is the best and Batman is nothing but a Republican with a nice belt, well, I can't find that part anymore. But what it shows is Superman battling some villain, and the villain asks Superman why he keeps saving the human race when they're so damn annoying. 'Who am I to impose my morality on them?' Superman asks, and I had to bounce up and down in my chair chanting 'Yes, yes, yes.' It was such an awesome moment. It just shows what an intellectual Superman is, that he thinks about all the things he does and why he does them. Batman, on the other hand, is out for revenge and teaching Gotham City to be more like he thinks it should be" (Chromey 2009b).

Plenty of people disagree with Jodi's reading of Batman, of course, but her point about Superman is a common one, which has the strange position of also sitting at the center of a frequent complaint about him. She's writing about a conversation in *All-Star Superman* 9, in which Superman is criticized by other Kryptonians for not remaking Earth in his own image. One thing people find fascinating about Superman is that, despite his physical superiority, he chooses *not* to impose his will on humanity at large. He could take over the world, but he doesn't. The complaint flowing from this is that Superman, as the apex of moral rectitude, is boring. It's a superficial complaint, ignoring the numerous times that Superman has made morally questionable choices.[6] It also speaks to a different aesthetic; certain people prefer antiheroes, or at least heroes whose flaws overshadow their strengths.

The morality at the heart of the character is not the only aspect worth debating. When discussing the characters with children, Jodi can refer to their powers: "'If you were stuck in a fire who would you want to save you, Batman or Superman?' 'Superman,' he says without any hesitation.' "He can fly.' 'Ha,' I say and point at him. 'That's because Superman is better'" (Chromey 2008). But she can also point to a moral superiority, or at least a morality that matches her own. The character resonates in more than one way.

Jodi does not identify herself as a Superman fan. She was more interested in Wonder Woman as a child, and became fascinated by Superman in her twenties. She identifies with him in part because as Kent he is a reporter; Jodi studied journalism. She associates him with the First Amendment. Despite sharing a love for writing, she feels less of an affinity for the Kent side of the character. Her affection is for Superman. "The older I get, the more I like him, the more I identify with Superman," she told me. "I find the more I read, the more I identify. I'm the only one from my set of parents. He's just for me." Implicit in this statement is that this component resonates for her personally. She is fully aware of the fact that others find the character resonant, and she knows that, for many people, Superman fandom is deeply rooted and their knowledge of the character dwarfs her own.

If fandom is in part defined by a social component (Bacon-Smith 1992; Jenkins 1992; Kleefeld 2009), it is also defined by esoteric knowledge, as is any folk group (Brown 1997). Jodi lacks both the esoteric knowledge of the character and the social component that would define her as a fan. She admits as much; the character, however, is sufficiently important to her that she has modified her body with his emblem. This tattoo, in turn, has led her to reconsider her role in various situations. Having a tattoo marks a point in her life, but having the tattoo changes how people perceive her (Sanders 2008: 53). It is just like speaking an opinion in that respect. People must react to it.

So, Jodi's Superman chevron reflects her perception of herself, as a half-sister. Superman is alone; his status as an alien cements that facet, despite the existence of others who have arrived his home planet over the years. People who share this feeling of solitude are able to identify with that element of the character. But, interestingly, Mark Waid points out that Superman was never a character to be identified with in this manner: "Before about 1985, no one ever whined that they 'couldn't relate to Superman.' You weren't supposed to relate to Superman. That's what Clark was for. He was our touchstone. The half of Superman which readers can actually relate to because we all (Jesus, especially comics fans) want to believe that even though we may be put upon and bullied by the world from time to time, we know what those who pick on us or look down at us don't—that if they could see behind our glasses, they'd see a Superman" (Singh 2003). Waid's statement is not really testable, since we cannot conduct fieldwork in the past. We should, instead, consider his essay as an interpretation of the character. Yet Jodi does not identify with Clark Kent specifically. She identifies with Superman because, to her, the important elements are his morality and a feeling of solitude.

JEFF RAY

Superman's polysemy attracts a wide variety of fans. With Jodi, the character's singularity is a resonating factor. For Jeff Ray, a number of aspects come together to cement his interest. I met Jeff at a library at Indiana University. He worked at the circulation desk, and as I checked out some books he noticed Superman on a cover. He asked what I was doing, and I told him about this project. He said he really liked Superman, and wondered if I was doing anything with the Christopher Reeve films. He told me that his brother was handicapped, and the two of them really got to like Superman because of Christopher Reeve's accident; in 1995, the actor (who portrayed Superman in four films from 1978 to 1987) was paralyzed from the neck down in a horse riding accident. He told me a story that day, about the time he and his brother met Superman in Illinois:

"We made our mom take us to the Superman Celebration in Metropolis. And that's my . . . I was about eight, I think, and that's when I realized Superman wasn't real. It's because we were able to meet Superman at a local truck stop. He comes in, he's dressed as Superman, but he's got a moustache and a beer belly and a wedding ring. And even as an eight-year-old, you know, it didn't fool me. I was like, 'That's not Superman.' That was the day, I tell people, I realized my childhood was lost because I realized Superman wasn't real. I didn't care about Santa Claus or anything like that. But I realized Superman wasn't real. And I remember [*laughs*] my mom shut my fingers in the car door as he was walking out, I was trying to wave to him, and I was like, 'Superman, I need help!' And he didn't come to help me or anything. And I was like, 'Yeah, this guy's not real.'"

That realization did not, however, diminish his appreciation for the character. Jeff agreed to talk more about Superman, and we got together several times. Jodi is more interested in the comics than the television shows or films, but Jeff doesn't read comic books; his one brief attempt was in 1992, when he read the "Death of Superman" storyline, wherein a monster named Doomsday kills Superman in battle. It was a poor entry point: Jeff didn't like the story, and he hasn't looked into them since. "Doomsday ruined all comics for me," he said.

Jeff stated several times that, before we talked, he didn't realize how much he liked the character. He hadn't reflected on it much. The manifestation of his interest, it seems, waxes and wanes with the prominence of Superman in media, coinciding with events such as the development of a new feature film. He filled our conversations with references to the films, less frequently to television shows, and to Superman's appearance in other aspects of popular culture with which he is familiar. His thinking about Superman is grounded in the stories he loves, and he relates the ideas we discussed directly to scenes in the films.

Jeff told me, "One of my earliest memories as a child is, I had a Superman cape. I always used to put that on and jump off the couch and pretend I was flying. We had stuffed dogs, and we'd put it on the dog and pretend the dog was Super Dog. We loved Superman." The "we" is a reference to his brother, Joseph, who was born with cerebral palsy. "He's actually legally blind, too. Growing up, I don't necessarily know this as a fact, but I know that being handicapped he looked at Superman and wished he could do those things Superman could do. He really idolized Christopher Reeve, especially when

Christopher Reeve got in his accident and became paralyzed. He looked at
him as kind of a hero trying to overcome his paralysis and trying to live
his life handicapped. So it's just kind of ironic that his hero was Superman
growing up, and Superman became handicapped."

Joseph played a major role in Jeff's appreciation for the character, and
is in part responsible for his continued interest. "I thought at first it was
my age group [he was thirty years old when I interviewed him in 2011 and
2012], with the movies coming out, but no one my age really cares about it."
At an age when many young boys are discovering sports, Joseph couldn't
participate. So, Jeff played sports but also kept up with Superman because it
was something to do with his brother. And his brother was always watching
the movies.

Discussing 1978's *Superman: The Movie*, Jeff said, "Just everything from
the movie to the music is iconic. I still get . . . I was telling people that the
opening scene is just iconic, where they show the original comic. Then there's
the opening credits. I get goosebumps thinking about it. That was the scene
where me and my brother would just jump on the couch and pretend we
were flying." Jeff still watches the movies with some regularity. Although his
interest hasn't been reflective, it does evolve. His opinions on the movies have
changed, and he is aware of this: "It was really weird. As a kid, the second
one [*Superman II*, 1980] was always my favorite, and now as an adult, it's
the first one by far. As a kid, you know [director] Richard Lester came in
and completely changed the formula and the timing of the film. It became a
comedic film. In the first one the only comedic aspect was Gene Hackman.
Christopher Reeve was a really good actor and he had his moments, but
comic relief was Lex Luthor and Otis. The second and third one with Lester,
the whole thing just kind of seemed . . ."

"Slapstick," I said.

"Yeah, exactly. Slapstick. But I liked it as a kid. The second one has a lot
more action. The first one is a really great story and really well done. As a
kid, you don't really appreciate that 'cause it's kind of slow. I would always
fast-forward a lot, especially through the Smallville things. It dragged on and
I didn't like when his dad died."

The death of Jonathan Kent has always troubled him. It was a deciding
factor in his choice to stop watching the television show *Smallville*. "I quit
watching after the episode when his dad died. I tried watching after that,
and that was when it just went downhill. I don't know if this is just weird
. . . If you look at it, Superman lost his parents, and he lost his adopted dad
on Earth, so I don't know if that's why me and my brother related with him,

too. It's because he didn't have that in his life, either. I don't know if that's coincidence, or . . ."

He trailed off, and I didn't fill in the silence. He moved on quickly. He identifies with Superman because the absent fathers reflect his own parents' divorce and the subsequent absence of his own father for several years. While that aspect of the character resonates for him, he doesn't like being confronted with the trauma of it happening.

Jeff sees a sadness in Superman, one related to the character's loneliness. To Jeff, this sadness is connected to the character's mythical complexity: "When you look at the Superman story, you think it's simple, but it's really not. I didn't realize how much Superman correlates with the story of Jesus. It's the journey of becoming and knowing who you are, losing your parents, they didn't really show it in the first movie. He does his pilgrimage, and it's the same amount of time Jesus did it. There are a lot of religious aspects to it.

"There's nothing like that in [other superhero] stories. There's not this religious background, where it's deep in the background, but if you study and look at it, there are a lot of comparisons, but you don't find that in Spider-Man. Just because they are human. While Superman may not be human, he's not vulnerable, but everyone around him is. So he can never get close to them. That to me is one of the saddest things about Superman. It's one of the saddest superhero stories around. Because he's all alone. He has no one else here like him.

"Like they're saying, it was in *Kill Bill*.[7] There's a really good monologue. I love that speech where [Bill] says: 'Batman is Bruce Wayne's alter ego. Spider-Man is Peter Parker's alter ego, but Superman's alter ego is Clark Kent. That's his made-up persona.' So, to me, it's really sad 'cause he is all alone, he doesn't have anyone else to talk to. It's kind of cool in the Singer movie [*Superman Returns*, 2006] when they have him flying above Earth, just sitting there with his eyes closed, just listening. There's so much he could do. But there's not really enough of him. Just having all that power, and you can stop some things, but you can't do everything. He hears everything going on, but he can only do so much."

He recognizes some of the same elements that appeal to Jodi Chromey, but their resonance for him is not as clear. I asked whether or not he feels lonely. He said no immediately. Then, after a few seconds' thought, he amended his statement:

"Sometimes lonely, but not really. I don't know, kind of. I have friends, but I only had one girlfriend in my entire life. I feel like I'm alone because, of all my friends, I'm the only one who likes Superman. When I watch the movie, I'm usually watching it alone. The day that Christopher Reeve died, I rewatched *Superman* and I just started crying. In my opinion, he was the perfect Clark Kent-Superman."

Throughout our conversation, Jeff returned to the same topics. Christopher Reeve. 9/11. Helping people. The first arises from his association of the actor with his brother. The second arises because he recognized it as marking a turning point in larger social discourse about heroism. The third is the seat of his conception of the character—Superman's defining trait. I asked Jeff what, if anything, about Superman could not change. He said, "Truth, justice, and the American way. That he's morally good. Always does the right thing. I think that's one thing I like about him—there's not a bad bone in his body, unless you get red kryptonite in him. I didn't always have a father figure in my life, and he's kind of like the father I wish I had. He'd be there for you, you know."

A month after our first interview, he suggested I come back for a lengthier talk. When I did, I was surprised at what happened. Even before I had the chance to turn on my recorder, Jeff asked me about how comic book writers approached the character—did they come to it cold, having just been given some research material in the form of old Superman comics, or did they have a system for the character worked out already? He was getting at an interesting idea—are Superman comics writers Superman fans? The answer is generally yes, but not always (Mark Waid, whose perspective on Superman will be important in Chapter 3, is a good example of a Superman fan who went on to become a Superman writer; Josh Elder, Chris Roberson, and J. Michael Straczynski, all quoted in this book, are others). That wasn't the end of Jeff's inquiry. It soon became apparent that he hadn't invited me back because he had important philosophical points to make about Superman. Instead, he really just wanted to talk about more with someone who had thought about Superman like he had—philosophically, emotionally, intellectually. My initial interview had reminded Jeff of how deeply he appreciated the character, and since then he had begun to reflect on that appreciation and the various meanings of Superman. To this end, he told me, he had engaged his friends and coworkers in conversation. These conversations, however, were not satisfactory. He didn't find a matching enthusiasm. So, when I came to get some books, he invited me back.

My second visit was more a conversation than an interview, and it lasted much longer. I talked as much (perhaps more) than I listened. He asked a lot about comic books and about my own interpretations of Superman's motivations and what he should be like. He asked me what I had asked other people I've interviewed for this project. But one question seemed of particular interest to him—namely, what did the writers have to say about Superman's teenage years after the death of his father and before he moves to Metropolis to assume his role as a superhero? "What was he like, in between those years?" Jeff asked.

Jeff was trying to fill in the twelve-year gap in the narrative told in *Superman: The Movie*. In essence, he was trying to learn the story of Superman as a hero's journey. Scholars such as Lawrence W. Levine (1992: 1395) have noted the tendency of audience members to fill in gaps in a text, and that this is often a central aspect of folklore: "In this manner, folklore encourages listeners to become not merely participants but even creators of meaning when the message is not explicit; to project themselves into the text in order to invest the empty spaces with meaning (Levine 1992: 1386; see Utley 1945 for a similar discussion on the topic of the Bible). Yet the pervasive presence of popular culture, the tendency of writers, producers, and editors of a story like Superman to fill in these gaps in an official way, can discourage this sort of audience participation. The television show *Smallville* engaged in precisely this sort of activity focused on Clark Kent's teenage years, and Jeff found the result unsatisfying, albeit enjoyable. I had mentioned an interview with the writer Josh Elder, which prompted Jeff to ask, "Did you ever bring that up to him about his interpretation of what he went through in those years? Maybe he wasn't always this, 'I'm here for good and I should be saving other people's lives.' Because in the original *Superman* movie, you know, when he was a kid right before his father died he seemed kind of angry. Because he had all these powers and he couldn't show them off. And it wasn't like he wanted to show them off to save people. He wanted to show them off to get the girl, Lana Lang. Because everyone saw him as being this wuss nerd and he's like, 'No, I'm all powerful, what are you talking about?'"

Jeff was searching for the development of Superman's morality and the means by which he discovered his role in the world. "I want to see him progress to Superman in the suit," he told me. Although *Smallville* dramatized precisely this progression, it remained unsatisfactory, possibly because it took too long. Jeff tried to watch that series' final episode, wherein Clark Kent finally dons the traditional costume and becomes Superman, but stopped before it was over because he didn't like it. Our second conversation seems to confirm my idea that he didn't like being confronted with the dramatization of being separated from a father figure. He was also aware that the mood of the show changed after Superman's father died. As I learned, he thinks that the death of Clark Kent's father should have ended the show. "To me, it doesn't feel like *Smallville* anymore, because he's not a child." In Jeff's view, the death of Jonathan Kent should make Clark grow up, and being grown up, he should become Superman.[8] The fact that the show took five more years to make Clark Kent become Superman is disappointing to him.

He again stressed how much he liked the character, and how little he had thought about it prior to our interview. I asked him if this was a renewed interest, or if it had been there all along and had simply gone unnoticed. He said, "That's what's weird. I don't think it's a newfound appreciation. I think it is more of a self-realization where. . . .[9] When you get older, you tend to look back on your life, and you start to reflect more. After we talked, when you kind of made me think about this stuff, and I started reflecting, and I was like . . . I was in this history club growing up and I was like, 'Yeah, I'm in it, whatever,' but I was thinking about it in my life and it was a huge part. When I started thinking about it, I thought, 'That's a really huge part of my life. And to this day, when I watch the [*Superman*] movies, I get goosebumps. It makes me want to be a kid and I want to stand up on the couch and jump off the couch and act like I'm flying. I think that doing this interview just made me realize that I might be one of these guys in the future who has a whole room for Superman one day, you know. I might be that guy. If I had disposable income, I would buy a Superman outfit. I would buy one of the costumes from the movie."

Here Jeff charts a course of interest in the character that springs from the realization of a lifelong appreciation. Jeff insists on emphasizing the realization of his love for the character, and there seems to be no need to argue the point. However, that does not mean that realization cannot change the nature of the appreciation of the character—or perhaps the affinity for him. With Jodi, getting a tattoo cemented an affinity, but it also led to written explorations of public displays of the self, especially in presentation of sexuality. A change in discourse—getting a tattoo—causes a subsequent, and perhaps unintentional, change in the topic, from existential to sexual. With Jeff, a change in the discourse—transforming from unreflexive to reflexive—leads to a change in the topic: Superman shifts from being an examination of relationships with other people to an examination of how one finds a place in the working world.

The recurrent topics of our first conversation were largely unexplored when we met for our second talk. Jeff was even more focused on Superman's sadness. He said that Superman is alone, but a more apt term might be *unique*, and that uniqueness comes with an existential burden that can lead to depression. In Jeff's interpretation, Superman craves the company of those like him, and in this Jeff's affinity resembles Superman's existential uniqueness. Jeff's continued interest in the character derives from his own uniqueness within the circle of his friends, which comes in part from his appreciation for Superman. When we talked, he was at a crucial moment in his life. He had recently finished school, and though he worked in his field—he has a master's degree in library science—he was in a position, he told me, that offered little opportunity for advancement. Something needed to change soon, and our conversations possibly offered an opportunity to examine the notion of change in his own life.

Jeff had been among other students, and now needed to leave that realm for the more solitary job search. This would explain his curiosity about precisely the same moment in Superman's life, when he must make the decision about how to proceed at a time when, after the death of his father, things must change for him. Beyond the simple catalyst of our conversations, his situation in life at that moment gives the character new resonance.[10]

KRISTINA JOHNSON

I met Kristina Johnson at the Superman Celebration in 2010. She has two Superman tattoos, one on her wrist and one on her shoulder. She placed the wrist tattoo high enough so that jewelry wouldn't cover it.[11] She got this tattoo in 2006. It wasn't her first tattoo; she'd gotten the Superman chevron on her upper arm when she was eighteen. The wrist tattoo shows the Kryptonian symbol for *hope* as depicted in the television show *Smallville*. We talked for a bit at the Celebration, but we further communicated via e-mail, since she had recently lost her hearing. As with many of my interviews, I began by asking her why she likes Superman. She wrote:

> My attachment to Superman runs kind of deep, and I have struggled through a couple of very hard times with the help of Superman. My mother died when I was a toddler, and my father has always been emotionally unavailable. In general, I didn't have much guidance, and the social structure of my family is a pretty big mess. I think I've always been a "seeker" type of person, always trying to find a role model. I was very close with my grandmother, but she died suddenly when I was 15 (I'm 32 now [in 2011]), which was very hard on me because she was kind of the glue that kept me from falling apart. As any teen does, I was struggling with identity issues and typical teen

'fitting in' issues. My grades suffered, and I became very depressed to the point of considering suicide. It was about that time when the TV show *Lois & Clark* started, and that's when I became a die-hard Supermaniac. I don't know exactly why the show grabbed me at just the right time and in just the right way to really change my outlook. As "super" as Superman is, he also is very human and has the same insecurities and struggles with making the right decisions. For lack of any consistent role model, I substituted Superman. Whatever I may struggle with, I can find guidance through the ideals of Superman. Cheesy? Maybe, but it's what works for me.

Kristina lived in Connecticut, and there she had trouble finding people with whom she could share her enthusiasm for Superman. But unlike Jeff Ray, she sought out people online. When she found online communities, it was "a dream come true." She is currently a member of, she estimates, a dozen online message boards, but only participates in two or three with regularity, including the Superfriends of Metropolis.[12] In addition to meeting for the weekend of the Superman Celebration, she also extends her association with many of these people to other times of the year. She writes, "Any one of us will tell anybody who asks that we're all family. We are supportive of each other's successes and hardships. We are connected in many other ways than just being Superman fans, and we talk about all kinds of stuff besides superheroes and comics. We arrange all kinds of meet-ups throughout the year to stay in touch. Many of the members have become the very best of friends, and I certainly have gained so much from having met these people. It was shortly after the 2008 Celebration (my first trip to Metropolis) when my health took a very harsh turn and I lost my hearing. I have several other neuropathies that affect my balance and the use of my hands/arms. I also have numbness throughout my head/face and sometimes severe muscle spasms that cause joint pain in my neck and shoulders. The people of the forum, whom I had only met once just a couple months before, were (and still are) my biggest source of support with regard to my hearing loss and physical limitations."

For some people, such as Kristina, the social world that exists with Superman at its center can be more important than the character himself. Nonetheless, the character is still important. I asked Kristina which version of the character she regards as definitive. She replied, "I grew up with Chris Reeve as Superman. When you say Superman, I always picture him. He was modest, and understated, not a forceful personality in the suit. In the years

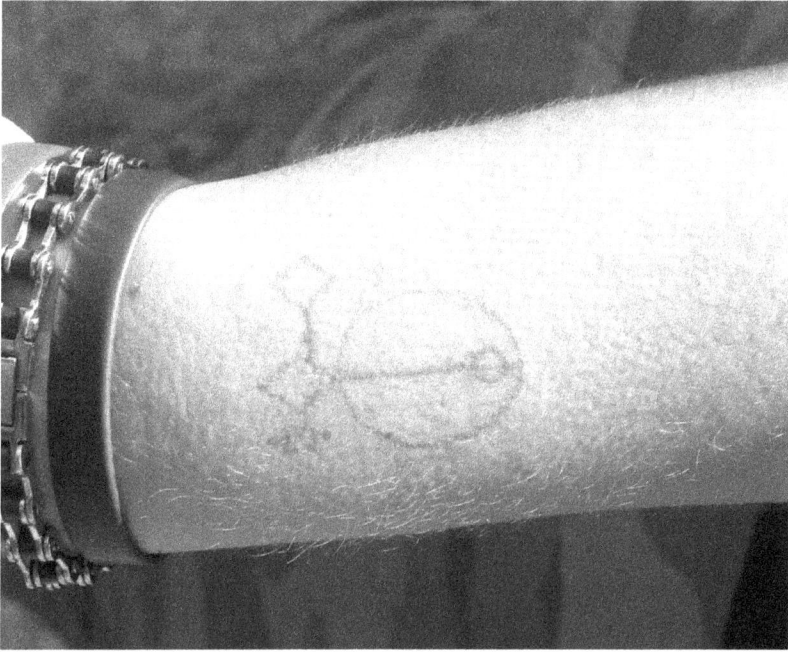

Kristina's wrist tattoo: the Kryptonian character meaning "hope," as seen in *Smallville*. June 2010.

following his accident that left him paralyzed, Reeve became a real-life Superman by doing so much to promote the research that has helped improve the quality of life for people with paralysis."

Her statement has several components worth unpacking. First, Christopher Reeve's portrayal is important because it was the one she became familiar with as a child. She grew up with the movies; she considers them to belong to her generation (she acknowledges that a new generation will have a new Superman; her conceptualization of myth allows for reinterpretation with the passage of time).[13] Second, as an adult, she can look at the actor in the role and evaluate the performance. Reeve didn't attempt to put himself in the role, but instead allowed the character to dictate his performance. Acknowledging the role of the actor in creating the character, she also looks beyond the character to the life of the actor. This is common enough, especially with Superman. Reeve himself noted how he became identified with the role in a manner far beyond typecasting. A particularly telling anecdote in his book *Still Me* (1998), about a trip he made to Hollywood after his paralysis, is worth quoting:

During my stay in Hollywood I entered hotels and buildings through garages, kitchens, and service elevators, and met cooks, waiters, chambermaids, and maintenance crews. Many of them said they were praying for me. Others looked me right in the eye and said, "We love you, Superman. You're our hero." At first I couldn't believe they meant it. Then I realized they were looking past the chair and honoring me for a role that obviously had real meaning for them. I didn't feel patronized in any way. Clearly a part I had played twenty years ago was still valued. The fact that I was in a wheelchair, unable to move below my shoulders, and dependent on the support of others for almost every aspect of my daily life had not diminished the fact that I was—and always would be—Superman. (Reeve 1998: 194)

Despite this conflation of actor and role, Reeve felt himself to be merely a "temporary custodian" (1998: 200) of Superman, and, like Kristina, he notes that the character should be interpreted anew from generation to generation. In *Still Me*, Reeve stresses that the Superman he portrayed was right for the time, though not for everyone all the time.

I bring up Reeve in part in reaction to Kristina's reference to him, and in part because his portrayal became relevant in light of her struggles. For Reeve, the most important aspect of the character is not heroism, but friendship. He refers to the scene in the 1978 film where Lois Lane interviews Superman on a balcony. There's little braggadocio there, he notes, little of the macho heroes of the previous decades. Instead, in the late 1970s, Superman represented a change in the masculine image. "For me this scene illustrates the difference between the two eras. When Lois Lane asks, 'Who are you?' Superman simply responds, 'A friend.' I felt that was the key to the part. I tried to downplay being a hero and emphasize being a friend" (1998: 196).

This is precisely what Kristina was looking for. As a teenager, she found that friendship in the character. As an adult, she used the character to find others with the same interests. She has become good friends with Michelle Lyzenga, whom she met at the Superman Celebration in 2008. I met these two women together (and will have more to say about Michelle's appreciation for Superman in Chapter 4). I bring her into the story at this point because Kristina's friendship with her has overcome the distance between them. When they met, Kristina lived in Connecticut and Michelle lived in Indiana. They kept in touch online, especially through social media such as Facebook, and Michelle is one of the people whom Kristina meets at times outside the Celebration.

Tattoo placement and content is markedly gendered. Clinton R. Sanders notes that women most frequently tend to get tattooed on their chests, while men get tattooed on their arms (2008: 50–51). Kristina placed a tattoo of the Superman chevron on her upper arm. Further, according to Sanders, women get tattoos as decorations, while men get them as markers of identity, particularly of masculinity. He describes three meanings of tattoos: they mark affiliations, symbolize a person's unconventionality, and serve as personal decorations (2008: 57). Sanders stresses the social aspects of tattooing, and rightly so, but he largely ignores the private, though visible, component of having a tattoo. He comes closest to addressing it when he concludes his chapter on "Becoming and Being a Tattooed Person" with the following: "The decision to acquire a tattoo is not only a decision to alter one's physical appearance; it is a choice to change how the person experiences him or herself and, in turn, how he or she will be defined and treated by others" (2008: 58). Sanders, approaching the subject from a sociological perspective, is right to emphasize the interpersonal orientation of the tattoo. Nonetheless, the intrapersonal experience of the self is critical to understanding the tattoos described here,[14] and though this is not just relevant to the genre of tattoos, its importance there is obvious. Mary Kosut, in her examination of the narratives people tell about their tattoos, points out that tattoos can be a message to the self (2000: 86). Everyone I've spoken to about tattoos has stressed their own perception of the tattoo above the perception of others, in part to decorate the self. The tattoos of Superman, I have found, go beyond aesthetic interests. They function as communication with the self, of controlling the self, as Michael Featherstone noted (2002: 2). Kristina makes this point with a comment about her shoulder tattoo: "The \S/ on my upper arm was the first tattoo. I picked the location for pretty much the same reason as the one on my wrist. I wanted to be able to see it. I'll never get a tattoo anywhere on my body where it won't be visible to me."

Having the symbol of hope tattooed on her wrist, where she can always see it, represents both her response to her own struggle with hardship and the support of the community she found through love of Superman, a community that has embraced her with open arms. The tattoo's visibility means that Kristina intends to deliberately communicate its message beyond herself. Although she only mentions the visibility to herself, the visible tattoo is always part of social interaction (Kosut 2000). It is *hope* that, in part, enables her to cope with newfound difficulties such as her neuropathy. Her Kryptonian tattoo, visible on her arm, makes a statement about her condition as well; her hearing impairment inevitably comes up in social interaction with new people, though it is something she could conceivably try to hide. Tattooing, as we have seen, can be a way to express a person in control of her body, often in the wake of physical or emotional trauma. Having a tattoo on publicly visible skin makes sure Kristina won't hide her condition. People ask about tattoos, and the reasons for getting them. By referring to her tattoo in the context of her neuropathy, Kristina is taking control of both her own body and of the narrative of her own life. She is exceedingly confident that she can find treatments to render many of her difficulties irrelevant. She is learning American Sign Language, despite neurological issues that affect her use of her hands, so that she can continue to communicate. To this end, she has even organized online ASL practice sessions with some of her friends. In 2011, she moved from Connecticut to Indianapolis, where she was accepted into the Museum Studies program at Indiana University-Purdue University Indianapolis. At a time when hope might be hard to come by, she finds it in the story she has been thinking about for years. The wrist tattoo, though added prior to her troubles, serves as a positive way to ground her ongoing story in her body (see Kosut 2000: 90). It can also be seen as a response to the changes that her neuropathy effects on her body. The tattoo's permanence subverts her neuropathic degeneration. While her body changes beyond her ability to keep it the way she wants, the tattoos—marks of her choosing—remain.

As with Jeff and Jodi, there has been a demonstrable evolution in Kristina's thinking about Superman. With hope as a thematic thread, we can see that Superman has served as a role model, showing her the way one ought to respond to adversity. He filled a role once occupied by her grandmother. But there are other facets to her appreciation for the character. One is obviously the notion of a being with godlike abilities who nonetheless has similar "insecurities and struggles" as she does.[15] His struggles affirm her normalcy, assuaging her "fitting in issues." But as her struggles change, so does the hope she finds. Now, with health issues, she looks to Superman as not only an inspiration through the stories told about him, but through the help provided by a social circle that would not exist without him. The online communities she has joined provide her with the support she needs to persevere through her difficulties.

GOOD TO THINK WITH

Through the examples in this chapter, we have seen that contemplation of Superman is also in part contemplation of the self and the roles that one can find in society. With Jodi and Kristina, this contemplative function has been made manifest in their tattoos, which alter the body as a means for marking the self at a specific point in life, but, inevitably, alter the presentation of the body to the self and to others. Marking the body in this way leads to further contemplation of the self. For Jeff, this contemplation has no outward manifestation. I have never seen him wear a Superman shirt, though he has a single box of memorabilia he keeps under his bed. If it does become visible, he said that it would be in the form of a collection, the display of which alters the environment to match the mental conditions of the individual in a specific way.

By looking at tattoos, we are reminded that superhero stories are all about bodies (Bukatman 2002). The superhero origin is often a tale of transformation from an average or below-average physical stature to an unrealistic physique. The tales themselves are stories of physical prowess leading to battle—a contest between bodies. Other stories frequently depict the transformation of the superhero body, sometimes into something grotesque (there are, for example, stories in which Superman is transformed into a monster). The body is on display in superhero stories, so much so that Michael Chabon has noted that the superhero is in effect naked (2008: 20). Aaron Taylor notes much the same thing, but goes further to remark on the distorted image presented in the art of superhero comics. Taylor sees the representations of the body in superhero comics as complex, as strangely other: "The superhero comic is a literature that represents a site of departure for typical ways of thinking about and categorizing the body" (2007: 347). The superhero body, according to Taylor, is fractured in the process of storytelling because of the framing of the comic panels (which rarely portray the entire body of any character), but it is reassembled through the process of reading. The reader becomes an active participant in not only the story but in the construction of the superhero body. Thus, the superhero body can be a projection of the readers' bodies, particularly when it comes to gender (2007: 348–49).

In the three case studies presented in this chapter, we see a very different notion of the use of superheroes in regard to the audience's bodies. For Jodi Chromey and Kristina Johnson, Superman is relevant in relation to their bodies not because of the specific physical characteristics depicted in the complex of stories about him (which include the life of an actor who portrayed him), but because he allows for the contemplation of one's self and body in relation to familial, social, economic, and pathological realities. They are not projecting themselves onto Superman's body or seeing how they wish to be; they are, instead, seeing possibilities. And that, in the end, is what this initial foray into case studies has been: a glimpse into the possibilities opened up by fieldwork and the folkloristic perspective on Superman. From here, we move on to examine how people use Superman to craft their lives in ways outside the body, looking at philosophy and, preliminarily, morality.

TRUTH MEANS MANY THINGS

LOOKING AT SUPERMAN FROM A FOLKLORISTIC PERSPECTIVE ENCOURAGES us to ask what people do with the character in their own lives, as opposed to looking at the official stories told about him in mass media. To answer this question, I asked people what aspects of the character they admired. The most common response singled out Superman's morality. This led to another question: How has Superman's morality influenced your own? People had trouble answering this question, for a variety of reasons. For one thing, the application of one's morality is a difficult thing to make concrete. Most people aren't required to make moral decisions on a regular basis. In this chapter, I will explore some specifics regarding how people expressed the influence Superman has had in their lives, and in particular through a conversation with comics writer Josh Elder. To set up a context for understanding their answers, I want to examine a philosophical approach to understanding fiction, and for that I will use Hans Vaihinger's attention to the useful fiction, what he referred to as the mode of "as if."[1]

Vaihinger synthesizes a great deal of previous philosophical scholarship on the value of fictions; "namely, that 'As If,' i.e. appearance, the consciously-false, plays an enormous part in science, in world-philosophies and in life" (1911: xli). These fictions are indirect routes to philosophical, mathematical, scientific, and legal goals; they are make-believe in the service of philosophy, and Vaihinger's philosophy is made concrete and grounded as we spend time "finding our way about more easily in this world" (1911: 15). He includes all of religion in the "as if" mode, seeing value in the thought process though not subscribing to it himself. Following Kant, he even bases true morality on fictions of this kind. In other words, our highest ideals come from the fictions (not always stories, but often enough) we create. Superman is one such fiction. If the value of Superman as such a fiction were not obvious from the stories themselves, it will become so in the way people put the stories to use.

Scholars such as Sigmund Freud (1989) and Joseph Campbell (1959) have picked up this idea of "as if" and applied it to mythology. Following Campbell, we might consider mythology as akin to play, as Campbell does when he argues for it as the basis for the meaning-function of myth. By operating in the "as if" mode, myth operates the same way play does.[2] Campbell describes the realm of myth as "the world of gods and demons, the carnival of their masks and the curious game of 'as if' in which the festival of the lived myth abrogates all the laws of time, letting the dead swim back to life, and the 'once upon a time' become the very present" (1959: 21). Campbell suggests that "such a highly played game of 'as if' frees our mind and spirit, on the one hand, from the presumption of theology, which pretends to know the laws of God, and, on the other, from the bondage of reason, whose laws do not apply beyond the horizon of human experience" (1959: 28). The issue Campbell doesn't confront is whether or not this sort of play is acknowledged as such. It is an important issue for Vaihinger, who writes that creators must consciously distinguish their fictions from reality, and that "as practical fictions we leave them all intact; they perish only as theoretical truths" (1911: 49). If fictions are not acknowledged as such, they become hypotheses and thus inhibit real philosophy. If the analogy becomes perceived as reality instead of as fiction, then fictions cease to be useful. "Man lives by imagination," writes Havelock Ellis (1923: 140), but only so long as it is recognized as such.

The notion of imagination being tied to the "as if" mode has been applied to play. Lawrence K. Frank, writing in "The Validity of Play," characterizes imaginary play as a way for children to pare down the world to a manageable size—the "as if" principle in application. In play, a child builds up an "'as if' world" that results in self-discovery (Frank 1979: 73). According to Frank, adolescents and adults can also turn to this sort of activity as recreation. This will become relevant in Chapter 4 as we take a look at the Superman Celebration.

More recently, Michael Saler has explored the "as if" mode in studying both the authors and fans of popular fiction (namely, the works of Arthur Conan Doyle, H. P. Lovecraft, and J. R. R. Tolkien). He refers to "modern enchantment," a response to the disenchantment produced by the Enlightenment worldview. For Saler, the virtual worlds in which certain people take part allow for a "strategy of embracing illusions while acknowledging their artificial status" (Saler 2012: 13). In this, Saler aligns with Vaihinger; both remind us that fiction can be useful. We will return to Saler and to the relationship of play and myth in the form of ritual in Chapter 4 as we look at the participants in a festival devoted to Superman, and to "as if" in general when examining its role in myth in the conclusion of this book. Vaihinger included science among the endeavors in which the useful fiction has been successfully employed, and to that field we now turn.

SUPERMAN AND SCIENCE

According to Vaihinger, the willingness to acknowledge the fictiveness of an idea means that, in the final equation, the "as if" component will be jettisoned in favor of reality. He was working, largely, within the realms of science and law, where the maintenance of the fictive frame, once its point had been made, would prove detrimental to behavior. The notion of Superman has inspired a number people to pursue science as a career.[3] In the early twenty-first century, a number of popular presses discovered that readers enjoyed seeing how popular movie and television franchises explored academic issues such as philosophy, psychology, and science. Superman proved to be an ideal focal point for all of these subjects, and especially for science.

Three notable books utilize superheroes to demonstrate scientific principles. James Kakalios, in *The Physics of Superheroes*, derives lessons in physics from the operations of superheroes, lessons that he has used in his own classroom. Kakalios deals with Superman in only a few chapters. *The Science of Superheroes*, by Lois Gresh and Robert Weinberg, likewise devotes little of its space to Superman. *The Science of Superman* by Mark Wolverton, however, is solely focused on aspects of Superman. Interestingly, the three books take different stances on the relationship of real science to superheroes. Kakalios, for example, wants only to educate us. He's willing to allow for a singular miracle that grants superheroes powers if that will then render physics interesting to his students. In arguing for the validity of his method, he points out that his students' need for attention to "real-world" application of science and math vanishes the moment he declares that they're going to understand principles of inertia and friction by studying Superman or the Flash (2009: 2). This is the philosophy of "as if" in action, demonstrating the value of fictions not only as a method of thinking, but also as a means of maintaining interest.

Gresh and Weinberg seek to demonstrate that none of Superman's powers are feasible for humanity to attain. Wolverton wants to show just the opposite; he writes as if everything Superman can do in the comics will be made possible some day through a combination of evolution and technological advancement. This notion of humanity becoming like Superman also inspired writer Grant Morrison, who has taken a caption from issue 1 of *Superman* to heart: "It is not too far-fetched to predict that someday our very own planet may be people entirely by Supermen!" (quoted in Morrison 2011: 114). Morrison looks to the ideas of the comics from decades past and sees them as possibilities. He goes on: "The superheroes may have their greatest value in a future where real superhuman beings are searching for role models. When the superhumans of tomorrow step dripping from their tanks, they could do much worse than to look to Superman for guidance" (2011: 116).[4] Wolverton and Morrison have taken the "as if" component of fiction, of Superman fiction in particular, and used it not as a logistical device for understanding the world but as a paradigm for the pursuit of scientific and philosophical progress.

MAKING SUPERMAN REAL

I've talked to a number of people about how Superman has influenced them in an attempt to elicit memories of particular instances when they thought about the character as part of either an ethical or moral decision. It was difficult to get people to offer specifics. Answers tended to be general; comics writer and editor Chris Roberson's reply (via e-mail) was typical:

> I don't know that I can point to a specific circumstance where the example of Superman led me to make a decision or to choose a particular course of action. To do so would be like asking a fish to point out his favorite drop of water. He can't, because he is surrounded by it to such an extent that he doesn't even notice it anymore, and that's what it's like for me and Superman's influence. He was one of the most powerful examples of morality and fairness that I had growing up, so much so that I think he provides a huge part of the foundation on which my sense of right and wrong is based.

I contacted Roberson because, at the time, he was writing the monthly *Superman* comic. His appreciation for the character runs deep. In an interview with the *Statesman*, Roberson made the following comment: "I believe in Superman the way a lot of people believe in Jesus . . . I believe that he is real and that he matters. The fact that he's fictional doesn't really enter into it."[5] This comment was picked up by many news sources related to comic books. Roberson was asked about it during another interview, and he expanded upon his initial statement:

> The fact that they're made up doesn't mean that they're not real. They're fictional, but they matter. . . . Far be it from me to judge anyone else's beliefs, but you could make the case that a lot of fervently

held—and for many centuries—beliefs were made up and now they matter. I feel the same way about Santa Claus. I mean Santa Claus is a thing where we collective know that he doesn't exist, or at least everybody over the age of eight, but we make him exist because of the way we act and the things that we do.[6] We do the things necessary to make Santa Claus real. And I think Superman is important because of what he stands for. Not . . . not, 'Will Superman save me in a burning building?' I questioned a lot of the discussion that happened after 9-11. About like, 'I wish there was really a Superman in the world who could have stopped this.'[7] Because you're thinking about it backwards, you're thinking about it wrong. Superman exists to motivate us to do better. Not to save us, because he doesn't exist! Anybody that has read enough Superman comics never has to pause to think, 'What Superman would do in this situation?' I mean we should all have WWSD bracelets that we wear, because you *know* what Superman would do. You know when faced with any moral dilemma or any ethical quandary what would Superman do. It's obvious. Whether or not we choose to do it, we have Superman there as an example to lead us.[8]

Roberson made these remarks in response to the question of why he was qualified to write Superman stories. By stating that he reveres the character, he was reassuring fans of his qualifications to write the comic book.[9] He implied that his consideration of the character and the themes of the stories is part of what makes him qualified. "He shows us how to be better people ourselves by being the best person he can be" (2011: 26).

Roberson's statement that people "do the things necessary to make Santa Claus real" implies that he thinks we should do this for Superman as well. The choice of Santa Claus is interesting in this context, largely because the similarities between Santa Claus and Superman have come up elsewhere. I first encountered the comparison when Jeff Ray mentioned that learning Superman wasn't a real being constituted the "end" of his childhood. He placed it in the same categories of revelation as learning that Santa Claus isn't real. Later, I found a similar statement by Superman writer Mark Millar, in the introduction to *Superman vs. Hollywood* (2008: V). These men had believed Superman was real during the early years of their childhood. Mark Waid (1993) lists some of the superficial similarities between the two characters—a home in the arctic, unbelievable powers, and an effect on children. In the comics, even in the television show *Smallville*, Superman sometimes performs the duty of Santa Claus by delivering presents to children around the world ("Metropolis Mailbag," *Superman*, vol. 2, no. 64; "Lexmas," *Smallville* episode 5.9).

There is a difference, however. When Roberson mentions that we do the things necessary to make Santa Claus real, he is no doubt referring to the fact that parents sustain the illusion for their children. They sometimes equivocate when asked directly about Santa's existence. They discipline their children by using threats about Santa delivering coal instead of presents. Above all, they put on a show to demonstrate Santa's presence in the house by placing presents under a tree and eating cookies left out by their children. They act as if he is real so that their children will believe. With Superman, this is not the case.[10] Yet there is still an effect on the lives of people who appreciate the character. What's unique here is the response to the argument that the fictional quality of Superman makes him irrelevant. Roberson argues that many figures are believed in but are not real (he's talking about legends); regardless of fictiveness, it's the way they affect reality that matters.

Roberson's comments point to the level of saturation Superman stories have attained in his life. In fact, this saturation makes it difficult to pinpoint any memories. The character's influence isn't even noticeable. The phrase "What would Superman do?" has become common enough, yet it's still hard to pinpoint situations in which it is applied. I found a couple of examples of specific personal experience narratives about the moral influence of Superman. The first is a story told by writer J. Michael Straczynski when interviewed about his writing career in 2008. At one point, the interviewer asks Straczynski about acquiring a piece of artwork by Superman artist Curt Swan. After describing the first piece he bought, Straczynski tells the following story:

> One time, at Chicago Comic Con, I heard someone shout "Stop him! Stop him!" and saw a guy [a thief] running down the aisle in my direction. The crowd split like the Red Sea and I helped tackle him, holding him down for the cops. At one point the organizer came over to the shoplifter and told him the guy from *Babylon 5* [a television show Straczynski created] just tackled him. Suffice to say his reply is unprintable. After they'd hauled the guy off, he asked me why I did it when I could have been hurt. I pointed to this huge cut-out of the Curt Swan Superman, which was where I had been standing, and I said, "How could I have been standing in front of that and done nothing?" (Taylor 2008)

The interviewer asks what appeal Straczynski finds in Superman. Straczynski mentions his troubled upbringing before discussing the topic of moral influence:

> My sense of morality and ethics came from the Superman comic books. I maintain those ethics to this day. You treat people decently, big and small. And you come to the rescue when there's a chance. Two or three years ago, there was a high school in Hawthorne, New Jersey, that was losing their financing for their arts program. Kids were scavenging in dumpsters for wire and hangers to use for art and sculpture. I heard they were going to run a little, tiny convention at the high school to try to get the arts program back. I heard about them, went down there directly, made some calls including to Joe Quesada and next thing you knew Marvel was involved, DC got involved, there were big-name guests and auctions for heavy duty art. It became a huge thing. It was the right thing to do. That's what Superman taught me. (Taylor 2011)

Straczynski takes the example of Superman and funnels it into his own efforts to provide for a larger community. He follows Superman's example in not letting wrongdoing go unpunished—notice the implication that other bystanders do nothing to stop the thief in the phrase "the crowd split like the Red Sea."

Others have written about specific moments when Superman had an impact on their lives. Mark Waid, for example, writes about his troubled teenage years and how Superman guided him toward a better adult life. He calls Superman a father figure (2005: 4), and says that Superman, specifically watching the first *Superman* film in 1979, changed his life. Waid describes himself at the time as "bright but violently self-destructive. . . . My life was a wreck, I had few if any friends, no one I trusted to look for guidance of any sort, and I was staring down the barrel of a future that had no direction and held little hope" (Waid 2009). Then, Waid saw *Superman: The Movie*:

> I sat down for the 3:20 show, the film started, the music swelled—and the instant that giant S-shield boomed onto the screen bigger and brighter than I ever could have imagined it, I was transfixed. And when Superman took to the skies for the first time, in that moment I found the hero I'd needed. It didn't matter that he wasn't real. What mattered was that he cared about everyone in the world, without ex-

ception, without judgment. . . . I'd walked into that theater with a very
short future ahead of me, and I'd walked out feeling safe and inspired
in Superman's orbit. Without that, I can promise you that I would not
be here today. (Waid 2009)

Note here the emphasis on the medium in which the story is told—not
just on the fact that he's sitting in the theater, but the combination of the
film's score (also mentioned by Jeff Ray in Chapter 2) with the size of the
projected image. He's awed by the magnitude of the Superman insignia, an
image he is already familiar with; here, however, he finds it in a new context.
Likewise, there seems to be some significance in the fact that a real human
being portrays Superman in flight. Waid had already read the comic books,
but they didn't have the same effect as watching the film. The combination of
magnitude, music, and the connection to reality provided by the cinematic
photography of human beings served to amplify the story's content. Medium
matters.

Waid's ideas about Superman have evolved. When employed as a writer
at DC Comics, his editor challenged him with writing a new version of
Superman's origin story. Specifically, the editor asked him to address the
question of why Superman does what he does—in other words, why does
he devote himself to saving people? The result was a story called *Superman: Birthright: The Origin of the Man of Steel*, but Waid also used what he
learned to write an essay called "The Real Truth about Superman." In it, Waid
concludes that when Superman saves other people, he is in fact acting in his
own self-interest; he wants to become part of a community in Metropolis,
so he helps the people in that community. His powers put him in a position
that requires him—in order to fully realize them and fulfill his need to use
them—to rescue people from danger. Because of his powers, Superman can
only be true to himself if he helps others. Waid's interpretation arises from
a paradox he finds at the heart of the Superman story:

> Superman has, since his creation, been a shining example to read-
> ers everywhere of the virtue of selfless heroism—but he has accom-
> plished this by acting in his own self-interest. . . . In helping others,
> Superman helps himself. In helping himself, he helps others. When he
> comes to the aid of other people, he is exercising his distinctive pow-
> ers and fulfilling his authentic destiny. That, of course, benefits him.
> When he embraces his history and nature and launches out in the
> one set of activities that will most fulfill and satisfy him, he is help-

ing others. There is no exclusive, blanket choice to be made between the needs of the individual and the needs of the larger community. There is no contradiction here between self and society. But it's a bit paradoxical in a very inspirational way. (2005: 10)

Waid has used Superman to explore one of the tensions that informs folklore: that between the individual and the collective. This tension is implicit in both Straczynski's story and in Roberson's comments—Superman reminds us of the obligation we have to help others when we can. From those relatively short examples, I turn now to a deeper examination of the way Superman can affect an individual.

DEAR SUPERMAN

On April 18, 2013, Josh Elder posted the following to Facebook:

It's Superman 75th anniversary today. All of you who know me—at all—know how much Superman means to me, how much I believe in the character and what he stands for. But here's a story many of you probably don't know. . . .

I was on the J train heading to JFK Airport after the MOCCA[11] convention in NYC. It was summer and the train was hot, sticky and way overcrowded. A brawl broke out as two women attacked a third for her seat. It quickly escalated as two men got involved. Bystanders took pictures with their phones, while others at least called the police, but no one was doing anything.

Then one particularly deranged individual started lashing out at everyone around him, including a little girl who couldn't have been more than six years old. I was taller than him, but he was broader, more muscular and clearly, you know, crazy. I was scared, so I froze. I knew someone should do something, but I lacked the courage to be that someone.

Thank goodness I was wearing short sleeves that day. I looked down at the Superman symbol tattooed on my bicep, and that made the decision for me. I tackled Mr. Crazy and managed to restrain him until we reached the next station where he, along with the other brawlers, was promptly arrested by the NYPD officers who were there and waiting for our arrival.

Mr. Crazy had worked me over pretty good, but I'd had a lot worse. On the other hand, the children he'd threatened were bawling their eyes out. They were safe now, but they didn't feel that way. Their parents tried to console them, but to no avail. And again, no one else in the train car did anything.

Thankfully I still had copies of one of my issues of The Batman Strikes left over from the show. As it happened, it was the one guest-starring Superman. I gave each child a copy and within moments the tears were gone. They were smiling and laughing and making their parents read out loud to them if they didn't understand the words.

It was the single most amazing moment of my life.

Superman matters only to the extent that we let him matter. If you love Superman, then be Superman when others need you to be. It won't be easy, it may even be painful, but it's so, so worth it.

You're stronger than you think you are. Superman believes that, and so should you. (Elder 2013)

The similarity to Stracyznski's story is striking: the crowd, the inaction of those around them, and the visual cue that prompts a selfless intervention. The presence of an image associated with Superman almost forces action in the service of others. We see this in Straczynski's reference to the Superman cutout after the incident was over, and in Josh's phrase, "Thank goodness I was wearing short sleeves that day." If he hadn't, would he still have intervened?

In 2008, Josh fulfilled a lifelong dream with the publication of issue 44 of The Batman Strikes. He had been the regular series writer, and the editors had asked him to incorporate Superman into the issue. With "A Tale of Two Cities" (Elder et al. 2008), Josh's first Superman story saw print. He says that it was his favorite issue of his run, and that he got to do some exciting things with the characters; however, this is not the most important of his Superman stories. That story was published by DC in 2013. It's called "Dear Superman."[12]

Josh wrote "Dear Superman" several years before its publication. When I interviewed him, I began by asking the broadest question possible, "What is the appeal of Superman?" I didn't even need to ask another question. What he gave me was essentially an autobiography that took Superman as a focus. It begins in his childhood, continues through his education, to his professional ambitions, and circles back to his childhood as he gets to the meaning of Superman and how "Dear Superman" reflects and shapes his worldview.

"If I were to psychoanalyze myself," Josh began, "and say the reason why I like Superman so much . . . I mean, for one, the comics and the movies were omnipresent when I was very, very young. The earliest memory, the earliest real memory I really have is wearing Superman pajamas, with the cape, and jumping off the furniture pretending to fly. Seriously, my earliest real memory. That being the case, Superman has been in my life forever, as far as I'm concerned. And beyond that, I grew up as a pretty lonely kid. I was an only child, and my mother was a single parent. I grew up without a father, and in many ways Superman was the father I always wished I had, and the man that I wanted to grow up to become, and I think that, psychologically, I know that's a pretty common trope—an outside attachment to superhero figures, to icons of masculinity when you don't have a father in the house. And for me Superman represented the best of all that, rather than like a sports star or any other superhero characters. Superman was perfect. Everything that I wanted to be, and in many ways the way that I saw myself was Clark Kent, and what I wanted to be was Superman. And this question of what is power . . ."

I interviewed him at the table where he sat as a special guest of the Superman Celebration. At this point, and occasionally throughout our interview, some people came up to talk to him about his Reading with Pictures project. When we got back to the interview, he picked up on the idea of perfection:

"I mean, I guess the idea of Superman, I think Alan Moore said it best in many ways, where he describes Superman as this man who came from the sky and only did good.[13] And I think that's beautiful. He's a science fiction Christ figure." He goes on to describe how Superman got him reading comics, which "metastasized" into a love for comics in general. His use of the word *metastasized* offers a clue to much of the context and subsequent meaning of Superman for Josh. He had more or less stopped reading comics until the age of twelve or so, in 1992, when Superman was killed. At that point, Josh started collecting comics in earnest, and began to see the extent of the Superman mythos. "I was a hardcore kid, but the internet didn't really exist yet. I just didn't know how deep this rabbit hole went that is Superman in the comics.

"And then my senior year of high school, I had to do a term paper report on the topic of my choosing. So, I did the history of Superman, and basically the importance of the character, as kind of an argument of why Superman is the most important fictional character of the modern era. And that I also used as the basis for my speech for the speech team. And so I got a lot of mileage of my Superman research. For the purposes of this, I ended up seeking out every book on Superman that had been written at the time. I gained this immense knowledge of not just the character's backstory but also everything that went into making it, the politics behind it, the Siegel and Shuster lawsuits and everything. I started reading real criticism about the character."

He brings up a number of books, in particular the collection *Superman at Fifty* (Dooley and Engle 1987). Reading this, Josh began to understand the character on a new level: "I realized that no other fictional character could even hold a candle to, again of the modern era, to the cultural significance of Superman. And I really become fascinated by what that meant and wanted to know more about that and delved deeper into it. And that was the beginning of my big-time Superman fandom . . . In college I became known as the Superman guy. I got that in high school, too. That became kind of like my thing. And you know the comic guy, too, but even more so obsessed with Superman and wanting to emulate Superman. When I'd be standing, I'd do, I didn't ever mean to do it, but I'd stand in that kind of pose [*arms akimbo*], or that pose [*arms crossed*] a lot. That was just how I'd stand. And all these things kept creeping into my life. Superman really just burned itself into my existence. I identified and imprinted on the character in a significant way. And there are certainly worse models to imprint upon than Superman.

"I took that, and when it came time to begin thinking about professionally writing, I started by writing a Superman story. And I wanted to write a Superman story that wasn't just a beat-'em-up or something like that. I wanted to write one that I could give to someone like my mother, for instance, who understood that Superman mattered to me but didn't really understand how much Superman mattered and why. And I wanted to write a story that I could give to her and say, 'This is it. This is why this character means something to me in a real way.' And it was about a little girl who's dying. Well, we don't say that she is, but she's sick. She writes a letter to Superman, care of Clark Kent at the *Daily Planet*. And the story's called 'Dear Superman.' He shows up at her window and knocks on it, on the third story, and takes her flying all over the world. They have a snowball fight in the Himalayas. They build sand castles at the Great Pyramid. She teaches him how to play chopsticks in the Sydney Opera House. And they have all these fairy tale moments with Superman as the star, as the Prince Charming of the story I guess, or the Fairy Godmother. And then he takes her to the Fortress and shows her all the wonders that he's acquired across the galaxy. And she says to him, 'With all your power why can't you save me?' And he has to tell her, 'Well, there are some things even I can't do. And

I'm sorry. But I was here for you, wasn't I? Did you have an amazing night? Didn't you get to fly and do amazing things?'"

We were interrupted briefly by people with questions about his comics. When we came back to the subject of Superman, he picked up his train of thought without prompting.

"So, I guess the way the story all came down was the end. Superman says, 'I can be there for you, I was there for you, I'm here for you right now, and that's all I *can* do.' But the point of that exchange is that when you're dealing, especially when you're a child and you deal with someone who is ill or dying, you feel very weak and powerless and helpless and guilty because of it. And these are things that we learn how to get under control, but children can't accept that. It's very difficult for them to deal with this thing and deal with the lessons of the immensities of life and how there are things that are too big for us or our parents, who we think can do anything, or doctors who we think can fix anything, or God, who . . . 'Why are you doing this? If you can do anything, why did you choose to do this?' It's a big thing. But if you can then confront them, saying that even Superman is in the same boat as you. The most powerful thing you can imagine, basically, and he can only . . . He's powerless, but he's not, and that's the big thing: That he's not actually powerless. He does what's within his power to do, and you can do that too. You can't take someone flying around the world, but you can do something. You can be there.

"The flip side then is he says to her, 'I came from a world called Krypton where everyone is dead. And I'm the only one. But they're not gone because, well, here they are [*he gestures to himself.*] When you die, you won't be gone, because here you'll be, and everyone who's ever cared about you will never, ever forget you. You'll never go away.' And so it's kind of a retort to both of these things that, especially when you're a child, that are difficult to deal with. Your own death and the death of someone else, the illness of someone else. And he takes some sand and fuses it into glass with his heat vision, and blows it cool with super breath, and it's this Superman symbol with a 'C' in it. The girl's name is Connie. She's named for my mother. And he says, 'I made this for you because you can't leap tall buildings in a single bound, or run faster than a speeding bullet, even with the weight of the world on your shoulders, you still have the strength to carry on. That's why you're my superhero.'[14]

"It was, we felt it was a really powerful story, that said real things, that used Superman in a way to do good in the world. That encapsulates person- ally my view of what Superman should be. If you're going to do a Superman story, it should be a story that inspires goodness in the world, as Superman

From *All-Star Superman* Issue 10, written by Grant Morrison, drawn by Frank Quitely, and colored by Jamie Grant.

does. I think my favorite moment in all of the Superman canon is when, in *All-Star Superman*, Superman is talking to Lois Lane and he overhears a girl saying, 'I'm going to jump.' Like talking to her suicide counselor. And she's trying to get there in time and you know the counselor won't make it, and she's like, 'I'm hanging up now.' And Superman says [to Lois], 'I have to go,' and he flies off. And he stops her [the girl about to commit suicide] and says to her, 'You're much stronger than you think you are.'

"In that one sentence, I think everything Superman is, is summed up in a beautiful way. In that here's this, again, perfect man from the sky who chooses to walk among us and be one of us and humble himself so that he can understand the human condition and be a part of the human condition. It's not that he pities us, and it's not that he is just lonely and seeks company. It's that he genuinely thinks we're amazing. He genuinely thinks that we are stronger than we think we are. And if he believes that of us, maybe it's true. I guess, and you know, this is common, in a Christian refrain, if God loves you then you're worthy of being loved. And if Superman thinks you're strong, then you are. Because who knows more from strength than Superman? And if he thinks you're special then you are. And he thinks we're all special."

Josh had been talking about his ideas about Superman in general, in ways that could apply to anyone reading a story. He talked of common, if not universal, experiences. Now, he began once more to talk about his own life: "So, I guess, I mean to me it's a chance to use fiction to tell a huge and beautiful truth. And Superman's done that in my life. That story that I wrote was written about my own feelings when my mother had cancer when I was eight years old, and I had to take care of her. She was convalescing in our home for close to a month after a substantial surgery, and there was a very real chance that this was, you know—she would not pull through. And she did. My mom's a tough lady, and it takes a lot to put her down. But it was frightening and terrifying. I wrote that story to answer those [questions], to be there, I wrote that for eight-year-old Josh.

"And about two years after I wrote that story, I was diagnosed with cancer. Clearly I'm fine now. The hair came back in. It looks great. That story literally helped me. I went back and reread it and said, 'This is true. It was true when I wrote it, and it's true now. And I'm going to live my life as if this story is true. I'm not going to give up. I'm not going to. There are things I can't fix, there are things I can't solve. But what I can, I'm going to continue to do. You never surrender to despair, you always keep trying, you always keep flying.' You know, and that story helped me, when I needed it. Superman helped me when I needed it, and so I guess when it comes to what does Superman mean to me ..."

He had begun to directly address the question I asked nearly an hour before. Someone came to ask about one of his comics, and when we resumed our conversation, I indicated that I thought he had been about to sum up what he had been talking about. He said, "I would say that Superman to me is ... a lot of the feelings and a lot of the positive connections and connotations that I have for Christ, I also have for Superman. I feel they overlap in so many ways and in many ways I've read ... I went to church, I went to Sunday school, I've read the Bible many times over, but I've lived with Superman more than I have [with Jesus]."

After a pause, he amended his statement: "Not to say that I worship Superman or anything. But everything that's great about Christ as a character, or about Moses, or about any of these sort of deliverer characters who are human but transcend that, I think Superman embodies that for the modern era." Josh describes Superman as a "secular savior. It's a beautiful story. It's a story that the world needs. I know, being a Superman fan, I know Superman has made a difference in my life. He's made me a better person. He's helped me through difficult times. And I know he's done the same . . . I mean, this whole town [Metropolis, Illinois] is a testament to the fact that the character really does mean something beyond just, 'I think it's cool and it's fun.' It's something real. And it sounds silly when you talk about it in terms of how important the character really is. You sound silly. But it's true and it's real. It's certainly real to me, and I think it's real to a lot of people here. And what I want, what I think of Superman in my professional career as I hope to write Superman, I hope to be able to use the character to tell stories that I know will matter to others in a way that Superman matters to me, and do that for other people. Because it's a beautiful thing I want to share. Superman is a secular savior figure. He's necessary for the modern world. I think if he didn't exist we'd have to invent him.

"The universe can't survive without the idea of Superman, but Superman himself isn't that important. Even in his own universe the fact that he's there physically isn't as important as the fact that the idea of him is made real. That's what matters. And the idea that is, I think the greatest, that, 'You're stronger than you think you are,' and 'You can all fly with me. One day you will,' is the most important story of the modern era. Of the modern world. However it comes out. Superman is one prominent example. The story that drives civilization in the modern era, and that's good for it, is that we'll all fly one day and we're all stronger than we think. And Superman is the iconic embodiment of that."

Josh and I talk more throughout the weekend, about specific stories, especially *All-Star Superman*. Looking at his statement in retrospect, it's remarkably well-structured. He began by talking about his professional life, worked his way into a general interpretation of Superman, moved into his personal life, back to a general interpretation, and finally incorporated his personal experience and interpretation into professional Superman stories offered to the reading public. He speaks as a man who has triumphed over cancer physically and psychologically; his use of the word *metastasized* early on reflects a genuinely healthy adaptation to the reality of cancer—he gives a positive connotation to a word whose denotation is negative.

Josh relates battles with cancer—both his own and his mother's—without much overt emotional display. His voice never cracks, nor does he need to pause when dealing with his own illness or with the memory of his mother's. We can attribute this, at least in part, to the writing of the "Dear Superman," which reveals itself as personally cathartic. The story—as he tells it to me on this occasion—has several meanings in his own mind, reflecting different points in his life. The earliest, when he originally wrote the story, reflects a young boy coming to terms with the possibility of his own mother's death. But it's not about the fear of being an orphan. Superman could easily be conscripted to this purpose—using it to find strength in the face of this adversity and seeing that being an orphan does not determine the course of one's life. A context-less interpretation of "Dear Superman" could easily come up with this reading: A son, Superman/Josh, is telling his mother that it's OK to die. But as he tells it now, it seems more like an apology to his mother: a son, Superman/Josh, telling his mother that he's sorry he can't save her, but he'll make the most of the time they have now.

As Josh moved to a different phase of his life, "Dear Superman" became more than a story he "wrote for eight-year-old Josh"; it became the story of overcoming the emotions that he felt as an adult, and as such it's for adults as well as children. It comforted him as he dealt with his own illness. He frames his interpretation initially as a general statement, but again and again he corrects himself, or perhaps more accurately amends his words to personalize them. He refers to "dealing with your own death or the death of someone else" but then corrects himself and says, "an illness of someone else." Naming the girl in the story after his mother is the most obvious example of this, but the character's name also no doubt reflects his own opinion of his mother. When he writes of Superman saying the girl is his superhero, he might as well be talking to his own mother.

"I'm going to live my life as if this story is true." Let's focus on the phrase "as if." In this statement, Josh is not aligning himself with Beaudrillard's fabrication of the real from the unreal—"to reinvent the real as fiction, precisely because the real has disappeared from our lives" (1998: 311)—but rather he is taking an interpretive stance on an idea. He does not "desire to enter imaginary environments," as Lancaster characterizes some fan activity (2001: xxiv). The difference is important, and it separates the performance of folklore from the performance of other fan activities, such as those discussed by Lancaster. Lancaster's fans immerse themselves in an imaginary entertainment environment (2001: 30) as a concrete manifestation of an artistic and sensible appreciation of this world. For Josh and, I would argue, for the fans at the Superman Celebration, it is a way to engage with the world rather than a way to appreciate it. The fans make the Celebration and the community of Metropolis their own, as we'll see in the following chapter, through their involvement in the planning process for the Celebration, and through their devotion to it over time.

Josh's Superman story dramatizes one of the pivots of his life. If we cast him as Superman in it, telling his mother that he is doing all he can for her, it reveals another side of Josh's interpretation: that it's OK to accept weakness. The statement "You can all fly with me. One day you will" is how he characterizes what he calls the most important story of the modern era. That last part is vital; we're not there yet. Unrealized potential lies at the core of the story and is key to understanding the fictive component of Superman—why we must believe in the make-believe. We must live as if it's true, because that's the only way it can become true.

DISSENTING OPINIONS

We have looked at people for whom Superman is meaningful, who apply his story to their lives, and who use him as an instrument for finding their way about more easily in this world. For others, the character cannot serve this purpose, and the reasons for this state of affairs are many. Dennis O'Neil, who wrote Superman comics during the 1970s, finds no affinity for Superman stories. He didn't enjoy writing about Superman, he writes, and he offers a hypothesis as to why:

> A writer must find a way to make a character symbolically real for himself. You've got to connect somehow, and the route to the connection is through your own deepest dreams and fantasies. Now, my fantasies are quite modest, generally concerned with human perfectibility. I might imagine myself training and training until some glorious autumn morning I run the New York marathon in 1:59:59 and receive a gold medal and admiring glances from three or four not-really-unattractive women. It won't happen but it could, to somebody, some day; it is, remotely, possible. I have never fantasized about having inhuman power conferred on me by an outside agency, nor shared what psychologists saw is a common wish-fantasy, that of having been born to high station and misrouted in infancy; not for a second have I believed I was ever a baby prince spirited away by a wicked

serving girl. Tremendous unearned power and exalted lineage are a lot of what Superman is about, and those are not my dreams. Writing Superman stories, I was operating on craft, professionalism and technique, and in the end they weren't enough. Not for Superman. I couldn't find a connection with even a vastly scaled-down version of this demigod; I couldn't locate his symbolic reality. (1987: 56)

These are precisely the same concerns expressed by another comic book writer, Steven Seagle, who wrote Superman for a year. Subsequent to that writing assignment, he wrote a partly autobiographical comic book called *It's a Bird* . . . about how he worked through the idea that he could write Superman. At the beginning of the story, Seagle's sentiments toward Superman echo O'Neil's: "The truth of the matter is, I have no Superman stories. There's no access point to the character for me." But he goes further: "For anyone if they ever really think about him. Too much about him makes no sense" (2005: 13). Superman, he insists, "doesn't hold water in the real world" (2005: 31).

It's a Bird . . . has two intertwined plots. First and foremost, it tells the story of Seagle coming to terms with his family's history of Huntington's disease and the possibility that he might one day contract it. Second, it is the story of Seagle's exploration of Superman as he comes to an understanding of the character that allows him to write the series. These thematic threads combine into a meditation on human vulnerability. It's also a story about secrets and relationships and how a person can behave erratically while maintaining a core identity. It's about having to deal with family history, especially when that history is not pleasant.

It's a Bird . . . includes twenty short stories that explore elements of Superman, including his costume, his status as an outsider, his courage, his devotion to justice, perfection, and the nature of fiction as an escape. This last—the escapist element of fiction—provides Seagle with the means to fully understand and accept Superman. He thinks back to his childhood, when his grandmother's diagnosis revealed his family's susceptibility to Huntington's disease. His parents gave him a Superman comic book to occupy him as they talked over what had happened. He overheard their conversation and became aware of their realization that their children might contract the disease as well. He describes reading the comic book: "I let the story take me into it . . . as the pages rolled by, I bought into the crisis . . . believed in the danger . . . and at the end, though I never would have admitted it . . . I was emotionally invested. I wanted to turn the pages and know what was going to happen next. Which is the lesson stories can teach life. There's always a 'next.' Always. That's what Superman is all about. To remind us that we have hurdles . . . but as long as we keep jumping them . . . we're in the race" (2005: 119).

Seagle voices many concerns that trouble some people: Superman's "fascism," his reliance on power, the silliness and unrealistic nature of the stories. Henry Jenkins, in an online essay, labels another: that Superman is too perfect to be interesting (Jenkins 2006; see Chapter 5 for more on this). Analyzing Superman becomes a way for Seagle to think about these things in the real world. What's interesting is that Superman's insurmountable power was not the primary factor in Seagle's contemplation of the character. He began by criticizing Superman for his power, but in the end the character transcends that criticism and Seagle is able to see the way that Superman dramatizes the human condition, particularly its vulnerability. O'Neil does not engage in this sort of analysis; he's more concerned with his own (and, presumably, his readers') ability to relate to Superman, which could be why the character does not resonate for him.

Superman provides a way for people to examine their lives, not because of his powers, but because of the way he is just like everybody else. Life events lead to reinterpretations of expressive, traditional forms, which are then used to cope with life events. Vaihinger viewed fiction as valuable only up to the final reckoning, where it would be removed from equations and from philosophy. Following Vaihinger, Lon Fuller notes that the true danger lies not in forgetting that fiction is fiction,[15] but in taking a single element of fiction out of its theoretical context (1967: 119). Decontextualizing an element of a fiction exposes the fiction as absurd; Fuller uses an example from mathematics—negative numbers, he writes, are ridiculous on their own (you can't have -5 of something) but make perfect sense within an equation. Such is the case with Superman. Michael Saler notes that virtual worlds, such as those created in Superman stories, "provide safe and playful arenas for their inhabitants to see the real world as being, to some degree, an imaginary construct amenable to revision. As a result of collectively inhabiting and elaborating virtual worlds, many [fans] become more adept at accepting difference, contingency, and pluralism: at envisioning life not in essentialist, 'just so' terms but rather in provisional, 'as if' perspectives" (2012: 7).

Saler characterizes attention to virtual worlds as an adaptive strategy for the real world. The context in which Superman's absurdity is rendered not merely normal but adaptive is not the context of the fictional world that he inhabits, but the context of real-world behavior. It is the context of interpretation and application, in which fans find and respond to an emotional core of the Superman stories. Among the science writers utilizing Superman in their books, Mark Wolverton makes much of the idea that humanity can one day approximate the powers of Superman. Grant Morrison theorizes the same idea. Josh Elder, J. Michael Straczynski, and Mark Waid all employ Superman as a means to contemplate morality and moral action in the real world. Superman becomes a paradigm for how things ought to be. In these thoughts, we can see a perspective that places Superman not in the "as if" mode but in the "ought." It's the difference between living as if the story is true and living in order to make it come true.

- 4 -

CELEBRATING SUPERMAN

AMONG THE MANY GENRES OF INTEREST TO FOLKLORISTS, RITUAL HAS EN-joyed a rich history. Its long-standing association with myth stimulated debate for many decades.[1] According to proponents of the myth-ritual school of interpretation, myths originate as explanations of rituals. In other words, people perform certain rituals, and in order to validate or justify these behaviors they invent stories indicating that the rituals have their origins in the workings of the gods or ancestors. This theory was extremely popular in the early twentieth century. Nonetheless, it was a profoundly flawed theory, as demonstrated by Joseph Fontenrose (1966), and has been largely rejected by modern scholars (though its tenets linger, see Hansen 2002). Superman's origin on a summer night in Cleveland as Jerry Siegel lay in bed unable to sleep has nothing whatsoever to do with a ritual of any sort. The story of that night is often told these days,[2] and it has grown beyond the character.

Ritual is nonetheless relevant because Superman has become associated with rituals. First and foremost, there is the ritual of the comic book collector. This ritual can be most simply described as a regular trip to a comic book store to purchase comics. There can be any number of reasons for which this ritual is performed (i.e., numerous possible functions), but the fact remains that the acquisition of comic books has distinctly ritualesque (Santino 2011) qualities. Sean Kleefeld (2010) describes these qualities: their calendrical recurrence, which commonly happen once a week or month; their social component (also stressed in Pustz 1995) as fans gather in the store to talk; their efficacy; and links to overarching ideals or institutions. My own research trips to comic book stores confirmed what I had known from reading comic books myself: the ritualesque elements of reading comic books are both prominent and important. I interviewed people who make the trip to the store weekly to buy comics, who feel strange and out of sorts when they have to miss a week. I was told (by employees) of people whose devotion approaches the religious in its intensity. I learned of a man, a police officer, who stops at a shop once a month to buy Superman and Batman comics. The reason, so he has told that shop's employees, is that it reminds him of why he became a police officer in the first place.

The rituals of buying comic books, or similar rituals of watching a film or television show, encompass more than just Superman stories, of course. In this sense, so does a comic book convention. Matthew Pustz, in *Comic Book Culture* (1995), explores the culture that has grown up around comic books, employing a modicum of ethnographic enquiry. Pustz analyzes both the sorts of people who read comics and the sorts of stories that comics tell, giving each roughly equal weight. He discusses comic book stores as well as conventions, letters pages, and websites. Bill Schelly (1995) writes of the early years of fandom development, in which Superman fans played an important part. Gerard Jones (2005) demonstrates how large a role fans played in the origins and development of comic books—and the large role that Superman played as well. These sorts of contexts, however, are both too general and too specific for present purposes. Note that these are fan enterprises, and limited to the narrative mode of comic books, for the most part. Because Superman spans narrative media, and because his appeal extends well beyond comic book fans, they are too specific. But there is a context where the multiple modes in which Superman stories are told, and where the casual consumer mixes with the devoted fan in the ritualesque performance of cultural expressions based on Superman: the Superman Celebration in Metropolis, Illinois, to which I devote the rest of this chapter. To keep the analysis grounded in concrete experience whenever possible, I will focus largely on Superman fan Brian Morris.

METROPOLIS LIES AT THE SOUTHERN TIP OF ILLINOIS, RIGHT ON THE OHIO River. Its residents number something less than seven thousand. The town was founded in the 1830s and named in anticipation of it becoming a large city. The Celebration began in 1979 and occurs annually from the second Thursday through Sunday of June. Every year, Brian and his wife, Cookie (rarely known by her given name, Carol), travel to Metropolis for the Celebration. Brian, though heavily involved in the festival, occupies no formal position in its organization. A committee of local residents organizes Celebration events, led by co-chairs Karla Ogle and Lisa Gower during the years I attended. The Celebration is based on Market Street, running three blocks north from the courthouse. The location has changed over the years, but now seems rooted there. Rides and some food vendors, which used to flank Market Street to the west, are now located in a field nearly a mile to the east. There are other events, such as a softball game and a road race, held in other locations. Fans organize less-public activities elsewhere, at restaurants, the local bowling alley, and other businesses. Some events are also held on the riverboat casino.

The Superman Celebration is in most ways like any festival that occurs in small towns across the United States. Its structures are typical: opening ceremony, ritual, drama and contest, feast, dance and music, and concluding event (Stoeltje 1992: 264–65), though the actual form of these activities varies from year to year. In other ways, the Celebration resembles a comic book convention. In *Comic Book Culture*, Pustz offers a description of such events and their traditions: merchandise dealers, socializing among fans and professionals, film screenings, panel discussions, and costume contests (1995: 159). The Celebration features all of these. It is rooted in the local, an opportunity for residents and entrepreneurs to take advantage of an influx of people, and for political work to be done. But it is also an extra-local event, as people from outside the community come and act not merely as tourists but as event organizers. They are active participants; they are performers of the festivity. This makes the Superman Celebration rare, if not unique, among small-town festivals. Certainly the Celebration is not unusual for its utilization of resources outside its boundaries—traveling food vendors, rides, and games are perhaps the most common examples. The Superman Celebration has these, but outsiders also participate in organizing events. These men and women are volunteers who take it upon themselves to ensure that the Celebration meets their own ideals.

"It started out as a one-block celebration with a sidewalk sale, a few food vendors, maybe a band, our local Baptist minister getting into the Superman suit," says Rebecca Lambert, former chair of the Celebration committee, in the documentary *Heroic Ambition* (Cranford 2010). The Celebration expanded, and now draws tens of thousands of people from all over the world. Its layout has gotten larger, the variety of events and activities available has increased, and the length of the Celebration has extended. The Celebration Committee hires an official Superman to work during the Celebration. At the time of this writing, that role is filled by Joshua Boultinghouse, who won a nationwide competition for the part. The influx of people, the concomitant increase in monetary flow, and the participation of outsiders in the organization of the Celebration has led to some tensions, tensions which are in part dramatized and assuaged by the Celebration, particularly through the opening ceremony.

The Celebration officially begins with the opening ceremony, held at five o'clock on Thursday afternoon. By this point, the vendor carts and other tents have already been set up along Market Street, and the rides are open for use. People have been milling about Market Street for a while already, waiting for the event to begin. Some of the fans from out of town have in fact arrived the night before. The city has prepared itself for the infusion of tourists. There are a larger number of yard sales than usual. There are Superman-themed sales at many businesses, and advertising features Superman and other superheroes.

Already we can see a bit of the tension. The local businesses cater to out-of-town tourists. Theoretically, the more of these, the better business will be. However, many of the locals, including entrepreneurs, are aware of the dangers of continued expansion. The documentary *Heroic Ambition* revolves around this potential conflict. This film chronicles the time Scott Cranford (also the film's producer) spent as the official Superman, particularly his final year in the position. It also serves as a general introduction to the festival, featuring interviews with many of the prominent figures. Several of these people reflect on the changing nature of the Celebration, and the continual need to find a balance between stagnating and becoming too large. Steve Kirk, a fan who comes from California to be part of the Celebration every year, wonders, "Is bigger better? I don't know that it is." Jim Hambrick, a Metropolis resident who owns the Super Museum, comments, "You don't want to lose the small-town charm." Put this way, the tension seems to be less between expansion-stagnation and more between corporatization-local interests. In this, the entire community, both locals and the fans, seems united.

Still, that union can be a tense one. I overheard several of the out-of-town fans commenting on how they were concerned about the opinions of locals. Fans value the Celebration as a chance to commune with those who share their interests. The words of Hugh Troyer, recorded in *Heroic Ambition*, sum up the sentiment nicely: "When I'm at home, I'm the Superman fanatic. When I'm here, I'm just one of the guys." He articulates the "alternative social community" described by Henry Jenkins (1992: 259), a group united by their relationship with a common text. I heard similar statements many times while I was there, and the idea was perhaps best characterized by Cookie Morris when she told me that the Celebration is "a place your passion can call home."[3] Because the Celebration provides an opportunity to realize this sort of community, the fans want to maintain a good relationship with the locals. One of the ways they do so is reflected in the opening ceremony itself, during a folk drama that is produced and performed almost entirely by fans. This drama will form the focus of this chapter, as will one of the men involved in it, Brian Morris. I have chosen to focus on these elements of the Celebration—the opening ceremony and one participant—partly because, through them, we can get at the larger issues of the Celebration as a whole; and partly because to analyze the entire festival would occupy the rest of the book. Nonetheless, the festival as a whole warrants further description before focusing on the ceremony.

ATTENDING THE SUPERMAN CELEBRATION

The Celebration, like any festival, is an assault on the senses. The most striking elements of the Superman Celebration are visual. Of these, prominent is the fifteen-foot-tall Superman statue.[4] Facing Market Street with its back to the courthouse, it dominates the festival. It stands on a cement pedestal three feet high and some twenty-five feet across, shaped in the pentangle of the Superman chevron. A second, smaller pedestal on which Superman is placed, reads "Truth-Justice-American Way." Karla Ogle, who co-chairs the festival with her sister Lisa Gower, runs a flower shop within sight of the statue. She says that there are always people standing in front of it, posing for a picture. She has worked on floral arrangements into the small hours of the morning, only to glance out her window to see carloads of people unloading to take pictures. It's a place people stop on their way someplace else. During the Celebration, it is the site of various events, such as the opening ceremony and the swearing-in of Honorary Citizens of Metropolis. It is also a place where many individuals and groups pose, often in costume, for pictures.

The next things to strike the eyes are the costumers.[5] There are dozens of people who use the Celebration as an opportunity to dress up as a fictional character. A costume contest, held now on Sundays (there's one for children on Fridays as well), is not the only time when this occurs; at any moment from the opening ceremony onward, people are dressed in costumes. There is also a costume parade on Friday. With the costumers come people who want their pictures taken with the costumers. This can sometimes create a bit of a spectacle, as a circle forms around those having their picture taken. The circle, or often a semicircle, forms naturally as people get out of the way of the cameras but linger to watch and take their own pictures. Costumers pose, and often will crouch down to pose with children (often in costume as well).

A great many people bring cameras; one man told me his primary reason for coming was to take pictures of people dressed in costumes to show his friends back home. Many of the photographers are journalists. There are fans who document the weekend (Jamie and Ronda Kelly do so for the *Superman*

Looking north on
Market Street.
June 10, 2009.

Homepage website) for media, others just for themselves. The number of
people can be visually overwhelming, especially on Friday and Saturday.
There's not much standing around; the crowd is always in motion except for
the lines to get autograph tickets or meet celebrities. I never saw long lines
for food vendors.

Vendors line both sides of Market Street. There are white tents for events
at both ends of the Celebration grounds—called the Man of Steel tent and
the Metro tent—as well as the vendors' carts and displays. There's more than
food. People come to sell purses, sheets, incense burners, airbrush caricatures,
tattoos, dish TV, toys, jewelry, shoe inserts, vegetable peelers, wood carvings,
T-shirts, and other items. There are tents supporting local interests; in 2010,
there was one to save the Massac Theater, and another to support public
schools. There are also shows—a bike show, movies and television shows
played for an audience, an art show, celebrities doing signings, trivia games,

The Superfriends of Metropolis, 2010. Here we see gestural folklore as several of the people shape their fingers and thumbs into the pentangle of the Superman chevron.

and a re-enactment of the *Adventures of Superman* radio drama. Celebrities who have been involved in Superman productions are a big draw. Fans can meet them and have items signed, take photographs of them in front of the statue, and ask them questions as they sit under a tent.

On the other side of the tents are the buildings—stores, mostly, but also the Super Museum and a gym. Some of these are open businesses with posters inviting festival goers to come in, stressing support of the festival and of Superman. Other buildings are empty and visibly deteriorating. Karla told me that many are owned by out-of-towners who aren't interested in anything beyond rent, so they don't maintain the buildings. As a result, local businesses move away from Market Street to strip malls, where rent is lower and maintenance is better.

Of these buildings, the closest to the Superman statue is also the most striking. It is the Super Museum, which features a statue of Superman emerging from the wall of its second story. The façade is lined with Superman images as well, drawing attendees inside to the gift shop. Farther along the block one finds the building housing Artists' Alley and Writers' Way, where there is an art exhibit and tables for creators. Beyond that, at the end of the

Looking south on Market Street, toward the courthouse and Superman Statue. June 2009.

festival's location, is an unpainted bronze statue of Lois Lane. It's only slightly larger than life-size, surrounded by commemorative bricks. It was unveiled in 2010.

A block east, down an intersecting street, is the children's tent, called Smallville, where there is a pony ride and other children's activities. A mile beyond that, back toward the interstate, is the lot where the rides are located.

At night, things are calmer, with fewer people out. The field where the rides are constructed is well-lit. There are various activities that keep people around until about 10 p.m., but a bit earlier than that the lights on the vendors go out. The glare of the daytime sun has ceased, but the smoke from the barbecue vendors keeps going for a while. Inside Artists' Alley and Writers' Way are, depending on the night, film screenings or a costume ball. The screenings always feature professional productions, such as one of the Superman films or episodes from the television shows, but fan-produced films are very popular, so much so that a competition has been developed.

Aurally speaking, there's the pervasive din of the crowd. It's not overpowering; it's fairly easy to carry on a conversation during even the busiest times. The participants in events such as the costume contest or the opening ceremony use microphones, but can usually operate without them. In the center of the block, a loudspeaker sits atop a pole. Most of the time it plays music related to Superman (there are a number of pop songs, as well as the scores and theme songs from movies and television shows), but is also used to make announcements for upcoming events. Live music—including gospel, country, and karaoke—is performed in the tents at the ends of the street.

The sizzle of the food is audible, as are the clop of horse hooves near the Superman statue (for carriage rides). A machine in the homemade ice cream vendor's area backfires every few seconds. Certain comments from the crowd stand out. It's all hustle and bustle. Depending on the time of day, attendees might hear snippets of the trivia contests, or of celebrity interviews, or of a re-enactment of a radio broadcast.

There's less to say about the other senses. The overwhelming smell is that of food—barbecue, especially, but also funnel cakes and nachos. Beside the carriage and pony rides, the smell of horses overwhelms everything else, and since it is usually hot out, it's impossible to avoid the smells of large numbers of people moving around in the same hot place.

Food likewise dominates the sense of taste. The pork is popular, as are corn dogs and funnel cakes. One year, a local church handed out flavored ice. There are cold drinks available and free water in a tent near the Superman statue. There are lots of types of food (Karla deliberately tries to bring in variety): tacos, deep-fried Twinkies and Oreos, chicken, pizza, chicken wings, hot dogs, barbecued pork, and hamburgers.

As for touch, the most obvious stimulant is the heat. The occasional breeze diffuses the heat, but the only real place to go to get cool on the street is in the Artists' Alley and Writers' Way building. Inside, it's never as crowded as I expect it to be during the heat of the day, though I have talked to people who go there specifically to cool down. The outside temperature can exceed 100 degrees. It is a topic of discussion, and it is possible that people stay away because of the heat. The costumers provide another appeal to touch, as people request to touch the costumes and put their arms around the costumers for photographs. Lots of people touch the cold metal of the Superman statue.

Events occur constantly throughout the Celebration, from the opening ceremony on Thursday evening until everything concludes on Sunday afternoon. Only recently has there been a closing ceremony, though for some time there has been an effort to put on more events on Sunday to keep people around. Some of the performers, such as the bike riders and magicians, are on the schedule several times. There are regular annual events, such as the memorabilia auction and George Awards banquet, but each year features unique events, like the dedication of the Lois Lane Statue in 2010. The Metropolis Chamber of Commerce sends out frequent updates concerning special guests and program information. Regional and national news broadcasts often cover the Celebration, which has been featured on the Travel Channel. The goal is to bring in a large number of people. In this, it is successful, and to these people we now turn.

THE PEOPLE

The community that gathers together during the Superman Celebration does not exist in any tangible sense until the second weekend of June every year. This has a more profound effect on the events of the Celebration than it would if everyone lived within a short drive of Metropolis. Three types of people attend the Superman Celebration. There are locals, including residents of Metropolis and people who live close enough to spend a day there without arranging for lodging. There are people who come from far away who may not be devoted fans of Superman, but are present more or less for something to do, and who may or may not attend again. There are diehard fans who attend regularly and are interested in Superman beyond the Celebration. Karla Ogle agreed with my assessment of the types of people who attend: they encompass locals, casual fans, and devotees.

The first people I met were locals. I arrived having never conducted any extensive fieldwork involving festivals. I was overwhelmed. Hundreds of people swirled around me, everything called for my attention, and I couldn't focus. So I sat down. There were picnic tables in the middle of Market Street that year, and I found an empty one. I got out a notebook and could think of nothing to write. Then, some people sat next to me. They were eating corn dogs. I made conversation. They were from a nearby town, and had just come to meet some friends and have corn dogs. They hardly noticed that the festivity had anything to do with Superman. Soon, they were gone.

More people sat next to me. The next group, two women, had made the ten-minute drive across the river from Paducah, Kentucky. They were eating nachos. They had come to listen to some of the music, meet up with friends (also from Paducah), and enjoy the food. When I asked them about Superman, they looked at the statue and shrugged. Nachos took precedence. Soon they were gone, and more people eating corn dogs sat down. They were from Metropolis. Not long after, I got my bearings and went to the Chamber of Commerce, where Angie Shelton introduced me to some people and recommended I meet several others.[6] But as the weekend went on, I would occasionally sit down to see who sat near me. They were always people from a city or town close to Metropolis, and always there for reasons unrelated to Superman.

That is not to say that none of the locals are Superman fans, but there are few whose level of interest rivals the diehard fan. Jim Hambrick, owner of the Super Museum, moved to the city because of the name. Another fan, Catherine Busbee, moved to the town for the same reason.[7] Thus far, these two are the only fans I have discovered who have relocated because of the town's name. They complicate the typology I'm developing here a bit, but since there are just two of them, the complication is negligible.

I also met casual attendees, some of whom drive several hours to attend the Celebration. Many are there just to take pictures of people in costume. Some dress in costume, too (I met one man from Chicago who rented a gorilla costume for the weekend). Often they will come once but not return. Two men from Detroit who I met in 2009 did not return in 2010. Generally, casual attendees are not active online, and they know few people, if any, at the festival. They are less immersed in the esoterica of Superman; though they may read comics, it is more likely that they know the character in other media. Sometimes the experience of attending the Celebration makes a devotee out of them.

Let's define the devoted fan by regular attendance—or at least the desire to come—and an interest in Superman that extends beyond the level of mere consumption; there must be an emotional investment. Some who would attend annually live too far away to make regular attendance financially feasible. Regular attendance aids in forming social bonds that lead to communication beyond the Celebration, most often via the internet. These fans know each other. Many of them have helped shape the course of the festival by becoming involved in planning it, though none are members of the committee. Some of them book time for performances and help decide which celebrities are invited. These fans are, for the most part, not locals. Devoted fans come from all over the world. The 2010 festival featured a world map on which attendees were invited to put pins in their places of origin; dozens of countries were represented.

The devoted fan, however, isn't necessarily a devoted Superman fan. We can see this in the examples of Bob and Michelle Lyzenga, father and daughter. Bob is a devoted fan of the character. He grew up watching the *Adventures of Superman* television show and reading the comic books, but his special fondness is for the Fleischer Studios animated Superman short films. He always thought it would be neat to have a full Superman suit, though he never even had a store-bought cape as a child when he pretended to be Superman. His love of comic books led him to become a graphic artist, though he now is a minister. He lives in Lafayette, Indiana, so the drive to the festival takes only a few hours. He started coming because he likes Superman, but he continues to come because it's a time to spend with his daughter Michelle. Neither his two sons nor his wife attend the Celebration.

Michelle doesn't really qualify as a Superman fan in the way that many attendees of the Celebration do; she admits as much herself.[8] She began coming to spend time with her father, and continues making the trip for the same reason. They both also attend because of the community of friends they have developed (I met Michelle and Kristina Johnson [see Chapter 2] together). Michelle's association with Superman comes through her father. Her earliest memories are of watching Superman cartoons with him. Yet she didn't immerse herself in the character until she was throwing his fiftieth birthday party. For this, she did a lot of research so she could write questions for a trivia game.

I focus on Michelle and Bob because they are typical of the community that has grown up around the Superman Celebration. Some of these fans are part of online communities centered on Superman websites, such as the Superfriends of Metropolis, the Superman Homepage, or the Superman Super Site. These fans plan activities for their stay in Metropolis, such as bowling, trips to specific restaurants, and hotel gatherings. Interestingly, there is overlap between many of these communities. They utilize the Celebration as an opportunity to maintain and renew social and familial bonds. During the 2011 closing ceremony, Brian Morris dressed as Perry White to participate in a brief skit in which he talked with Superman and Lois Lane, fending off the threat of an evil aspect of Superman. As the drama drew to a close, Brian delivered the following speech:

"Lois, we just spent the four best days of our year here in a town that many of us consider a second home. People come here to meet with celebrities. Other people just come to escape the pressure of the real world for a few days. Many of us come to hug old friends, and many of us leave with a lot more. But as the sands of time run out on this year's Superman Celebration, we take the best of the event with us, and that's the spirit of friendliness that the people of Metropolis give to each and every one of us. Isn't that right? And not only that, but we owe it to the people of Metropolis and are reminded by them, to say nothing of this guy right here [Superman], we should always uphold the principles of—say it with me—truth, justice, and the American way. If we share that with everyone around us, throughout the rest of the year, then the Superman Celebration never truly ends, ever."

This sums up the devotees' sentiment toward the festival. For them, the activities put on by the committee are merely a starting point. They organize their own activities, which appear on the schedule, and they get together once the day's events have concluded, often in hotel lobbies and rooms. The anticipation and planning for these events begins months in advance.

There is, it must be said, a fourth category of people who attend the Celebration. These are the committee members. They are all locals, yet they are heavily involved in the Celebration and attend every year. Through this exposure, they become well-versed in the lore of Superman, often being able to discuss minutiae with devoted fans. Even among the committee members, though, there is a range of knowledge and involvement. They are all volunteers, since Karla Ogle opted to make the position of chair a nonpaying one when she took over. Some become involved because they are pursuing careers in event planning or tourism.

All these sorts of people congregate in Metropolis during the second weekend of June. The event lasts Thursday through Sunday, and it begins, officially, with an opening ceremony on Thursday evening. This ceremony offers participants an opportunity to welcome people to the town and to demonstrate, in ritual drama, the importance of Superman to their communities.

THE OPENING CEREMONY

As at any festival, folks attending the Superman Celebration perform a variety of folklore. According to the text on the back of the 2009 program, "The Superman Celebration started similar to many small-town festivals—except that this one included a mock bank robbery and Superman appeared to save the day." This statement signals the Celebration's similarities to and differences from other festivals. In recent years, the opening ceremony has taken place on the pedestal of the Superman statue, behind the courthouse and overlooking Market Street. The ceremony combines announcements of interest with bit of folk drama (Abrahams 1972) starring Superman and other characters from DC's superhero stories. Before the skit, members of the Celebration organizing committee, the mayor, and other figures of local or regional prominence take the stage to say a few words. There follows the drama, which is far longer than the opening remarks. Finally, a ceremonial ribbon is cut and events officially begin. There were about fifty people watching the festival in 2009, but I estimate that more than a hundred showed up in 2010, much to the delight of the performers. Even more attended in 2011.

The drama had been a component of the opening ceremony during its inception, but for some time it had not been performed. I was unable to find out why or precisely when it stopped. It started again, however, due to fan interest.[9] Fan involvement is what makes the Superman Celebration an uncommon festival. The institution of an official Superman brought national attention in 2000, when newspapers picked up the story of the search. Scott Cranford won the first contract and became heavily involved in the opening skit. He chronicled the process of creating one of them as part of his *Heroic Ambition* documentary. From the single example offered in that video, it is apparent that Cranford used the drama in part to discuss larger issues, such as environmentalism. After Cranford's time as Superman, Steve Kirk, Stephanie Perrin, Andrew Chandler, and Brian Morris became heavily involved with the skit.

I met Brian Morris[10] in 2009 because of his involvement in the opening ceremony. After seeing the ceremony, I inquired about it at the Chamber of Commerce and was introduced to Brian. In the midst of a hundred people in a crowded room, Brian was glad to talk. I asked general questions at first, trying to get toward the reason he liked Superman. He immediately mentioned the secret identity, which he sees as a way to look at the human condition. "It's a comment that any of us could be Superman," he said. "We all have someone else in side us. Look past the glasses and see the amazing person inside." The inclusion of glasses in the ensemble of a hero was novel in the 1930s, and it continues to resonate. Glasses are a good example of the sort of idea that Superman embodies: that the limits of the human condition, such as poor vision, can be overcome. So, it's not surprising that Brian, who wears glasses, ends his initial statement about Superman with the comment, "I'm an optimist."[11]

Brian is a devoted fan. He has a Superman chevron tattooed on his left wrist, a place that could be covered up if his job required it, but he intends someday to extend it up his arm with depictions of other versions of the chevron. His current tattoo shows the five-sided chevron, red and yellow, about an inch across. The *S* is most appropriately viewed by others when his arm is upright, a result of the fact that the tattoo itself is meant for him. He chose the orientation so that it looks correct from his viewpoint. When I asked to photograph it, he took a wide stance and held up his arm to give me the best view. His position in this photograph closely resembles the position

Brian K. Morris showing his tattoo, just after the opening ceremony. June 9, 2010.

of someone flexing a bicep, demonstrating a meaning of the tattoo and what it represents: Brian's strength. In showing it, he holds his fist aloft.

Brian has thought through Superman in ways a casual fan or a disinterested person would not. His knowledge is encyclopedic. When talking to him about the character, I found that he would preface any reference to a story with its writer (and sometimes its artist or editor), its issue number, and the era in which it was originally published—either its "age" (Golden or Silver) or the decade. This sort of knowledge is not uncommon among fans, but the regular application characterizes Brian's devotion and his conversational style.

Compare this sort of devoted, detailed fan knowledge to that of Karla Ogle and other members of the Celebration committee. When talking to the members of the committee and others who work in the Metropolis Chamber of Commerce, I quickly discovered that none of them qualify even as casual fans. Their interest in the character extends so far as it is required to make the Celebration run smoothly. Lisa Gower's comment sums up the common attitude; rather than being a fan of the character, she said, "I'm a fan of our town." Karla shared this sentiment, yet she demonstrated an extensive

Dough Hubler, Josh Boultinghouse, Steve Kirk, and Stephanie Perrin pose as Non, Superman, Zod, and Ursa after the 2010 Opening Ceremony.

knowledge of the character, developed by a decade of experience organizing the Celebration. As we talked one night, she rattled off the names of creators (though not issue numbers). She talked of actors who had played in the television shows and films. She knew a lot about the history of the character, but it all revolved around the Celebration. She only knew the creators who had been guests at the Celebration. She had met and gotten to know them sufficiently well to determine who would be welcomed back in the future. Her knowledge of attendees eclipsed her knowledge of creators. Dozens of people greeted her by name as they walked by us that night. She would return the greeting, calling them by name as well. She knew details of their lives: where they lived, how many years they'd been coming, facts about their family. She, along with other committee members, attends the Celebration's social events and some of the parties. The fans often give her gifts, which she accepts graciously. Hers is a practical knowledge of the character and stories. It is professional. Her personal interest, she confessed, is *Gone with the Wind*.

Here we have two people with vast knowledge—cultural capital—of the character and many opportunities to employ it. Karla employs that

knowledge in service of the Celebration, which is for her a political and
economic enterprise. For Brian, the same knowledge is social and personal.
The thrust of Brian's life owes part of its trajectory to Superman. In his
own words: "Superman has pretty much infused my life." The content of the
knowledge is vital. The same cannot be said of Karla, for whom the content
is incidental. It stems from the name of the town, given in 1838, a full century
before Superman was first published.

Brian has been attending since 1999, when he read about the auction that
occurs each year. He and his wife came, at first just for a single day, driving
back home to Champagne the same night. Over the years, they have extended
their stay; they now arrive on Wednesday night and leave Sunday evening.
Within their first few years, they began volunteering to help with the auction.
This soon translated into helping with other aspects of the Celebration. Now,
Brian aids in writing the drama that accompanies the opening ceremony—
since 2010, the closing ceremony also contains a dramatic skit.

The drama incorporates the official Superman, but fans play all the other
roles. Brian describes the process by which the fans create the story as collaborative; however, based on what the group has decided, he has occasionally
been responsible for the script itself. Everyone performs without the benefit
of a script onstage (at the request of the committee), and for the performances I have seen, no help has been required for lines. Brian estimates that
90 to 95 percent of the lines adhere closely to the script. The actors take their
roles seriously.

This analysis will focus on the 2010 ceremony, with some reference to
those in the years that precede and follow it. During the four years when
Brian Morris has been involved, the players have been a relatively stable mix
of people. Superman was played by Josh Boultinghouse. Lois Lane was played
by Stephanie Perrin in 2008, 2009, and 2011. In 2010, Stephanie played Ursa,
so Michelle Lyzenga took her place as Lois. Michelle told me that she was
a bit nervous when she was asked to play the role, but Stephanie convinced
her that it wouldn't be a problem. All she had to do was try her best, and
everyone would love it. This was true; kids came up to her and asked to have
their picture taken with her after the show. In 2010, Steve Kirk played Zod,
and Dough Hubler played Non. Andrew Chandler (who also contributed to
writing and directing the 2011 opening skit) played Lex Luthor. John Gleckler
played Mind-Grabber Kid and co-wrote the 2010 opening skit. The characters
don costumes, made specifically for them and often worn during other times.
Lois Lane is denoted by a woman's business suit with a skirt and either a

press pass or a notebook, sometimes both. Lex Luthor is defined by his bald head. Superman wears the costume that comes with the role, provided by the Committee.[12] Other characters wear costumes mimicking those worn in movies, television shows, or comic books.

The drama itself lasts several minutes, and it forms the bulk of the opening ceremony. The ceremony sometimes includes local business as well. In 2010, Lisa Gower delivered a speech commemorating O. D. Troutman, who had been heavily involved in the Celebration for years and had passed away during the previous year. Once this business was concluded, Superman and Lois Lane came to the statue, ostensibly to begin the ceremony, but what happened was in fact the drama. The members of the committee stood in the background while the actors performed the drama that built up to the cutting of the ribbon. The drama always incorporates a variety of characters from Superman stories. In 2010, it featured Lex Luthor and the villains from the 1980 film (Zod, Ursa, and Non), as well as the obscure comic book character Mind-Grabber Kid. In it, Lex Luthor tried to capitalize on Superman by filming him fighting with super villains. Instead, Mind-Grabber Kid defeated the villains with his ability to control minds. While the villains danced under his control, Superman delivered a speech about how the Celebration is very much a group effort:

"As a member of the Justice League, I know what team efforts can accomplish. Think about the Celebration, for instance. It wasn't put together but just one person, but the collaborative efforts of many different people. The Metro Chamber of Commerce, the local volunteers, the emergency staff, policemen, the vendors, business owners, and the very special guests that share their stories and talents with us all to enjoy, we're all part of the same team that makes the Superman Celebration so great for people near and far to enjoy together. Even the criminals can work together as a team. And when we work together for truth, justice, and the American way, there's nothing we cannot accomplish." After additional dialogue with the villains, he continued, "I could have stopped all of you myself, I've done it before. But sometimes it's nice to know you have a helping hand."

The villains exited, defeated, and Superman concluded: "And now, finally, thanks to the efforts of everyone involved, I officially open up the thirty-second annual Superman Celebration." As Karla Ogle spoke briefly about the events to come, particularly the unveiling of the Lois Lane statue, the committee members stretched out a ribbon. After Karla introduced those who were still onstage, Mayor Billy McDaniel was cued to cut the ribbon. The committee, performers, and mayor moved off the pedestal, and were soon replaced by people who wanted to get their picture taken in front of the statue.

Superman's speech emphasizes the benefits of community. As Beverly Stoeltje notes, the opening ceremony of a festival "usually displays the existing social structure and confirms the values dominant within the community"[13] (1983: 241). The community is not merely the population of Metropolis; the fans have a large hand in shaping this particular festival. The fans come from elsewhere, so they lack the bond of geography. They have an emotional investment in the festival proceeding smoothly. They also want to mix well with the local community. This desire is displayed in the drama of the opening ceremony. The local members of the festival committee conduct business, introduce themselves, and remain onstage for the duration. The fans perform most of the roles in the drama. They perform between the audience and the committee members, who in 2010 danced with the villains under the control of Mind-Grabber Kid. At the end of his speech about the importance of the community, Superman calls attention to the help given by Mind-Grabber Kid, a truly obscure comic book character (he appeared in *Justice League of America* issue 70, in 1969). This has the rhetorical effect of involving the entire community in Superman's efforts.[14] When Mind-Grabber Kid comes to the stage, the actor breaks the fourth wall to tell the audience what comic and issue number his character appeared in. This includes everyone in the fan group by imparting the kind of esoteric knowledge that is one defining trait of fandom.[15]

There's a lot going on in the opening ceremony. It qualifies as "ritualesque" (Santino 2011) in that it displays some of the transformative efficacy of ritual while not being dominated by this quality. The drama is the focus. Myth-ritual scholars would be interested to see Superman annually enact the defeat of evil and the community renewal that takes place onstage. It lacks any association with calendrical rites or customs, no reference is made to crops or fertility—and Metropolis is not a farming community. Yet there's vital symbolism being enacted, the maintenance of the political social status quo in the face of its violation by a villain.[16] This is explicit in the actions of the characters. Also explicit, however, is the dramatization of relations between distinct but intertwined communities.

The social structures on display are a dialectical combination of the local and the global. The syntagmatic structure of the opening ceremony—which includes a largely fan and extra-Metropolitan group of people putting on a drama that is embedded in attention to local interest—relates to the physical layout of the dramatic arena: the local Committee members (and mayor)

The cast of the 2010 opening ceremony drama. Left to right: Stephanie Perrin, Dough Hubler, Steven Kirk, Josh Boultinghouse, Michelle Lyzenga, John Gleckler, and Andrew Chandler. Photograph by Brian Morris.

stand behind the fan performers, who direct their attention to the audience, made up of locals as well as out-of-town fans. The content of the drama invites everyone in the audience to become more than just a consumer at the festival; it invites them to join the fan community and gives them the same kind of knowledge valued by those already initiated.[17]

In this way, the drama during the opening ceremony also articulates a certain tension (Stoeltje 1983: 242) that is present in the Celebration—the tension between the locals and the fans. The documentary *Heroic Ambition* demonstrates the tension through the words of various members of the committee and the fans as they discuss the benefits and drawbacks of expanding the Celebration. In recent years, it has exploded in popularity, a fact reflected in the increasing number of people staying for Sunday events. Not everyone is happy about this, and I have heard fans express some concern that the locals don't want it to continue to grow. Stoeltje also indicates that, for modern Americans, contests and competitions have replaced the folk drama as a means to articulate societal tensions. Competitions held during the Celebration include a road race, a softball game, a washer pitching tournament, and costume contests. However, the tensions between the local and the fan communities, between the wish to expand the Celebration and the fear that it will grow too large, are absent from these competitions. This could reflect the fact that the tension isn't particularly strong. No one I talked to, local or out-of-towner, expressed any wish for the Celebration to once again become a more intimate festival.

The dramatic component, as the production of fans who live outside Metropolis, can be seen as a subjunctive idealization of their relationship with the town itself. They want to establish and maintain a relationship that allows them to contribute to the festival and make it the experience they seek, so they portray a mutually beneficial relationship of Superman with those around him.

The ritual of the opening ceremony has a potentially transformative effect on the audience, as we have seen, but it has a very real transformative effect on the city, which is made most apparent in the 2009 opening skit, wherein Superman convinces Lex Luthor to help save the day. Once that is done, Superman says, "Lex, why don't you just calm down, relax, and let all these fine people enjoy the festivities for the next four days." Luthor says, "OK, fine, enjoy your little Celebration. But come Monday morning, start looking over your shoulder again." Luthor agrees to cease his criminal activity until the Celebration ends. It is marked as the "time out of time" (Falassi 1987) that Marianne Mesnil characterizes as "a break with everyday life, a time that is qualitatively different and perceived as separate" (1987: 189). The community thus changes from a small town of some seven thousand people to a bustling throng of tens of thousands. The transformation began days earlier, as tents and rides were set up. The ritual gives official sanction to it.

Stoeltje contrasts festivals with rituals; the latter attempt to control meaning while the former explore and experiment with meaning (1992: 262). But festivals can incorporate ritual into their unified whole.[18] The opening ceremony of the Superman Celebration is the most ritualesque of its various components. Other events, such as the dedication of the Lois Lane statue, the costume contest, the dances and auction, have ceremonial qualities, but they lack the function of rituals—they mark occasions instead of providing opportunity for transformative performance.

The opening ceremony combines ritual and play—a ritual is performed by people putting on a play.[19] These two modes of behavior are, as Frank Manning notes, complementary and contrastive: "Play inverts social order and leads toward license, whereas ritual confirms social order and is regulated" (1983: 7; see also Handleman 1977). They are complementary, not binary, opposites. While, as Manning notes in the same passage, the modern world seems to favor ritual, here play, in the form of a play, is foregrounded but embedded in the words and actions of commencing the Celebration. In a ritualized ceding of control of the city by the local organizers, fans from outside the community are given the stage. The mutual benefit of the situation is apparent in the increased attendance of the opening and closing ceremonies. As the fans get what they want, such as a chance to perform and demonstrate the meanings of the Superman myth that are important to them, the local community benefits. The more the local community benefits, the more welcoming the Celebration will be to outside fans.

For many locals and fans, the play factor is of primary importance. In the previous chapter, we saw how play—in the "as if" mode of action—can provide a valuable logical tool for working through various sorts of problems. But Lawrence Frank reminds us that play is also restorative; it is recreation. Each year, the opening ceremony, in which adults get onstage and make-believe for the audience, signals that the dominant mode of the weekend is play. The Celebration provides a chance for everyone to engage in the sorts of renewal and recreation activities that are part and parcel of festivals (Frank 1976: 75).

The transformative effect of the opening ceremony highlights what might be of great concern to locals—the need for the festival in the first place. Of the locals, only Jim Hambrick and Karla Ogle mentioned the deterioration of Market Street, but it is a widespread concern. Locals must negotiate the need for external contributions the town's economy. Carole Faber (1983), in studying Old Home Week in Mount Forest, Ontario, sees the same central tension—the locals are no longer in complete control of the economy. It is in this interest that another ceremony was performed during the 2011 Superman Celebration: the unveiling of the first plaque in the Walk of Heroes. By placing a series of chevron-shaped plaques in part of the sidewalk along Market Street (the plaques are similar to the stars on Hollywood Boulevard in Los Angeles), this project is designed to bring more people to the downtown area. The idea, though implemented by the Metropolis Tourism Commission, was brought to them by Steve Kirk. The first chevron bears the names of Superman's creators, Jerry Siegel and Joe Shuster.

Faber describes the structure of the Old Home Week festival in Ontario as resembling that of the rite of passage. Commenting on Faber's work, Frank Manning suggests that the rite of passage may be the common pattern for the community festival (Manning 1983: 10). I would not have agreed that this applied to the Superman Celebration until the addition of the closing skit in 2010. Its content returns participants to their regular lives, and the structure is closer now to the rite of passage than it once was. The questions then become: What transition is marked and eased by the rite of the Celebration? Who undergoes a change of social status? I have noted that the opening ceremony does transform the city streets into a place suitable for festivity, and it provides the opportunity for those uninitiated to become so, but those cannot be the reasons for the Celebration as a whole. I would argue that the Superman Celebration is less a rite of passage—though it may resemble one in structure—than a recurrent liminal/liminoid time for all involved (Turner 1969; Manning 1983). This play is taken very seriously by the participants, particularly those who must come from far away. Thus, ritual and play are combined in the opening ceremony. The semantics of play, according to Manning, "are open-ended, unorthodox, fragmented, and often highly individualized, enabling them to elude control and to transcend or subvert ideology." Ritual, in contrast, has a symbolism that "conveys a version of the social order that is meant to be believed, or at least acknowledged or adhered to, and over which society exerts control" (Manning 1983: 27). Together, they present a metaphor of change and innovation alongside a metonymy of stability and conservation. This duality must be retained for the festival to have any meaning.

For this apparent paradox, Superman provides an overarching symbol that fits perfectly. He is an adult who dresses up in the clothes favored by children at play. He lives out the dreams of childhood, particularly that of flying,[20] while doing his job of protecting his city. He embodies play in the most serious of circumstances. During the opening ceremony, the actors play, making light of the material of the superhero genre while at the same time performing a ritual that invokes themes and sentiments that are profoundly important to members of the community. Interestingly, despite the association of ritual and myth, the opening ceremony does not dramatize the aspect of the Superman story that is most mythical in content—his origin, wherein the infant Superman is placed into a rocket ship and sent to Earth. Instead, the skit dramatizes the defeat of villains, and always has. The origin, while offering potential for variation, still maintains a fairly rigid plot and cast of characters. There is little opportunity for humor—a valued component of the ceremony—or for the incorporation of new characters. Overcoming villains is a much more malleable story. It can involve other heroes as well as new villains; it allows for the inclusion of Lois Lane. Because of its flexibility, it allows the theme of community to become prominent.[21]

The skit incorporates humor that can be appreciated by multiple audiences. During earlier dramas, the plot was always the same: Superman would appear to stop a bank robbery. When the drama was reinstated, Scott Cranford wrote new scripts each year. Brian became involved in 2008, and he was onstage as an emcee for that ceremony. That year saw the introduction of the new official Superman, Josh Boultinghouse, incorporated into the skit. Also incorporated was a locally invented character, the Red Mullett. The story involved a confrontation with Bizarro, who wished to be the official Superman. He was defeated when Superman appeared. During the performance, Bizarro's nature as Superman's imperfect and opposite duplicate was explained. This serves the same function as the information about Mind-Grabber Kid: imparting esoteric information to the audience to include them in the group. The Red Mullett can also serve the same function.[22]

Both the fans and the organizers have endeavored to make the production more suitable to younger audience members. I asked Brian about this, prompting a response that demonstrated the extent to which he has thought this through: "That's one thing we try to approach with the skits that we do. We talk online about it and then somebody usually goes off and writes the skit and then presents it to everybody for feedback. And I, from my theater background, have trained to do stage fights. It's not something that you generally can get two people who have never done it to do well, or safely, which is one factor. Also there's the matter of what I call reproducible violence. We have a number of children here. You know how kids can get rambunctious, and if they like it they'll try to re-enact it. We don't throw any punches. In fact, this opening skit [in 2010, when some of the villains grab Superman by the arm] was the first time we actually had any sort of body contact with anybody. And it was fairly neutral. Most of the time it's just standing there posing, looking threatening, or verbally threatening somebody, but it's nothing that somebody is going to go out and hurt themselves doing later on. We're very aware that we're also doing it for children."

In the past, Brian's particular fandom has been less visual in expression, but more recently he has gotten involved in costuming. He often wears a Superman tuxedo made for him by his wife, Cookie. He has worn it to events held during the Superman Celebration, but when I saw and photographed him wearing it, he was attending the gaming convention GenCon, held in Indianapolis. The bright colors make him stand out and identify him as a Superman fan, but the form—a tuxedo instead of the Superman costume—makes him unique among the costumers. He also played Perry White in the 2011 skit.

There is another reason why the origin story doesn't fit the opening ceremony. It doesn't dramatize the values that most people find worthwhile in

Superman. As noted, the qualities that people appreciate about Superman are his values and morality. When asked to elaborate, they talk about sacrifice, altruism, and doing one's best to make the world a better place. The origin story does not include those themes. Placing the infant Superman into a rocket ship is not an act of sacrifice on the part of his parents, and it is often the only act committed on Krypton.[23] Once Superman makes the choice to be a superhero, the story resonates with people. This is not to say that elements of the origin do not resonate but merely that the rest of the story is much more powerful. Brian articulates the core of the character, and his appeal, nicely:

"When he's written correctly, in my opinion, he does embody self-sacrifice, of using your talent for a greater good, serving as an example for others. Too many people equate personality with angst. And Superman at his core, while he can feel a little of bit of angst, and there's a little bit of conflict in his past, Superman himself is not conflicted. He has a clear moral idea of how the world should be, and that is what he works for. At the heart of it Superman is not a conflicted character."

This is the importance of the content of the Superman skit, which remains constant from year to year (even before Brian's involvement). It's about what Superman does—not where he comes from—and this flows from his character. Brian has stated similar ideas before, as we'll see. With his involvement, the skit has developed into a story about the community as well. During an interview with Brian and Cookie in early 2011, I asked Brian what he thought of my ideas about the way the skits work to provide people with the esoteric knowledge to become part of the fandom, particularly with the inclusion of characters like Mind-Grabber Kid.

"Yeah, yeah," Brian said. "He's the benchmark for obscurity in comics."

I proposed the idea that the entire production was about being as inclusive[24] as possible.

"Creating a community," Cookie said.

Brian followed up on her comment: "Exactly. I've had a hand in—I've either written or had a hand in writing—all of the skits, opening and closing, since 2008, when Scott Cranford stopped being the town Superman, and one of my stated goals was that, whatever path you have taken to Superman, I will have something in there that is familiar to you. We had the nod towards the comic books. We also have the nod towards the movie, and the TV show. This year I've written the closing skit where I'm going to be Perry White. I, of course, have 'Great Caesar's Ghost.' I also have 'Great shades of Elvis' from the *Lois and Clark* show."

Brian in the
tuxedo Cookie
made for him,
Indianapolis,
October 16, 2010.

That's not quite a confirmation of my argument, but it comes pretty close. The idea of community in Brian's mind involves providing familiar ground for everyone, and his opening skits seek to accomplish that by being ecumenical rather than by providing common information. The former is his goal; the latter seems to happen organically.

CONVERSATIONS

People's preferences for Superman vary, but that doesn't matter at the Celebration; no version is favored. This allows attendees to make the festival a very personal experience. Fans with diverse interests get involved in a way that wouldn't be allowed at a celebration devoted exclusively to the films, or to the comics, or the television series. By participating in the Celebration's planning and organization, they learn about the festival itself, another subject of esoteric knowledge. At noon on the last day of the 2010 Celebration, I spoke at length with Brian and Cookie, along with their friend Sean Dulaney. Nearby, costumers were getting ready for the 1 p.m. costume contest. I asked a variety of questions about the character and each person's history with the Celebration itself. I noticed that each of them—and this applied to virtually everyone I interviewed at the Celebration—would begin by talking about how they had become involved with the festival, but would soon broaden the scope of their story to include the history of the festival itself. Sean, for instance, began with a discussion of how he heard about the festival, but was soon discussing the reasons for various events that occurred before he had ever attended.

When I pointed out this pattern—that when I asked people about their history with the festival, the answer turned into a history of the festival—and asked why that might be, Cookie put it well: "Ownership. We take a certain amount of ownership in making sure that we're having fun and that fun can be had. We take ownership of our own fun and we want others to be included in it. It's not being performed for a captive audience. Anybody can walk down the street, anybody can have fun here. If you come in the best costume, or just like some of the kids do, some fun costume, you're going to be admired. People will probably ask to take your picture. You'll be included. It's going to take work to be excluded." Sean and Brian agreed.

I commented that a component of ownership is knowing all sorts of things about the subject, to which Brian responded, "We're the type of people who take the watch apart to see how it works." Being a fan involves this sort of exploration, delving into the subject matter so deeply that knowledge of it becomes second nature. This facilitates discussion. I asked simple questions: What aspects of the character must remain constant? What are the stories you like the most? Brian, Cookie, and Sean would talk with each other, comparing stories and amending each other's comments. When we discussed the fixed and fluid parts of Superman, Sean characterized the character's evolution as follows: "It was just basically an evolution from social justice to moral justice. [Comics editor] Mort Weisinger realized, and I think [television producer] Whitney Ellsworth did as well, that the audience was kids. So, let's cut back on flinging emissions producers. Treat Superman like a young man, or a little boy."[25] Brian agreed readily. They had been discussing the Silver Age, which dates roughly from 1954 to 1980. At this point, Brian brought up the writer Alan Moore, whose story "Whatever Happened to the Man of Tomorrow?" (Moore et al 1985) more or less closed the door on the Silver Age by providing that iteration of the character with an ending in which Superman decides to kill one of his enemies. Superman feels that he had no choice in his action, but so great is his moral code that he feels he can no longer be Superman. He gives up his powers. Following this story, the character was given a blank slate, and his origin was revised. Despite the changes, what must remain constant, according to Brian, is simple. "He doesn't win because he is stronger, or faster, or does things we can't do. It's because he is morally right. Also he has a strength of character, at his core, that I think makes him unique. Also the idea that only criminals should fear him . . . He's basically a moral compass . . ."

Cookie interjects: "When he's being written correctly." Brian expands on the idea: "There are some writers who can't handle that. There's cynicism, and they think he should be written like Batman."

Sean takes up the point: "And the most ironic thing is, the most cynical of the writers in the comics—Alan Moore, Warren Ellis, Mark Millar—they are the guys who will almost fight you to the death to keep Superman written properly. Mark Millar wrote basically the kids version of Superman for the entire run of the animated series comic. And this is the guy who is writing *The Authority* at its worst. Who's writing the quote-unquote adult version of *The Avengers*."

Brian adds, "With the blood and the sex and everything . . ."

Sean continues, "But when it comes to Superman, [Millar's version is] the big blue boy scout."

Although they know Millar's stories, Brian and Sean don't respond to them in an emotional way. When asked about the stories they do respond to, they don't even hesitate: Moore's "Whatever Happened to the Man of Tomorrow?" and "For the Man Who Has Everything" (1985b), and Eliott S. Maggin's "Why Must There Be a Superman?" (1974). These three are widely acknowledged as some of the finest Superman stories. Brian describes "Why Must There Be a Superman?": "It was written by Elliot S. Maggin and plotted by Jeph Loeb, who went on to write some other Superman stories, and it was basically an explanation of why Superman should not interfere in everyday affairs. Which, at the time I read it, was nice because it set up that demarcation line between reality and . . . 'Why can't Superman stop Mount St. Helens? Why can't Superman save the space shuttle?' He's not supposed to. He can't take care of everything because we have to take care of some things ourselves. Which is not a bad lesson."

Brian then describes the impact that *Superman* issue 190 (Shooter et al. 1966) had on him. The issue is a fairly straightforward adventure story in which Superman battles four villains with elemental powers, but the context in which Brian encountered the story is important: "It was a comic that I bought on a trip with my parents, and I bought it with my own money. That was my twelve cents, and we were kind of lower middle class. My parents put me on a budget and everything. Getting that one comic was special. Plus, this was at a time . . . It was a full-length adventure, and this was a time when they were doing three or two stories in a [single comic] book. And suddenly it's like going from short shorts and a cartoon and a newsreel to a full-length motion picture. Give the story time to expand. It was just a fun story, with wacky art and everything."

The context and, surprisingly, the form are as important as the content. For Brian, that Superman comic became an index of, first of all, the degree of financial independence it represented. Second, it was a luxury in some sense, purchased despite his family's financial situation. Third, it was part of a memorable family experience. Beyond that, this particular issue marks the opening up of new storytelling possibilities. Prior to reading *Superman* 190, his experience had been with shorter stories between eight and thirteen pages. *Superman* 190 gains importance because of its commodity value (see Gordon 2012) and his ability to purchase it himself, which is increased because the story's structure—one long tale instead of several shorter stories—differentiates it from others within the same genre.

The association with childhood memories is important, as is the case of nearly everyone I have interviewed. Nonetheless, content is vital. Brian also points to the stories that demonstrate Superman's effect on real people, or rather, on people who are fictional Superman fans. He discusses a story about a police officer whose devotion to Superman inspires his fellow officers. And then he describes a story that he admits makes him emotional, though Superman does not even appear in it: "But the best one and the one that really does touch me emotionally . . . This boy is dying—you know, has a tumor. And the boy loves Superman. The father dresses him in the shirt and hat. And the doctor comes in and there's says there's no hope for him. All we can do is make him comfortable. And the father's distraught raising him by himself. And the kid is almost in a coma. And he wakes up just long enough to say, 'Daddy, I'm going to take care of this kryptonite inside me,' and goes back to sleep. And the doctor says, 'We can't do anything for him.' 'No, he said he's going to make it. Weren't you listening to him? Superman said he's going to win.' That's a hard story not to like."

He keeps back tears as he talks of it. This prompts Sean to bring up a story called "The Kid Who Collected Spider-Man" (Stern et al. 1984) which is about a little boy who wants to learn Spider-Man's secret identity. When the hero hears about him on the news, he pays the boy a visit, and does reveal his name and face. As Spider-Man leaves, we discover that the boy is dying from cancer. Sean finishes his summary with the following comment: "Really and truly, it's a Superman story." The way he says it, and the way Brian and Cookie agree, no higher compliment could be paid.

Brian has mentioned the stories that mattered to him the most as a child—the ones where Superman engaged in titanic battles with villains who challenged him on a physical level. But now, looking at the stories he mentions as most meaningful to him as an adult, he refers to those whose emotional or philosophical component overshadows the action. Sean's choices reflect this same shift, and we saw the same change take place for Jeff Ray in Chapter 2. For Brian as an adult, the Superman stories that matter the most are the ones that reflect how to live a good and moral life. As we sat in a restaurant for an interview in early 2011, he told a couple of stories that reveal the way he makes moral decisions. The first was a response to my comment that, although Superman is very much about fathers and sons, when Brian talked about Superman he never brought up his own father. At this, Cookie smiled. Brian began by referencing Cookie's reaction:

"She's smiling. She's heard this crap before. My father was a very strong parental unit. He was a comic collector back in his youth. So he encouraged me to read. Actually my mother encouraged me to read, my father encouraged me to read comic books because he related to them when he was a child. He told me stories about the original Captain Marvel, Superman, Captain America, Green Lantern, books like that. My father was very conservative, which I have evolved into, for better or worse. He was a very controlling figure, and there reached a point where I started developing a personality, and he didn't quite like that. Especially since I was not quite as conservative as he would have liked. I remember the first time I voted. The candidates were the University of Illinois governing board. At the time you could vote for the student representatives, I think it was. I didn't know anybody on the ballot, so I threw it away by basically voting communist and he got madder than hell at me. He was furious.

"My father and I eventually—especially back in the '60s and '70s, when I became somewhat of a hippie, which was not real popular in east rural Illinois—but he and I came to odds. And my father worked for the military. Starting in the late '60s, he worked with the department of the Army in education. He'd always been a teacher. Both of my parents were teachers, I married a teacher, my oldest friend is a teacher. The pattern continues. And my father went overseas to work with the GIs and came back with a girlfriend, when Vietnam finally fell. We were at odds with this. It boiled down to me telling him . . . He said he was going out east and I said, 'When you come back, you'd better come back alone.' And I told him in front of the whole family, which, of course, ostracized me from the male parental side of that family.

"So, that's why I don't talk about him a whole lot. Because after a certain point he stops being relevant in my life. But by then I'm old enough and make my own decisions. Which of course ties back to Superman. You know, Superman is partly about honoring his Kryptonian heritage, and through that the works of his father. I recognize that and hope I'm not trying to compensate for something. I also see Superman as a very strong, independent figure. Yes, he has Lois, yes, he has friends, but when he's flying into space to battle the Phantom Zone villains, he's pretty much on his own. He's strong not just physically but internally as well. And also he doesn't abuse his power.

"Getting back to my father, one time, somebody was roughhousing. One of my friends was roughhousing, within our core of friends. And he kind of got out of control. I was about six inches taller, considerably heavier, and a bit stronger than him, but I didn't want to fight him because I could hurt him. I basically pushed him away and walked away. And, of course, you get a couple of scrapes in this sort of thing. I come home and I've got a couple bruises, you know, my clothes were messed up. My father asked me, 'What did you do?' I said I ran away from a fight, basically, and he proceeded to wail on me. Because he thought that I should have stuck behind and beat the crap out of this kid. And I said, 'No, that's not what somebody who's stronger does.' I recognized that I had the physical advantage over this kid. And I think that probably contributed to my estrangement to my father, for some particular reason."

The important point here is that Brian's morality differs from his father's. He's not sure precisely why they've become estranged, but it is not one particular incident. He rejected his father's morality, and decided to shape his own, partly because of Superman stories.

The second relevant story came up because we were talking about the definition of myth. I point out that a myth is a story that some people would hear and think, "That's not just a story."

"That transcends a story," Brian adds. "That's an interesting point. Some of us, the Metropolis people, we talk about the spirit of Superman, the spirit of giving, the spirit of service to others, which again figures into religious beliefs. I found myself on Facebook, on the Superfriends page. With the recent flooding that's going through southern Illinois right now, especially through Metropolis, they're looking at a great deal of the city going under water. It's nasty, and some people were making jokes about it. Part of it is that my apartment long ago flooded, so I have great empathy for it. But I think it's just wrong to be making fun of this. A night or two ago I finally unloaded. I said, 'You just need to stop now. This just isn't funny.' I think I used the phrase 'spirit of Superman.' You know, Superman would not be cracking jokes about this stuff. Superman would, if nothing else, just be sympathetic. Of course he'd be building a bunch of moats and a series of locks and dams to filter the water away, but that's just my [love of] '60s Mort Weisinger stuff coming to the fore. To me it's just a whole series of abhorrent behavior that just wasn't fitting my worldview. And I realized that I was relating it directly to Superman. I don't remember anything in the Bible about 'Thou shalt not tease the locals about their flooding problems.'"

In these stories, we can see the extent to which Brian has internalized Superman. Thus, when it comes to telling his own Superman stories, he foregrounds his version of Superman and shares it with the Celebration. His version is supremely inclusive, focuses on community, and is aware of its own context. The emphasis on community is not limited to the 2010 opening skit. In 2011, as the villains are defeated with the help of another DC superhero (the Flash), Superman declares, "It helps to have help from your friends." This leads to the skit's conclusion, in which Superman says, "This celebration brings together people from all different walks of life. We have one common thread. Our common value for truth, justice, and the American Way." Brian, it must be noted, only had some input in the writing of the 2011 skit; the task was completed largely by Andrew Chandler and John Gleckler. The similarity of the message of Superman's closing speech, as written by other members of the same circle of fans, only serves to underline its commonality.

OTHER ASPECTS OF THE CELEBRATION

As would be the case with any festival, the Celebration features far too much material to discuss in a single chapter. I have chosen to focus on the opening ceremony for several reasons. It is a marked performance, able to be decontextualized or analyzed in terms of its function within the festival as a whole. It has a limited cast of characters, and it recurs so that variation can be studied. A similar folkloric analysis could be undertaken with the costume contest as its focus. Or the auction. Or the exhibition of the fan-made films. Or the swearing-in of the Honorary Citizens of Metropolis. Or the trivia contests. The costume contest seems particularly inviting, because the contestants are invited to pose and make a brief speech in character. This leads to several dozen short dramas. Performance has become as much a part of the evaluation as the costumes themselves. The costumers do not limit themselves to Superman, or even to characters found within the Superman mythos. Again, the dominant mood is inclusive. No costumes are rejected; everyone is applauded. Eclecticism and variety are valued.

We can also see this in the food consumed at the Celebration. Being focused on a character rather than on local produce, the festival lacks a defining food. Media sources like to point to funnel cakes and corn dogs as examples of the food consumed at the Celebration, but these are no different from any other festival held in the lower Midwest and upper South. People do come for these foods, but those who do so are the locals. Fans from out of town go to local restaurants to eat much of the time. The festival food from the vendors doesn't hold a lot of allure for them. Their main goal is to spend time with each other. Purchasing food from the vendors doesn't allow time or space for the social aspects of sharing a meal, so the fan communities have dinners together. These are often spontaneously organized, but some, such as the dinner that accompanies the auction and George Award presentation, are part of the Celebration. I happened to be talking to some of the fans at dinner time, and as several of them milled about, they decided to go to dinner. There had been some vague planning earlier in the day, but at this point it became a matter of finding out who was going to attend and where all of these people were at that time. There was a lot of standing around, inquiring to no one in particular about plans. Eventually, despite the lack of organization, everyone went to dinner at a local restaurant within walking distance, and I was asked to join them.

At dinner, there was virtually no discussion of Superman. The little conversation that did focus on the character involved a few comments about how much one of the fans, Alex Rae, who was new to the Celebration that year, looked like Christopher Reeve (he later won the grand prize in the costume contest for his portrayal of Clark Kent). I should not have been surprised at how little discussion of Superman occurred at any of the events. People didn't debate the comics, continuities, interpretations, or the values of the character. Instead, they shared their own creations, especially costumes and films. They discussed the events of the day, which events they planned to attend, and which they were looking forward to attending. They might have become friends for any number of reasons; as with many friendships, the reason it began becomes almost irrelevant. Some attendees were newly acquainted, but even these people didn't talk about Superman. Having come from different places, they talked more about their hometowns and regions than anything else.

The ceremony in which the mayor swears in the Honorary Citizens of Metropolis provides the most condensed opportunity to see the union of local and outside interests. In 2010, Michelle Lyzenga purchased an Honorary Citizen certificate for her father, Bob, as a birthday present. At 3 p.m. on Saturday, he participated in the ritual swearing-in on the pedestal of the Superman statue. He and fifteen others stood with the mayor to recite the oath: "I, Honorary Citizen of Metropolis, having been declared as such, by the City of Metropolis, Illinois, do solemnly swear to serve as an ambassador for the city of Metropolis wherever I go and to uphold the values of truth, justice, and the American way." For $20, anyone can become an Honorary Citizen. It is an opportunity to provide money for the local economy while demonstrating one's devotion to Superman and, more specifically, to the Celebration itself. Becoming an Honorary Citizen is a statement about an individual's participation in the Celebration and a willingness to share interests with other participants.

The festival is all about people sharing interests. Despite the lack of Superman-centered conversations that occurred where I was, the character binds the groups together. On more than one occasion, I heard people saying things such as, "At home I'm the Superman freak, but here I'm just a regular guy." This desire to participate in activities with those of similar interests drives the Celebration. The fact that the interests are varied—some are in it to benefit the town, some to further social goals, some as a chance for performance, some as invited guests—does not change the focus on the festival itself. This is the underlying unity of the Superman Celebration—its participants become involved in order to make it thrive. In doing so, they can achieve their own goals.

I HAVE, THROUGHOUT THIS CHAPTER, BEEN IMPLICITLY FOLLOWING ANOTHER scholar, Dorothea Wender, who wrote about "The Myth of Washington" (Wender 1984). She was being facetious, employing myth-ritual, psychoanalytical, and structural readings to illuminate stories and events surrounding George Washington (and the town of Washington, DC), connecting American folk history to the same sorts of data that mythologists treasure. Knowing that Washington is an historical figure, she can have some fun with the myth-ritual theory, which postulates that the myths are later fabrications that attempt to validate and explain ancient rituals. But we already know that

Superman is fictional, so the culmination of any such analysis cannot be as tongue-in-cheek as Wender's. The participants know he's fictional, but they still take him seriously. The combination of ritual and play evident in the opening ceremony can be characterized by the union of the moods of "let us believe" and "let us make-believe" (Handleman 1977: 187; Turner 1986, 126). The Superman Celebration unites these moods: *Let us believe in make-believe.* In this, the participants resemble the ironic believers in Sherlock Holmes, who, as Michael Saler describes, "were not so much willingly suspending disbelief in a fictional character as willingly believing in him with the double-minded awareness that they were engaged in pretense" (2003: 606). There's a rationality to the enchantment at work here, enabling adults to immerse themselves in the imagination without letting go of reason. Participants, especially devoted fans, choose to believe in the make-believe because it is useful. It provides a symbol.

We can see, in the symbolic forms performed at the Celebration, reiterations of the same meanings found in Superman stories. We have seen one Superman story performed in the opening ceremony drama. I have found in the drama that the tension between the local and the fan is simultaneously articulated and assuaged by a content that emphasizes inclusion above all else. The Celebration commends cooperation in the service of community—for locals who need it both for the tourism and as a break from the norm, for casual fans who want unique experiences, and for devoted fans who need it as a place and time to realize their otherwise imaginary community. Metropolis has other economic possibilities (a casino, a Revolutionary War fort, a Harley Davidson rally), and the fans have other locales at which to congregate (throughout the country there are comic book conventions, and many are attended by the same people who frequent the Celebration). Neither is wholly dependent on the other, but both are better off than they might be in other situations. In Superman their interests unite. This is reflected in Superman's speech during the opening ceremony. It is also reflected in the Superman stories.

Superman's initial role was as a proponent of social justice. He fought for those people who were being beaten by corrupt economic or social systems. As the superhero genre rose around him, he became part of a variety of groups. There is the Superman family, composed of Superman's Kryptonian allies and the friends and cohort of heroes he has developed on Earth. There is the Justice League of America, composed of other superheroes. In cartoons, Superman became part of the Super Friends. There's a bit of a disjunction here, since in popular usage to call someone "Superman" is to stress that person's independence and, above all, singular competence. This is most commonly encountered in sports, where nearly every different professional sport—and a great many specific teams—has a player called Superman for just this reason. Yet the language works to the advantage of Superman as part of a group—in fact, as the coordinating thrust of the group. He's meant to guide us as a group and as individuals. He works as an individual, but his function is directed toward the group. As such, cooperation is inherent in his character. This is in fact precisely the focus of the opening drama in 2010. The fan involvement demonstrates that the community is one of integration, wherein members from several different origins gather together to negotiate ways to make the moment when they can come together into their ideal.

I have here attempted to stress the inclusivity of the Superman Celebration. I do so because it was an early observation of mine, validated by interviews and apparent in the event's symbolic forms. I saw no boundaries drawn between who could or could not participate in any given event; the only requirement was willingness to do so. This is but one perspective, based on my decision to analyze the opening ceremony.

There could be a powerful book written about the Superman Celebration. It would treat the transformation of the whole town, not just of Superman Square and Market Street as I have here, and it would encompass the totality of events to offer a more complete analysis of the way the parts comprise the whole.[26] It would look at the role of the geography and the townspeople in determining what can be accomplished in those four days. It would examine the tension between locals and fans more fully, taking into account those who, perhaps, choose to leave town for that weekend. It would delve more deeply to find those who contest the performances. It would look more thoroughly at the role of celebrity, as well as those honored by the George Award and Lois Lane Award. It would take a closer look at gender, race, and ethnicity, as constructed by costumers and in other performances. It would take into account the concerns of families, particularly spouses of those with a devoted interest in Superman. It would see ways that the Celebration constructs itself as particularly American while inviting participants from other countries. It would account for the history, both oral and officially documented, and the development of the Celebration since its inception—what has changed and why. It would see the Celebration as a microcosm, and articulate the macrocosm it represents. This chapter can only scratch the surface.

- 5 -

METAFOLKLORE AND SUPERMAN HUMOR

IT SEEMS PROPER AT THIS POINT TO TAKE A STEP BACK TO OBTAIN A LARGER perspective. I have thus far presented a number of individual, sometimes idiosyncratic ways of looking at Superman. There is also a growing corpus of interpretive writing about Superman. Interpretive writers, many of whom are academic, offer ways of looking at and understanding the character that are grounded in theory, and many of them choose to focus on a specific aspect of Superman, such as his status as an orphan. It is important to test these theories by looking at what people for whom the story is meaning-ful actually find in the story; fieldwork can thereby provide a corrective to academic criticism (see Toelken 1990). The fact that Superman is an orphan (which ties him into the tradition of hero stories and has inspired the orphan status of a great many other superheroes) is relevant to his character and to interpreting him in a textual sense, but it is also significant that no one I interviewed used the term *orphan* when describing him. Jodi Chromey and Jeff Ray discussed the character's uniqueness, but that could arise from several factors in a character's backstory. The cause of his uniqueness wasn't relevant, possibly because neither Jodi nor Jeff is an orphan.[1]

It is possible that an interpretation of a character can influence how an au-dience sees a character. Thus, discussion of Superman's orphan status might lead a reader to explore it more fully and find a resonance he or she had not noticed before. This influence is a good reason to have several conversations with the same person, over long periods of time. While critical interpretive works can be fascinating, they reflect abstractions, not the contextualized meaning that folklorists seek.

In "Folklore as a Mirror of Culture," Alan Dundes writes that the study of folklore can be "a way of seeing another culture from the inside out instead of from the outside in" (1969: 55). Folklore consists of the creative expres-sions of a community, and quite often those statements are about particular aspects of that community. This chapter takes a look at American cultural expressions about Superman in order to grasp the broader, native perspec-tive on the character. The perspective from which to approach these cultural expressions derives from "metafolklore" (Dundes 1966), or folklore about folklore; that is, a performance of folklore that comments on either itself or other types of folklore. But this does not need to be limited to folklore commenting on folklore; folklore can comment on other forms of expressive culture—indeed, it can comment on culture in general. A good example of the sort of commentary that can be found in folklore is Elliott Oring's analysis of jokes that take as their subject matter the 1986 Challenger space shuttle explosion (Oring 1987a). Oring finds that, while the jokes' content concerns the explosion of a space shuttle, they work toward a criticism of media coverage that trivializes that disaster. He demonstrates that not only is folklore a mirror of culture, it is also a critique of culture. Folklore can be used to make arguments and to reveal the meaning that its performers find in another text or event.

SUPERMAN JOKES

Folklore about Superman comes in many forms. Earlier chapters described several of those, such as folk speech, festival, drama, and tattoos. But these forms do not offer an explicit comment on Superman. They employ aspects of the Superman story to make comments on other parts of culture; interpretations of Superman must be teased out of them and explored in conversation with the performers. Jokes, on the other hand, provide a good entry point into the cultural perspective on Superman. Steven Swann Jones (1985) uses jokes based on fairy tales to get at the meaning of the tales in much the same way that I intend to use Superman jokes here. While the jokes Jones studies bring out symbolic interpretations of the tales—meanings that were already there (we can see this in Jokes 1 and 2 below)—there are Superman jokes that offer a different perspective (Jokes 3 and 4). The latter do not focus on interpretations of the character inherent in the stories, but present "what if" scenarios that are not part of the official narratives. Whereas the fairy tale jokes under Jones's analysis make explicit certain metaphorical aspects of the stories they parody, Jokes 3 and 4 here offer humor based on things that Superman would not do. Nonetheless, the jokes about Superman, similar to jokes about fairy tales, "focus on and reiterate the major concerns expressed in the original story" (Jones 1985: 99).

This analysis of Superman jokes stems largely from online research. During interviews, I found that people knew Superman jokes, but that they didn't tell them out loud very much. I had trouble finding people who told these jokes at all. I had heard both 3 and 4 (though not 1 and 2) in oral tradition, but they seem only to thrive online, commonly on message boards.[2] Superman jokes abound on the internet. Superman appears in four joke types, which exist in many versions. Of those, two (1 and 2) are less about the character than they are about other aspects of culture. They use Superman as shorthand for something—politics and growing up, respectively. Joke 1 is perhaps the most recently invented joke (or at least the most recently circulating), and its content is overtly political. It requires a bit of sociocultural knowledge, not only about Superman, but also Pinocchio and Snow White.

JOKE 1

Pinocchio, Snow White, and Superman are out for a stroll in town one day. As they walked, they came across a sign: Beauty contest for the most beautiful woman in the world. "I am entering!" said Snow White.

After half an hour she comes out and they ask her, "Well, how'd ya do?"

"First Place!" said Snow White.

They continue walking and they see another sign: Contest for the strongest man in the world. "I'm entering," says Superman. After half an hour, he returns and they ask him, "How did you make out?"

"First Place," answers Superman. "Did you ever doubt?"

They continue walking when they see another sign: Contest! Who is the greatest liar in the world? Pinocchio enters. After half an hour he returns with tears in his eyes. "What happened?" they asked.

"Who the hell is Nancy Pelosi?" asked Pinocchio.[3]

As a comment on Superman, this joke is rather straightforward—he is a paradigmatic fit for a strong man. Theoretically, anyone known for physical strength could be substituted, just as anyone known for physical beauty could substitute for Snow White or anyone known for lying could fill in for Pinocchio. Interestingly, the other two fictional characters come from the genre of fairy tales—one stemming from oral tradition and one from literary tradition. All three characters, however, are part of widespread, indeed international, consciousness and are characterized by the qualities that are relevant here. Superman's strength counts among his key traits. Gerard Jones, in writing about why children need fantasy heroes and violence, notes that Superman's strength is especially appealing for kids in the first years of school. He finds something appealing for every age group, and his summation of his thoughts is worth examining at length:

When I was asked to write Superman material, I set out to try to understand how this one simple character could be so compelling to people from toddlers in Superman pajamas to adults who love the Christopher Reeves [*sic*] movies. I found that for preschoolers his one great power was simply being *above pain*. Pain is a central issue for young children—wondering how bad it will be, how to avoid it, how to be brave when it's inevitable—and Superman being attacked and defeating his foes is a comforting demonstration that one can pass through it and come out happy on the other side. As kids get older, they're more likely to value Superman just because he's *strong*. He can knock down buildings, throw jet planes around the sky, tear through the heart of a mountain; whatever seems insurmountable to a child he can do. By preteen years, fans become more interested in Superman's *secret identity*. Going through more complex social stresses, becoming aware of the need to maintain different personae among their buddies in the classroom and at home, trying to retain their fantasy lives without being "nerds," they respond deeply to a nearly omnipotent hero who can be endangered by no more than the revelation of his "real self" to the world. Many fans in their early teens see in the same hero the nexus and protector of a *community* of widely differing individuals: Lois Lane, Jimmy Olsen, Supergirl, assorted superheroes and aliens. Others love learning his decades-long fictional biography and real *history*. Adults respond to Superman most powerfully because he is, in one twenty-something fan's words, "an innocent individual who goes through the worst that a corrupt world can throw at him and comes through clean and pristine—while everybody else grabs hold of him and is lifted out of the swamp themselves." (Jones 2002: 223, emphasis in original)

Jones goes on to point out that Superman is "an organizing fantasy" that presents a world a person can master and understand. It has rules and interpretations.

The closest Jones gets to offering any sort of evidence for his statement is paraphrased words of one fan; he doesn't present his research methods. To be fair, his book is neither academic in nature nor about Superman. His points about who likes the character and why are merely digressions from his larger discussion of the consequences of children imitating the violence they see in fiction. Nonetheless, his points are intriguing. Jones argues that Superman offers psychological comfort at a variety of ages—a mechanism for coping with crises and reassurance that obstacles can be overcome. In this, perhaps, the character of Superman resembles the folktale characters with whom he appears in Joke 1, as analyzed by Bruno Bettelheim in *The Uses of Enchantment* (1977). Bettelheim, a psychologist, examines fairy tales to find their functions in the lives of children. Folklorists, however, have looked at the same materials in light of other age groups as well (Holbek 1987; Falassi 1970). Still, the appeal of Superman to children is strong. Another joke demonstrates the association:

JOKE 2

At his request, each morning 3-year-old Ray's mother pinned a bath towel to the back shoulders of his size two T-shirt. Immediately in his young imaginative mind, the towel became a magic blue and red cape. And he became Superman. Outfitted each day in his "cape," Ray's days were packed with adventure and daring escapades. He was Superman.

This fact was clearly pointed out last fall when his mother enrolled him in kindergarten class. During the course of the interview, the teacher asked Ray his name. "Superman," he answered politely and without hesitation. The teacher smiled, cast an appreciative glance at his mother, and asked again, "Your real name, please." Again, Ray answered, "Superman." Realizing the situation demanded more authority, or maybe to hide amusement, the teacher closed her eyes for a moment, then in a stern voice said, "I will have to have your real name for my records." Sensing he'd have to play straight with the teacher, Ray slid his eyes around the room, hunched closer to her, and answered in a voice hushed with conspiracy, "Clark Kent."[4]

Joke 2 lacks the paradigmatic structure of Joke 1. In Joke 1, any number of substitutions could be made, and have been made for the punch line. It is applicable to numerous situations, particularly politics. Joke 2 could vary paradigmatically by using any superhero with a secret identity in place of Superman. Superman is utilized because of his popularity among Ray's age group, and this notion is bolstered by the fact that every man I interviewed talked about pretending to be Superman as a child. Certainly other characters are imitated, but the widespread recognition of Superman makes him a good fit for the joke.

Joke 2 dramatizes the boundary between work and play and between stages of childhood development. Paramount in importance for our purposes here is the cape, which is the primary signifier of Superman. As Superman fan John Rinaldi told me, "The cape is important. It's a thing that helps him fly through the air. 'Cause we always put a towel around us and stuff like that. . . . You know what the interesting thing is, with the cape, it personified being a superhero. Nobody walks around with a cape. You need a cape to fly. If you didn't have a cape on, you can't make-believe you're flying. It just didn't work."[5] Michael Chabon calls the notion that the cape is essential "the irresistible syllogism of Superman's cape," a reference to the fact that Superman himself does not rely on the cape to fly, but that children equate the flight with the cape, especially in their play: "[Y]ou only had to tie a towel around your shoulders to feel the strange vibratory pulse of flight stirring in the red sun of your heart" (Chabon 2008: 13).

Superman is associated with childhood (as is the entire genre of superheroes), and to some extent, Joke 2 comments on this fact. Joke 2 uses school to signify growing up, and it simultaneously states the need for those who pretend to be Superman to cast aside the childish fantasy upon reaching a certain age and situation while presenting Ray—the character with whom the audience is perhaps supposed to identify—as cleverly subverting that need. We applaud him for it.

A MODEL OF PERFECTION?

This is a book about people who like Superman. There is, however, something more to be said about people who do not like the character. Such sentiments are prominent enough in American culture that entire internet message boards are devoted to disliking him. Henry Jenkins sums up this sentiment: "The reality is that Superman is and remains more of an archetype than a fictional character—too powerful to be really interesting, too bland to be emotionally engaging, and too good to be dramatically compelling. . . . At the end of the day, though, he feels like a museum piece" (Jenkins 2006; see also Grossman 2004 and Seagle et al 2004). Too powerful, too good; these qualities, for some, make Superman bland. Superman is perceived as being in some way perfect, and to many audience members, this is a detriment.

As an opinion, Jenkins's writing could be explored as a reflection of his own personality or aesthetic. As a statement of the character, however, it seems to reflect a perception of bad writing rather than a bad idea. Is Superman too good to be interesting? We find commentary on the notion of Superman's morality in two other jokes. In these jokes, and in much of the Superman humor in popular culture, Superman is not the moral exemplar that the comics and popular conception make him out to be. Instead, he's commits some of the most despicable crimes imaginable. Superman's imperfection is a very prominent strain of Superman humor, and it reflects the idea that perfection is impossible. The following joke was told to me by comics writer Dirk Manning at a comic book convention in Chicago in 2010:

JOKE 3A

One day, Superman's flying over the world, patrolling everything, and, you know, flying around like he does every day, stuff like that. And he happens to be flying over this one beach and he looks down. And he sees Wonder Woman lying there naked. She's just got this little smirk on her face, kinda laying there spread eagle, hanging out, just kind of doing her thing. And Superman's like, "Wow, man." Obviously he's been on a team with Wonder Woman. He knows Wonder Woman. They're both superheroes and stuff like that—you know, JLA and all that stuff. He's flying by and he sees her. "I finally saw wonder woman naked. That's just awesome."

So the next day he's flying over the world again, and he happens to fly over the same location. And there again is Wonder Woman lying there naked on the beach, you know . . . little smirk on her face . . . spread eagle. Says, "Wow." And for the first time this thought enters his head, like, "What if . . . what if . . ." But, you know, he's Superman. He's got to stand for the good thing, so he just keeps flying.

But sure enough, the next day, like a moth to a flame he flies over that same spot at the same time. And yet again there's Wonder Woman . . . smirk on her face . . . laying there spread eagle on the beach. And this time Superman thinks, "I am faster than a speeding bullet . . . what if . . ." He's like, "No, no, no! I can't think like that! She's my teammate! I won't, I can't do it!" And he flies away.

And over and over again this happens. Every day at the same time Superman flies over the same beach looks down sees Wonder Woman. And every day he thinks again more and more, "What if . . ." And the what if's turn into, "Maybe I should."

And one day he's flying over and he sees Wonder Woman down there lying on the beach . . . spread eagle . . . little smirk on her face . . . things like that. Finally, he just snaps. He flies down there, boom-boomboomboomboomboomboomboomboom! Just starts banging her as fast as he . . . dadadaddoo! Real quick, boof! And then he's gone again. Superman flies away. And, of course, Superman's feelings on

this topic at this point are a subject for another time altogether, because we go to Wonder Woman. She's on the beach. She opens her
eyes. She says, "Did you just hear something, like a whooshing noise
or something?" And the Invisible Man says, "You know, I did. And all
of a sudden for some reason my ass really hurts and it's bleeding like
a sieve."

Superman attempts to rape Wonder Woman but unintentionally rapes the
Invisible Man. In this variant, Superman commits this crime after a period
of introspection, which reflects the way the culture at large contemplates
the nature and moral character of Superman. This introspection is, however, rarely spelled out so clearly. Manning's variant is the most elaborate I
encountered; the joke can be rendered very succinctly:

JOKE 3B

Superman's flying around one day looking to save stuff, when he no-
tices with his incredible vision, Wonder Woman on a roof top. She's
touching herself quite ummm . . . intimately, in the nude. So Superman gets this crazy idea that if he flew down there at super speed,
he could umm . . . do his thing, and leave without her even noticing.
So he does . . . he's in, he's out . . . completely undetectable. Wonder
Woman, after seeing a big gust of wind says "What the heck was that?"
The Invisible Man says, "I have no clue, but my ASS is killing me!!"[6]

The difference in length (426 words vs. 96 words) is not empty elaboration.
Expansion enables Manning to establish context for Superman. I attribute
some of his elaboration to the presence of the recorder; not only is Manning performing for posterity, but he is also performing for an unknown
audience. I had explained my project, and he knew that his version of the
joke might be read by people who knew little about Superman. This is why
he includes details about Superman's relationship with Wonder Woman;
they serve as an aside, a parenthetical interpolation to the joke. I attribute
some of the length to the fact that Manning, having digressed from the plot
of joke, is repeating some information as he figures out where he left off.
Much of the elaboration—the sound effects, for example—can be attributed
to the specific performance for the recorder, but there's more to it than that.
In Manning's longer variant, Superman experiences a moral and existential
crisis. We might say that, because his character is so fundamentally moral in
nature, any moral crisis is for Superman an existential crisis. In Manning's

joke, Superman contemplates whether or not he should take advantage of the situation. He knows what's right, but ultimately chooses to do wrong.

I've spoken with many people about this joke; it's usually the only Superman joke they know. Its concern with Superman's morality is obvious, yet this is not what the punch line is about. So it seems reasonable to wonder if Superman's morality is really what's at issue here. Several interviews play this out. I talked with Matt Traughber, who runs a comic book shop in Bloomington, Indiana, called Vintage Phoenix. He had little to say about the joke, but his one comment was interesting. He said that the common complaint made by comic book fans is that, in the fictional universe where Superman lives, there is no character called the Invisible Man. In other words, it doesn't meet the standards of continuity. Yet the joke is not about the continuity, either. The appearance of the Invisible Man seems to be one of the two ways the joke impugns Superman's moral character. The first is the rape of Wonder Woman, the second—which is possibly only implicit—is homosexual sodomy. Both of these stem from his powers, which enable his moral transgressions. Another joke takes up the same theme of an immoral Superman:

JOKE 4

A guy walks into a bar on the top of a very tall building. He sits down, orders a huge beer, chugs it, walks over to the window, and jumps out. Five minutes later, the guy walks into the bar again, orders another huge beer, chugs it, walks over to the window, and jumps out again. Five minutes later, he re-appears and repeats the whole thing. About half an hour later, another guy at the bar stops the first guy and says, "Hey, how the heck are you doing that?!" The first guy responds, "Oh, it's really simple physics. When you chug the beer, it makes you all warm inside and since warm air rises, if you just hold your breath you become lighter than air and float down to the sidewalk." "WOW!" exclaims the second man, "I gotta try that!" So he orders a huge beer, chugs it, goes over to the window, jumps out, and splats on the sidewalk below. The bartender looks over to the first man and says, "Superman, you're a jerk when you're drunk."[7]

This joke has many variants. While Superman's presence remains constant, the other two participants range from a barfly and bartender to a Canadian and an Irishman (in that variant, Superman is at first referred to only as an American). Joke 4 often begins with the common opening of "a guy walks into a bar," and the final line sometimes varies by using "asshole" instead of "jerk" to characterize Superman. The location is sometimes at the top of a cliff, rather than a tall building. And the explanation (or lie) Superman gives for how he's able to survive the fall varies as well, from a strange updraft resulting from the architecture to no explanation at all. The variations seem less important than the fixed elements: Superman is drunk; Superman lies to a presumably innocent man. The lie is bolstered by a demonstration of Superman's powers. The victim is convinced that he can reproduce Superman's feat, and he jumps to his death. The third person present delivers the punch line, and it's important to note that the punch line includes the revelation of Superman's identity and that he's drunk.

I had a lot of trouble eliciting any oral literary criticism about this joke—or about any of the jokes. Scott Bayles, whose story is told in Chapter 6, knew of Joke 4 and said he didn't like this (or Joke 3) precisely because they present Superman in a negative light. He wrote to me, "I've never been a fan of [Joke 4], I think, because it portrays Superman as very human and flawed, representing the worst of humanity rather than being the altruistic symbol of hope that the character was evolved into over the years. I prefer Bill Cosby's Superman routine; the one where he's changing clothes in the phone and a police officer comes over and tells him to step outside. Superman says, 'But officer, I'm Superman. Can't you see this red S on my chest?' The cop replies, 'I'll give you red S and black eye if you don't get out of that phone booth!'"[8]

Jokes 3 and 4 are precisely the sort of tradition we should expect to develop alongside a myth: the double aspect that laughs and scoffs at the sacred deity. In this tradition, Superman embodies his opposite; where official versions present him as moral, Superman in the jokes is immoral. Mikhail Bakhtin, who explored precisely this phenomenon, writes, "At the early stages of preclass and prepolitical social order it seems that the serious and the comic aspects of the world and of the deity were equally sacred, equally 'official'" (1968: 6; see also Morreal 1989). This is especially true in the case of Superman. Valerie D'Orazio, who worked for DC Comics, writes about the sacrosanct way the company treated Superman: "There was a sense that we were to avoid any scandal relating to the company or the characters at all costs—that nothing should darken the aura around Superman in any way, directly or indirectly" (D'Orazio 2008).[9] With this sharp division between the sacred and the comic—things you must not laugh at and things you may laugh at—and between the official and the unofficial, it seems fitting that the official Superman stories treat him as sacrosanct while the folklore (the unofficial stories) sometimes villainizes him.

What, then, are the jokes saying? It's tempting to see in Joke 4 a comment on the phenomenon of kids jumping off high places with a Superman cape on, crossing the line between pretending to be Superman and mistaking fantasy for reality, transforming play into ostension. This is the subject of another bit of Superman folklore. Actor George Reeves—who died of a gunshot wound in 1959—was reported as having killed himself. Newspaper headlines alerted people to this immediately following his death; "TV's Superman kills self," read the *New York Post* headline on June 16, 1959. Rumors soon spread that Reeves had taken hallucinogenic drugs and, believing himself capable of flight, had leapt from the top of a hotel. It was also rumored that he killed himself out of grief over so many children having gotten hurt or killed trying to fly in imitation of him. While kids do get hurt imitating Superman in this way, such accidents are not very common.

Just as, in Elliott Oring's analysis, "dumb-blond jokes are not about blonds" but instead "evaluate and make foolish values associated with traditional images of women" (2003: 66), Superman jokes are not really about Superman. These jokes dramatize issues centered on morality. They comment not on the issues themselves but on the dramatizations represented by Superman stories. Where the Superman stories reveal, commonly, a "perfect man who fell from the sky and did only good" (Moore 1986: 1), the jokes subvert the possibility of moral perfection. They show a Superman who uses his powers for trickery, self-service, and crime. Of particular relevance is the notion that Superman's perfection extends from his physical nature to his moral idealism. These two aspects of the character intertwine, since his moral perfection is bound to his physical power. If not for his power, his morality would be no more important than that of any other being. With great power comes the ability to affect great numbers of people. Superman could conquer the world—yet he does not. The jokes are, in this way, also a comment on the nature of heroism. Superman inspires people to act as he does. The ramification here is that he must do the right thing because other people will follow his lead. Joke 4 places the rhetorical crux of this in a physical act—people will imitate his power of flight, just as they will imitate his morality. When he leads them astray, the results are disastrous.

TWO CARTOONS[10] ALSO DEPICT THIS IDEA. THEY INDICATE THAT HUMANS cannot imitate the abilities of Superman. The first parodies the commonly seen "caution signs" posted in hazardous areas. It portrays a man in free-fall from the roof of a building. Next to the cartoon drawing are the following

Mother Goose and Grimm, by Mike Peters, August 17, 2006. © 2006 Grimmy, Inc.-Distributed by King Features Syndicate Inc.

words: "Caution You're Not Superman." A second cartoon depicts the same idea. A man in a superhero costume, compete with cape, shouts, while leaping from a building, "AM GOT THE POWER!!!" The three panels show him running, then leaping, and finally flying with a halo over his head, denoting his demise.

Superman represents heroic and ideal perfection, and these jokes judge the pretense to perfection. We detect their message in the fate of the anonymous victim who follows the drunken Superman's lead, only to fall to his death. We find the victim again in other cartoons, performing the same ill-fated leap. The victim is a normal human serving as a proxy for the rest of us. Superman is a handy referent, an allusion that carries the connotative thrust of perfection. Jokes 3 and 4 depict imperfection in physical and moral ways—since these aspects of the character are inextricably bound—and in doing so they articulate a widespread notion about perfection and imperfection: To be human is to be imperfect, as often expressed in the proverb "To err is human, to forgive, divine." Since Superman is perfect, to imitate him is to go against human nature. Those who do so are doomed to failure.

Another strand running through Superman humor depicts him using his powers for selfish, sometimes licentious reasons. This time, it's his X-ray vision. Humorous depictions of Superman typically show him doing two things with his powers: cheating at poker and seeing through clothing. There seems to be something of wish fulfillment going on in these cartoons, as well as in the jokes; flight and X-ray vision are common enough fantasies. The difference is that in the cartoons, Superman either gets caught abusing his powers or feels so guilty about it that he confesses. The humor comes from the tension arising because he is caught, but we might also interpret it in a way that suggests a view of human nature that does not include freedom at

Off the Mark by
Mark Parisi,
January 21, 2002

such a level of unencumbered libido. The humor hinges upon the audience responding, to some extent, with a level of sympathy for Superman doing such things—as if to say that any of us would do so if we had the chance. The relevant point is that Superman does not.

ON THE COUCH

The argument above deals mostly with people trying to be like Superman. Plenty of examples of humor hinge on Superman experiencing the same problems as the average person. This theme is exploited for comedic purposes in several ways. The first is psychological. Danny Fingeroth's *Superman on the Couch* (2004) exemplifies this theme, at least in its title and cover. The book's analysis does not discuss the dysfunction of superheroes, but its cover image depicts a generic superhero modeled after Superman lying on a couch while a Freudian analyst takes notes about his possible neuroses. Similarly, the promotional photograph for the documentary *Confessions of a Superhero* shows Christopher Dennis,[11] one of the subjects of the documentary, dressed as Superman, lying on a couch. No therapist is present here, but the image invokes a therapeutic session.

A number of single-panel cartoons bring the theme to fruition. In one, the creator of which I could not trace,[12] a cartoon image shows a superhero (mostly identifiable as Superman, except for the mask on his face), head held in despair, asking his therapist, "When is it *my* turn to be rescued?" Another cartoon, an installment of *Off the Mark* by Mark Parisi, implies that Superman makes the mistake of trusting people who are untrustworthy: A therapist offers Superman the advice, "You've got to stop trusting people as far as you can throw them,"[13] which has the nice layering of a joke about both Superman on a proverbial phrase. A third therapy cartoon, from Mike Peters's *Mother Goose and Grimm*, has Superman voice the curious complaint that "I have all these superpowers . . . but I still can't win the super lotto."[14] In other words, although he is the peak of physical perfection, Superman is still the victim of luck. The theme of Superman in therapy reflects Superman's imperfection. It invites us to notice that, though the character is physically and morally perfect, these things do not comprise the entirety of a human being.[15] There are other elements into which his perfection does not extend, such as mental health.[16]

There are indications that the economic stresses of the world are too much for Superman. Some cartoons reflect the changing nature of the newspaper industry, in which Clark Kent makes his career. In the comic books, Superman originally made this career choice because the newswire was the fastest way to stay informed of threats and disasters that required his attention. The advent of other media has made this seem quaint, which is a criticism often leveled at the character himself (as when Jenkins refers to him as "a museum piece"). In *Time* magazine, Lev Grossman notes that "he's a metaphor for America, but an outdated, obsolete America" (2004: 72). Cartoons reflect this notion that Superman is somehow out of step with the times. One such cartoon is set in the office of Perry White, editor of the *Daily Planet*. White holds in his hand a pink "layoff" sheet of paper, handing it to Kent while saying, "As you know, Kent, it's a tough time right now for newspapers."[17] In another, his career as a journalist requires him to adapt to working on the internet, prompting the thought that it's "not the same" as he looks at "daily-planet.com."[18] Other elements of the changing world provide the opportunity for humor. In some early stories, Superman habitually removed his business suit in a telephone booth prior to springing into action. By the 1978 film,

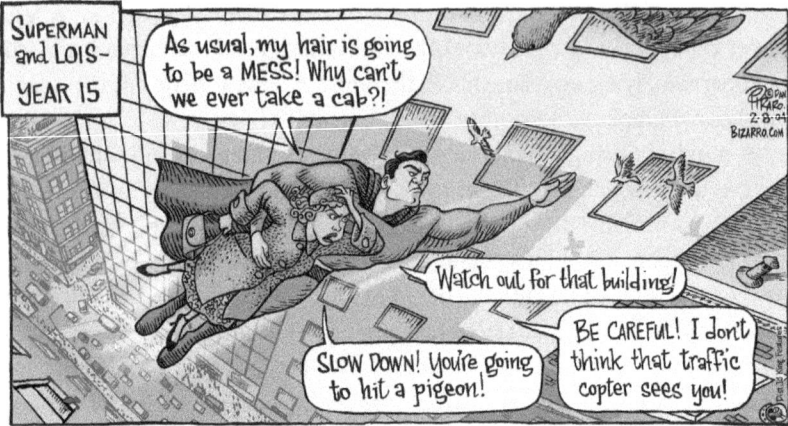

Bizarro by Dan Piraro, February 8, 2004.

this was treated as a joke when Kent paused briefly to look askance at one of the current phone "booths" that didn't feature even so much an enclosure to shelter the user. In *Rhymes with Orange* by Hilary Price, Superman is sitting at a bar with Batman and says, "Every corner there used to be a phone booth! These days I'm lucky to find a porta-john." Dave Coverly's *Speed Bump* reflects Superman's dissociation with current mainstream culture. In the panel, he sits in a lawyer's office, looking at a piece of paper. The lawyer sits across from him, mute. Superman says, in reference to the paper, "'Faster than a speeding bullet from a legally purchased and registered handgun' just doesn't have the same ring."[19]

Superman is also depicted as having romantic trouble. This does not arise because of outdated ideas of gender roles, as we might expect, but for other reasons. First, Superman's Fortress of Solitude—the arctic location where he goes when he's not working as a superhero or reporter—is used as a sign of his independence and thus for his aversion to commitment. In another *Mother Goose and Grimm* strip, Superman is on a date with a woman. As they clink together glasses of wine, something the woman has said prompts Superman to say, "Because . . . then it wouldn't be a Fortress of Solitude anymore, would it?"[20]

Other humor reflects the oddity of Superman's costume. In a *Bizarro* strip by Dan Piraro, one of Superman's dates says, "It's an impressive career and you've got a great body, but if we go out again, could you wear normal clothes?" In a *Mother Goose and Grimm* strip, Peters depicts Superman saying to his date, "Do you mind paying? Superheroes don't carry cash."[21]

If Superman is less than perfect as a date because of the trappings of the superhero genre, his marriage is marred by instead by human foibles, particularly the notion that "familiarity breeds contempt." In a cartoon captioned "Superman and Lois—Year 15," Piraro's *Bizarro* depicts Superman and Lois flying through the air. Lois talks incessantly: "As usual, my hair is going to be a mess! Why can't we ever take a cab?! Watch out for that building! Slow down! You're going to hit a pigeon! Be careful! I don't think that traffic copter sees you!"[22] It plays upon the negative stereotype of the nagging wife. In another cartoon with similar composition, *Pardon My Planet* by Vic Lee, Superman and his unnamed companion are flying through the air. She says to him, "You never take me anywhere fun."[23] The implication—that their relationship has become mundane and boring—draws its humor from the irony of that statement being made while they are in flight.

Physical imperfection is also a trope to be employed for humor. In one cartoon, Piraro depicts a morbidly obese Superman explaining to a friend, "All this time I thought my greatest weakness was Kryptonite. Turns out it was French fries all along."[24] In these cartoons, Superman's physical flaw is either old age or gluttony/obesity. This leads to a loss of powers. One cartoon shows Superman taking a pair of "ex-ray glasses" out of a box. The caption reads, "Superman turns 50." Age also leads to a less-than-perfect physique. In a *Mother Goose and Grimm* strip, a woman says to an overweight Superman, who is walking away from a fast food restaurant with a hamburger, "You don't have to supersize everything." Age can lead to dementia as well. In a *Far Side* cartoon by Gary Larson, captioned, "Superman in his later years," the character, wearing a hat and glasses, stands at an open window. He has turned back to his wife to say, "Dang! . . . Now where was I going?"[25]

A FINAL MOTIF IN THE HUMOR IS THE COSTUME ITSELF: CARTOONISTS OFTEN focus their humor on the "underwear on the outside" element that defines the superhero costume. One cartoon by Doug Bratton comments on the absurdity of the image by changing it a bit. In this, Superman's costume is the standard one, except that the briefs he traditionally wears have been replaced by boxer shorts. He has apparently ordered this costume instead of making it himself, and there has been a mistake. He says, "What the heck?! I ordered *briefs*, not boxers!! This just looks absurd!!!"[26]

Other cartoons follow the idea: Hilary Price's *Rhymes with Orange* shows "How Clark Kent Blew His Identity" by having him walk into the *Daily Planet* with his underwear on the outside of his everyday clothing. These cartoons point to the dysfunction of being a superhero, especially in social situations.

Speedbump by
Dave Coverly
May 12, 2009

Clothes are the most obvious manifestation of this, being outwardly visible.[27] Superheroes, the humor tells us, are not normal.

Taken together, these examples of Superman humor reveal that, to some extent, the character is indeed viewed as old-fashioned. In addition, the conventions of the superhero genre are seen as absurd, but the absurdity is accepted, for the most part. Much of the humor arises from putting Superman in common but difficult situations, especially the tribulations of marriage and growing old. These are situations that Superman doesn't have to deal with in comics or films. Although some versions of the character get married, the official story is not about making a normal marriage work. And, although he grows older, the official story is not about coming to terms with old age. Symbolically, the humor here is the same as that in the jokes: putting Superman into a situation that normal people have to face and letting the consequences bear the comedic weight. The cartoons about underwear being worn incorrectly provide the clue to understanding the overall gist of the humor. If Superman—perfect as he is in a moral sense—gets things wrong that every adult can do properly without trouble, then we need not worry about living up to his model.

There is a tendency in mythological thought to poke fun at the gods. It can be found as early as Homer's *Iliad*. This story treats the gods as above human beings but concerned with their fates. They intercede in wars and in love. Yet they also stand around making fun of Hephaestus and his marital difficulties with Aphrodite. Furthermore, the trickster figure, common cross-culturally, is constantly a figure of comedy. The Norse god Loki, a trickster, is frequently getting into trouble, and he makes fun of the other gods. Audiences are invited to laugh as Thor dons a dress and veil to disguise himself as Freya in order to retrieve his stolen hammer. We're invited to laugh at the preposterous things coyote does. Cartoons such as the above are certainly not far removed from the humorous stories of the gods.

SUPERMAN AS SAVIOR

And Superman *is* the equivalent of a god, at least in the popular imagination. If we didn't have Reynolds's book *Superheroes: A Modern Mythology* (1992), or the scores of other academic and popular books that proclaim as much, we would still have the words of television character Homer Simpson to make the equation clear: "I'm not normally a praying man, but if you're up there, please save me, Superman."[28] Superman rescues people from danger. A *Speed Bump* comic shows Superman drinking with another, anonymous superhero (or perhaps a psychologist dressed as a superhero). Superman says to him, "You save people from themselves? Man, that's a tough gig . . ."[29] These cartoons comment on the kind of hero Superman is. He saves us from external dangers, such as natural disasters and criminals, not from our psychological issues. Cartoons also use Superman to comment on the nature of heroism. They point out the limits of his actions. One example is a *Strange Brew* cartoon by John Deering, in which Superman is flying by a locksmith, who is wearing a cape. The locksmith says, "You really want to be a hero? Unlock a car someone left their keys in."[30] It is worth noting that the Bloomington, Indiana, towing company Chad's Towing has put Superman chevrons on the hoods of their trucks. A similar cartoon, also by Deering, features Superman flying while holding a criminal. The criminal says to him, "Shouldn't you, like, be doing something about the environment?!"[31]

Underlying these cartoons is the notion of superhero impotence. Superman cannot fix the environment, our psyches, or the economy. It's an impotence of the genre, explored most fully in a story called *Superman: Peace on Earth* (Dini et al 1998), in which Superman decides to ensure that everyone in the world has enough food to eat for one day. He meets many obstacles and must eventually leave the job undone. This story exposes the weakness of Superman, a fact recognized by cartoonists. A cartoon shows Superman, Wonder Woman, and Spider-Man looking at a picture of newly inaugurated President Barack Obama. Superman says to the others, "So you think he can save us?"[32]

During the 2008 presidential campaign, dozens of images could be found on the internet depicting Obama as Superman. The portrayal of Obama as Superman fits with Superman's association with hope and Obama's campaign slogan of hope and change. The idea of a savior in the White House was tantalizing given the economic difficulties experienced in the United States at the time, so images of Obama in the full Superman suit, and especially of him pulling open his button-down shirt to expose the costume underneath, were popular. These images use the Superman image, pose, and costume to invoke the idea that Obama could somehow (the specifics were not quite clear) save the country from the numerous problems it faced at the time. The equation of Superman and candidate Obama became a recurring theme in humor, extending even to a speech given by Obama himself. During the Al Smith Dinner on October 16, 2008 (an event where candidates traditionally give humorous speeches, poking fun at each other and themselves), Obama said, "Contrary to the rumors you have heard, I was not born in a manger. I was born on Krypton, and was sent here by my father Jor-El to save the planet Earth." When, inevitably, Obama's presidency didn't solve all the country's problems, people started pointing out that the expectations had been unreasonable. Since the analogy had been made so often—we understood Obama in terms of Superman—it only seemed natural that the rhetoric surrounding the continuing problems would remain the same. Obama ceased to be Superman, as evidently everyone had known all along. In July of 2009, Colin Powell said that he felt the president was doing well, though not perfectly. He said Obama couldn't possibly accomplish everything: "We didn't elect Superman, we elected a human being."[33] When asked if Obama was acting appropriately in response to a large oil spill, commentator Ben Stein said, "I don't think Obama's done much wrong. . . . Look, he's not Superman. He can't dive down into a well and plug it up."[34] The rhetorical use of Superman as a means to understand Obama shifts from optimism to realism. Optimism had its place in the campaign, when promises were key, so Obama was Superman. But when performance is at issue, those who are making statements want to offer a different perspective that reinforces realistic possibilities, so Obama is not Superman.

Superman humor is a way to comment on what it means to be a hero. The pairing of Superman with a locksmith points out that real heroism is what's possible in real life. When a criminal accuses Superman of focusing on the wrong problems (i.e., "Shouldn't you be doing something about the environment?"), it is a comment on the deficiencies of the superhero genre—that superheroes cannot solve *any* real-world problems. The popular tradition is critical of Superman, and it uses him to be critical of humanity at large. If the cartoons are commentaries on the nature of heroism, then the one in particular, by Nick Galifianakis, is a commentary on the people who are looking for heroes. Floating in the air near a man who is hanging by his fingertips on the side of a tall building, Superman says, "You know, at some point you really do need to learn to help yourself."[35]

A FEW FINAL THEMES

In many of the preceding examples of Superman in folklore and popular culture, we have seen people telling their own Superman stories. But with the uses of Superman in rhetorical expressions about Obama, we see people using Superman to make sense of other people. Superman is an interpretive tool, one about which some people spend a lot of time contemplating. In an episode of the television show *Seinfeld*, two of the characters, Jerry Seinfeld and George Costanza, discuss whether or not Superman has a superhuman sense of humor:

JERRY: I think Superman probably has a very good sense of humor.
GEORGE: I never heard him say anything really funny.
JERRY: It's common sense. He's got super strength, super-speed; I'm sure he's got super-humor.
GEORGE: Either you're born with a sense of humor or you're not. It's not going to change. Even if you go from the red sun of Krypton all the way to the yellow sun of the Earth.
JERRY: Why? Why would that one area of his mind not be affected by the yellow sun of the Earth?
GEORGE: I don't know. But he ain't funny.[36]

In the earliest comic books, written by Jerry Siegel, however, Superman regularly uses humor to ridicule criminals as he apprehends them. This has changed. He now rarely cracks a joke in the comic books. He's more likely to be funny in television shows, but even then such behavior is rare. Bakhtin writes about the history of the relationship between laughter and the sacred in Western culture. These two modes of behavior have sometimes been joined, sometimes been driven apart in official culture—in many cases, humor regarding something sacred is seen as sacrilegious. There is a related disjunction between folk and official culture, and that disjunction is often found at the point of laughter. This dichotomy in culture has long been recognized, but Bakhtin emphasized that the folk or vernacular element is often characterized by humor. He describes medieval parodies of scripture and ritual (1968: 77 ff.). It seems that Superman's tendency toward humor reflects this division as well. If he is merely a fictional character, there can be humor in his stories. If, however, he is something more, a myth perhaps, then he is not fit for that mode of storytelling. And the editors and storytellers who create the official narratives seem to have an interest in perpetuating the mythical component of the Superman story. Thus, in the official stories, Superman can inspire us and uplift us, but he can no longer make us laugh.

The humorists—the joke tellers and the cartoonists—see things differently. The parodies described by Bakhtin were often created by devout men, so the humor itself is no evidence of profanity. Likewise, Superman jokes and cartoons are not evidence of a dislike of Superman (though they may be appreciated by people who dislike the character). Instead, they represent the need for laughter in the face of "official seriousness" (Bakhtin 1968: 75) toward the character. That official seriousness finds expression in the dialogue between Jerry and George. Jerry Seinfeld, both character and actor, is a Superman fan. The character of George is not, though as an "everyman" in this situation, he articulates the common perception of Superman as humorless. Jerry, the devotee, sees at least the potential for humor. His occupation as a comedian might contribute to this view. As a comedian, Seinfeld stands opposed to the official reading of the character as sacred and thus inviolable. He allows humor to enter into the sacred realm. He represents the devotee who writes the parody—actually doing so in a series of dramatic commercials for credit cards in which Seinfeld starred alongside an animated Superman, which were played almost entirely for laughs.

The exchange in *Seinfeld* aims for humor, but it reflects the sorts of discussions that fans have about the characters (see Pustz 1995). It has become trite to describe the concerns of the average comic book fan as being about who is stronger, Superman or the Hulk, but these discussions have been a vital part of the fan community. It is an element of the folklore of superheroes, but it is also an element of how Richard Reynolds characterizes the continuity developed by superhero comic books—it's part of their appeal. When Reynolds discusses the continuity and mythology of superheroes, he distinguishes between "serial continuity" (which is the sum total of stories actually told as part of a comic book universe, such as those published by Marvel or DC) and "structural continuity," which is the combination of serial continuity and all the elements of the real world and its implications that must exist for a story to work within serial continuity (1992: 38–41). Continuity in comic books is the result of intertextuality, which leads readers to infer much more than actually happens on the page (such as characters eating regular meals or traveling). Such inferences lead to discussions over which character is stronger, more intelligent, or better in other ways. They lie beneath the humor as well, as people work out the details of the real-world implications of superheroes. Reynolds writes that the ideal fan envisions "an ideal DC or Marvel metatext: a summation of all existing texts plus all the gaps which those texts have left unspecified" (1992: 43).

This is good as far as it goes, but the processes by which these texts are envisioned are left unarticulated. Indeed, as far as I can tell, for every fan who obsesses over the metatext, there are hundreds whose affinity for the character is much more specific and limited, who may only care about one version of the character, and who don't worry too much about continuity. We have seen so far that Superman, in the popular consciousness, is a heroic savior, a moral exemplar, whose features are his immense strength, invulnerability, flight, secret identity, and costume. These are precisely the aspects of the character that are treated in humorous folklore and cartoons. They reveal that the elements of the story and character are elements worth thinking deeply about, and useful for examining issues of identity and heroism.

- 6 -

MORALITY

FOR A FINAL CHAPTER BASED ON FIELDWORK, I WOULD LIKE TO JUXTAPOSE the experience of two Superman fans, Scott Bayles and Josh Walgenbach. Unlike Chapter 2, in which we saw three points on the continuum of affinity for Superman, these two men have ideas about Superman that at first seem directly opposed to each other. Analysis will reveal, however, that both Josh and Scott use Superman to think through the same questions regarding morality, raising children, and relationships between themselves and their communities. Their experiences have led them to different conclusions regarding overarching issues, but the underlying internal discourse of these men shows how Superman has shaped them in remarkably similar ways.

Many people consider the most essential component of Superman to be his moral virtue, the values he holds and embodies through his actions. As you read the stories of Scott and Josh, consider a statement by Ben Saunders, to which this discussion will return: "For to the extent that Superman is defined by an absolute and *a priori* commitment to a finally unverifiable and unknowable good, he reproduces in himself the formal structure of all acts of religious faith. Thus, we might say, Superman's ethics are theological in form while remaining indeterminate at the level of content" (2011: 32).

SCOTT BAYLES

The concept of embodiment is a useful one when considering Superman. People like to dress up as this character. Through exercise and costuming, people make themselves look like him. Superman is a rare type of character who is known for his posture.

In Chapter 3, Josh Elder described his tendency to assume the poses that have become associated with Superman. This becomes part of the way people perform Superman. They create costumes to wear in public, and in those costumes they pose for photographs. Scott Bayles has been costuming

Scott sewing the trunks for his costume, Palmyra, Illinois, October 6, 2012.

since 2008, and his case presents an opportunity to see the process by which Superman can become part of a variety of aspects of a person's life.

When I arrived to interview Scott, he was working on a new Superman costume inspired by the costume drawn by Frank Quitely in the comic series *All-Star Superman* (Morrison et al. 2011). While his wife and three kids went about their business and played around us, Scott sewed the trunks, belt loops, and cape for this costume. He didn't have any other costumes at the time. He'd either sold them or "cannibalized" them to make others. Scott started making superhero costumes in 2008. He and his family lived near Metropolis, Illinois, and he heard about an attempt to break the world record for the most people in Superman costumes in one place at the Celebration that year. He made costumes for himself and his son so they could be part of the event. He knew a little bit about sewing from home economics in school, but that was it.

In costuming, Bayles follows a long-standing fan tradition. Among the earliest superhero costumers are Dick Lupoff and Pat Lupoff, who dressed as Captain Marvel and Mary Marvel for the 1960 World Science Fiction Convention (there were no comic book conventions at that time). There's a bricolage quality to their costumes, made from pillow cases, T-shirts, and rubber gloves (Schelly 1995: 19). They attended a masquerade, at which there was a costume contest. Although Dick Lupoff admits that the costumes weren't of high quality, he deems it a success: "[E]veryone just clustered around and wanted to talk about the costumes and the characters they were based on" (quoted in Schelly 1995: 20). Other costumers followed suit, and over time the available materials have become more and more workable as costumes have become increasingly elaborate. We can see that, even at the beginning of superhero costuming, it was a social, even familial endeavor.

Costuming is very much a Bayles family activity, but Scott makes the costumes by himself. His wife, Ashley, doesn't like working with spandex, which can be difficult. Scott doesn't mind the difficulty, and he does his best to make costumes with which he is satisfied. In this pursuit, he doesn't always adhere to a particular design from comics, film, or television. Heather Joseph-Witham discusses such adherence to standardized versions of costumes as an ongoing dialectic between fidelity to source material and fans' own tastes (1996: 16). Some fans strive to reproduce the source as closely as possible. Others, like Scott, prefer to treat the source material as an inspiration, a beginning point from which to proceed according to his own taste. Strict adherence is complicated by the fact that many versions of the costume are drawn and thus don't have to conform to physical limitations imposed by gravity and the contours of the human body.[1] Drawn costumes are idealized and difficult to replicate. The cape illustrates this point: As drawn in most comic books, it needs no anchoring to the shoulders of his shirt, nor does it need to obey gravity.[2] In creating a real cape, these factors must be taken into account. The cape must be made separately and attached with straps under the shirt of the body suit; if not done this way, it will either bunch up at the shoulder or fall out too easily. The cape material itself presents another problem. The suit and trunks are made of spandex, the weight of which makes it stretch and sag. Scott uses gabardine for the cape. It is lighter and does not stretch, but leads to another problem—the only red gabardine Scott has been able to find does not match the bright red of the trunks and boots, so he uses the closest he has and keeps looking for a better match. I've found that a great many costumes are works in progress of this kind, but that people will wear them as soon as possible. Costumers are always approaching their ideal look. Scott's first costume was, in his own words, "pretty terrible," but he kept practicing. In 2012, he chose the Quitely design from *All-Star Superman* in part to accompany his wife, who wore a costume he made based on what Lois Lane wears in the third issue of that story.

According to Scott, the chevron is one of the toughest parts of the costume to sew, largely because he has to take heat into consideration. Sewing another layer on the chest makes things hotter, and the June temperature in southern Illinois can reach 100 degrees. Scott's solution is to cut out the shape of the chevron from the body suit and sew the chevron right into it, with minimal overlapping layers of fabric. The chevron itself is fairly difficult to make. For the Quitely design, Scott traced the shape: "I took one of the comics where on the cover it was him pulling the shirt open and you can see the *S*. I blew that image up and traced it and made an exact replica of the way [Quitely] draws it." Scott says that the chevron is what holds the costume together, aesthetically speaking. "One of the reasons I've made so many costumes is, I've struggled to find the one iconic-looking chest symbol, because there have been so many different ones. For a lot of people, Christopher Reeve's is the main one, but I never liked it. The shape just didn't look right to me. And I think Jim Lee has done a real good one. I think the *All-Star Superman* one is the most iconic I've seen." Scott already has the chevron sewn onto the suit by the time I've arrived. He has neared the end of this costume. While I watch, he sews the trunks, commenting that they aren't exactly like the longer trunks Quitely draws, which resemble boxer shorts. Aware that there's an aesthetic among some fans that does demand strict fidelity to sources, he says, "I kind of like the brief version of the trunks better than the longer shorts-looking appearance, so I decided that I'll just forego that. You know, there's only so many people that would notice and say anything about it. So I figure if they complain I'll just say it's inspired, rather than a replica of it."[3]

Scott has trouble estimating how long it takes to make an entire costume, largely because he works on them in bits and pieces, rarely getting the chance to spend a full day sewing. He devotes much of his waking time to his family and work, and he has other distractions, including television and reading. "I would guess, and it *is* a guess, that it takes me probably about twelve hours. Assuming that I have all the material, and it's set up where I can just grab it and start using it. It's a guess because I do all my costuming here and there in spare time. Right now, our daughter, our youngest one, just started preschool. I don't like to do costuming and sewing and stuff when the kids are here. She is in school for one hour. Two hours, actually, but by the time you drop her off come back and then and go get her and everything. So, I've got one hour in the morning. I'll usually use that hour to do some costume-making. We get them in bed, if we're lucky, seven thirty, eight o'clock, if we're not so

Scott in the suit
he made in 2011.
Photograph by
Ashley Bayles.

lucky nine o'clock, and then I'll do a little more costuming after they're in
bed, maybe an hour or two then. And that's why it'll take me a week or two
to make a single costume, whereas if I just had the day off where I could just
sit down and do it, I could probably do it all in one day."

After making his first costume in 2008, he practiced his craft so that his
costume for the next summer in Metropolis would come closer to his ideal.
That year, 2009, he started to experience more of the thrills of costuming:
"I remember that year a little kid, a random little kid that I'd never seen,
wanted to have his picture taken with me. He ran up to me and hugged my
legs and said, 'I love you!' And so I was like, 'Wow that's the coolest thing
ever!' And that's when I decided we were going to keep doing this because
it's just great." Soon, his wife and daughters became costumers. They began
coordinating their costumes, appearing as members of superhero teams
such as the X-Men, the Avengers, the Justice League, and others. They even
organized efforts with other costumers at the Superman Celebration and

appeared in costume with friends during the costume contest. In 2010, they and some friends won the group category dressed as the Avengers.

Costuming has an effect on people, especially children. Scott has translated his costuming into something that he hopes to make a regular part of his life: visiting children at hospitals: "We do occasionally go to the hospital to visit kids," he told me. "We met a guy, whose name is Keith, who was in Metro[polis, IL]. He does a wonderful George Reeves version of Superman. He made his own costume and he perfected it over time. And he's just got a good look, you know? Physically, he looks a lot like him." Scott sometimes accompanies Keith on his monthly visits to hospitalized children, though he doesn't get the opportunity to do this very often. Because Keith dresses as Superman, Scott wears his Batman costume when visiting the hospital. He had not gone to hospitals to entertain children before he began costuming, but he and his family have been engaged in social activities more frequently since he took up this hobby, often involving his children: "This last year [2011], their homecoming theme was superheroes, and so we made costumes and [my son] Yeshua was in the homecoming parade in costume and Ashley rode with him. Year before that they had a book fair, and their theme for the book fair was heroes. And they had local heroes like a paramedic and a firefighter and a police officer and a marine who came in and read books to the kids at the book fair. And they asked Ashley and me to come, and we came as Superman and Supergirl and we read the *Superhero ABC*[4] to the kids."

In Scott's story,[5] we can start to see some of reasons why people engage in costuming. Pravina Shukla lists seven motivations, derived from her fieldwork: social, heritage, protest and spectacle, education, artistic creation, expressing one's individuality, and elective expressions (2015: 251–66). In the following discussion, I will focus on the artistic and social motivations. To approach the idea of making costumes as artistry, it's important to point out that the endeavor is also a way to make money. Scott sells costumes after he is done with them. He advertises these to friends in the costuming community, but he mostly sells them on the auction website eBay. He also makes costumes upon request, though he does not do this often. He asks a minimum of $300 for a costume without the accompanying boots, which he says are difficult and take a lot of time to get right. This is an increase from his original pricing of $150 to $200, an increase he instituted because of the high demand; he hoped it would decrease the number of requests. This didn't accomplish that goal, so he had to begin turning down requests: "I've recently started telling everybody that I just can't do it because it takes up

too much time." The most popular of his costumes has been Superman. He
has made roughly thirty of those. Some of them, sold to others, have gone
on to win the contest at the Metropolis Superman Celebration.

Scott makes Superman costumes as a way to realize his artistry, which is
reinforced by the response his costumes get when he wears them, but also
by the validation received when he's able to sell one, especially if a costume
he sells wins an award. This element is separate from Scott's performance
of a character while wearing a costume, though they are related. While he
and his family have entered the contest—and won—Scott has never entered
as Superman. The reason he gives is that, with his reddish hair, he doesn't
look much like Superman. He sometimes wears a wig to approximate the
character, dying his eyebrows when he does this. He also wears a homemade
suit underneath the costume to enhance his muscular definition. He doesn't
seem bothered by the fact that he doesn't fit the Superman profile. He doesn't
make the costumes for the prestige of winning a contest himself, though
he does seem pleased that his costumes have been awarded; he has other
motives.

Scott's motivation is also social, which is made clear by the reason he
sewed his first costume, mentioned above: so that he and his son could
participate in the attempt to break the world record for having the most
people dressed as Superman. He did it to become part of a community. Scott's
involvement with his church ensures that he has a community; family and
friends form extensions of that, but it is possible that Scott also wanted to
commune with others who share his interest in Superman and superheroes.
Returning to that same place year after year, Scott has built up a group of
friends, another community. Writing about the costuming of *Star Trek* fans,
Heather Joseph-Witham describes the public attention costumers get as a
primary motivation for the activity, and her comments apply to Superman
costumers as well. Joseph-Witham finds that costuming encodes meaning at
multiple levels, individual, group, and global. Costuming is a creative outlet,
and it provides a way to construct a meaningful experience. She writes that
these fans "see themselves as participating in a very special phenomenon,
and the uniforms they invent can aid them in feeling that they are outside of
time and in a fascinating realm.... Fans, like other people, look for a place
or a group in which they can express ideas that are important to them. What
some may find in belonging to a religious group or a body-piercing club, fans
find in fandom and in costuming" (1996: 30–31). In Chapter 4, we saw how
the opening ceremony of the Superman Celebration worked toward setting
the festival outside normal time. Costuming works toward that as well, as

does the presence of the same people—the Superman fans and the locals, who come back year after year. Costuming has provided the hub around which Scott has formed a community of friends.

But there are other reasons for costuming. What cemented costuming as a recurrent activity for Scott was when a child reacted strongly to seeing him dressed as Superman. Shukla writes about a "magic moment" experienced by many costumers, especially those who are members of the Society of Creative Anachronism, or whose occupation requires a costume at Colonial Williamsburg or to perform on the theatrical stage. The people whom she interviewed describe a moment in which they experience a deep connection to the past (2015: 191). They wear "a style of dress peculiar to another time or place," which enables them "to imagine or inhabit the past" (2015: 117). Superhero costumers may wear historical costumes when embodying a specific depiction of the character, and they may also enact their own past if they dressed up as the hero as a child. But I would say that the same sort of "magic moment" that the costumer experiences, the feeling of transformation that comes with wearing a costume and performing a character, happens in situations such as the one Scott describes about being approached by a child who couldn't contain the emotional rush of seeing a superhero walking down the street. The connection to the past isn't prominent in this situation; rather, there's a total immersion in the present. Yet the result is, essentially, the same: the costume becomes the identity. But, as Shukla points out, the costumed identity is not an alternate identity taken on by the costumer. It is a facet of the costumer's identity, what the costumer chooses to emphasize about the self. According to Shukla, "While ostensibly representing another character, the costume permits the exposure of an actor's truer self by highlighting a facet of his or her personality that cannot be fully realized in daily dress, a facet that emerges in the rendition of a complete human being with a biography, experience, and aspirations" (2015: 246). In this passage, she refers specifically to theatrical performance, but the wearing of a superhero costume also requires performance—for the camera, for the crowd, and sometimes even for judges (as in a costume contest, which, as we saw in Chapter 4, will often incorporate an element of drama and is conducted on a stage).

To Shukla's list, I would add service. As Scott told me, "If I'm going to make costumes and wear them out in public and have fun with it, I want to do something positive with it, too. And make a difference. And doing the hospital visits is one of the biggest things." In some ways, costuming is an indulgence for Scott, which he balances with service. It fits with his calling as a pastor. Superman does not form a large part of his ministry—he has limited it to one instance of a superhero-themed vacation Bible school, during which he taught children spiritual lessons derived from superhero stories; the first night he devoted to Superman, whom he presents as an analogue of Jesus, the son sent from above to save the world. I asked Scott to expand on the reasons he engages in this type of service: "I'm a little biased as a pastor and a Christian. I have a perspective where I feel I'm called to serve anyway. I think it crosses those borders no matter what somebody's background is because it's just the nature of superheroes. When you're a big fan of Superman, for instance, who spends all day every day saving people, or Captain America who does the same thing, or Batman who's fighting crime . . . The idea is . . . it instills in you this belief that you ought to be serving and helping other people. So the people who make the costumes and wear the costumes take that to the next level, I guess. They take it very personally."

In Scott's opinion, people who emulate the appearance of superheroes ought to emulate the morality of superheroes as well. "Growing up I had three major influences," he said. "My mom, Superman, and Jesus. And they've all stuck, for the most part. Superman has always been a favorite, and I guess the draw or the allure was just the ultimate hero kind of thing. He was self-sacrificing. He was altruistic. He did the right thing just because it was the right thing. The thing that set Superman apart from all the others was that he was basically invulnerable. Super strong, super fast, he can fly, and basically everything that you want to do he can do." These elements led Scott to want to be Superman, to the extent such a goal was possible. The character's influence has been subtle in his life: "It instilled in me at an early age the idea of helping other people and doing things that mankind as Superman would do. A respect for authority figures, you know, police officers, firefighters. I looked up to authority figures. He's one of those inspirational figures, when I think back to the Christopher Reeve movies, which I was unfortunately too young to see in the theaters." Scott sees Reeve's portrayal as the definitive Superman, even though the story deviated from his ideal version. It was the performance that mattered (and the music). But as we discuss the reasons he appreciates Superman, Reeve doesn't come up as much as other versions of the character, particularly that of comics writer and artist Dan Jurgens. Jurgens wrote and drew Superman stories during the 1990s and contributed to the "Death of Superman" storyline.[6] This particular story had a powerful impact on Scott:

"When I was thirteen, Superman was killed in the comics. That was a really cool story that came at the time I was just kind of discovering faith and what that's all about, too. The storyline is of him sacrificing himself to save the world, and then he's dead for a long time, they have this big long 'Funeral for a Friend' storyline, and then at the end of that he comes back from the dead. And what happened was, his father Jonathan Kent had a heart attack and died on the operating table. And their spirits met, and Jonathan encouraged him to come back, that he wasn't finished yet. And so Superman helped him to come back, and that's when Superman comes back to life again after that. That impacted, too—just the idea of this hero sacrificing himself to save other people and dying and coming back to life resonated with me as someone who was just discovering Christ and what that was all about."

The concomitant rise of his interest in Superman and Jesus allowed him to see similarities between the two stories: "There are Christ figures in all sorts of literature, and the more I grew into my faith and of course was continuing to grow in my comic book geekdom, too, I started seeing a lot more parallels between Superman and Jesus. There was stuff that I'm sure was intentional, stuff that wasn't intentional, but I still saw it." He has come to see the Superman stories as parables. "Jesus, every time he taught, he taught in these stories that he called parables. All of them were just fictional, made-up stories but each had a spiritual truth behind it, and the people who were listening closely would get the message. And to me, that's kind of what Superman is. There's a metaphor or a spiritual meaning behind the character. Obviously this doesn't apply to every story ever written or every comic that was published, but just the general story of this infant from the stars coming to Earth, being raised in a small town, by small-town parents, growing up to adulthood, and then starting this, you know, other life where he goes about doing good deeds and rescuing people and saving them."[7]

Scott recalls going to his local comic book store the day *Superman 75*, the comic in which Superman dies, hit the stands. He arrived late, and was worried that the issue would be sold out because the line of people waiting to buy it stretched out of the store, around the corner, and past the nearby grocery store. "But I went in and the comic book store owner knew me because I was there every week, so he saved a copy for me. I was so excited that I got that. It's the coolest thing. And it was emotional, I think, for a thirteen-year-old to read about Superman being killed. So that always stuck with me." As with the experience of so many when it comes to comic books, the story is only one important aspect. It's partly the artifact itself—a comic book that in this case came sealed in its own plastic bag—and the process of obtaining it; these things contribute to the creation of meaning. Scott's story of getting this issue contains a bit of fondness, not the least of which comes at the recollection of the store's owner holding a copy for him. The owner's consideration meant that Scott was an important part of that particular store. He was known by sight, name, and interests. He had become part of the event. Memories such as this fuel his interest to the present day. He admits that nostalgia, more than anything else, maintains his interest in the character. The new iterations of the story in film, comic books, and television don't appeal to him. Although he owns all the episodes of the show *Smallville*, he says he doesn't like them very much (especially as the show developed in later years).

Entering the Bayles house, I'm not immediately struck by the presence of comic books or superheroes. They're most prominent in his son's bedroom, which is decorated with superhero pictures and toys. Scott keeps his comic book collection in the garage. His costuming materials take up a closet in the bathroom. Yet the ideals of superheroes have infused much of the family's activity. Scott's three children will often dress up in costume to play, and sometimes he joins them. He encourages them to play together, to create imaginary scenarios in which they work together to defeat villains.

"What keeps me coming back to Superman," he finally decides, "is the hope that my kids have the same experience I did, and having that influence. The children's comics, the ones written for younger readers, tend to have that moral lesson, something to learn, and I like that about those comics." Bringing his thoughts back to costuming, he says, "But the Superman I grew up with is the Superman I want to portray."

JOSH WALGENBACH

As with Scott Bayles, nostalgia fuels Josh Walgenbach's current interest in Superman. But when he was younger, Josh admits, he had an "unhealthy emotional attachment" to the character. In looking at Scott's interest in the Superman, we saw that a Christian resonance boosted his burgeoning religiosity and fueled his fandom. While we will see some similarities here, one result of Josh's devotion to Superman moves in precisely the opposite direction.

Scholars have noted the necessity of myth. Lauri Honko states it thus: "Philosophers who have been eager to abolish myth have realized that a vacuum is immediately created if the contribution made by myth to culture is explained away. They have therefore tried to provide constructive suggestions as to what might take the place of myth and its place in culture" (1984: 43). The story Josh Walgenbach tells of his life is an example of this process. Rushing to fill the vacuum, in his case, is Superman. But Superman's presence is only intermediary. Josh's interest in Superman goes back to early in his childhood and is associated with his father: "My dad traveled a lot," Josh told me, "so sometimes he would bring me little gifts. I know now that he basically stopped at the drug store on the way home. This was when I lived in Wisconsin, a town of twelve hundred people. But I was just happy to get something from my dad. And he knew I liked superheroes, because I watched . . . I mean, I didn't really have comic books, but I watched *Super Friends* on Saturday morning."

Josh associates Superman and his father in another way, but it's important to acknowledge that these comics might easily have been something else. Their Superman content was almost incidental; as we have seen, the artifact matters as much as the content. Josh said of his father, "In the beginning I associated these Superman comics with my dad coming home, because he'd bring them to me. And I think that was part of why, initially, even if I didn't understand the stories I loved the objects so much. Probably the only superhero my father even knew about was Superman. So, I'm sure that's why he brought those, rather than anything else." He still has these comics, which his father gave him in the 1970s. They're digest-sized collections of earlier Superman stories called *The Best of DC.* Crime and social injustice had ceased to be the primary causes of conflict in Superman stories by the time these stories were published; under new editors, Superman stories grew in scope and began incorporating elements of science fiction, which Josh liked. He said of them, "I actually credit comics with getting me interested in science and engineering."

Superman stories resonated with his family life as well, particularly with his evolving view of his father. "My dad was kind of a stern guy and I was raised with these sort of liberal values. And my dad being a stern guy, I sort of only peripherally realized that he did really good things for some people and didn't want anyone to even mention it. My dad made a fairly good living in the '70s, and he would give really large sums of money to people who needed it . . . And it never really registered to me what he was doing, until later on. He didn't want anyone to talk about it. These were things you did, and you did them because they were right. If you have something more than you need and someone has less, you help them. That's just the way it works."

Josh grew up in a tightly knit community in Wisconsin. He acknowledges that knowing most of the residents was a good thing, but could also create problems. From this potential for turmoil grew his father's reticence about the help he gave. Josh begins explaining the situation, however, with what seems like a non sequitur: "He was really good at his job." He continued, "It's not that he didn't want any credit. If he had to accept help, and he did a couple of times in his life, it's embarrassing to have it acknowledged that someone's giving you help. And I don't think he wanted to do that to anyone else. You help people, and you don't talk about it because it's rude to the people you're helping." Josh sums up the point: "You help your neighbor, don't embarrass your neighbor. That's how communities survive. Farming communities are all dependent on each other. Even if you're competing by selling your crops or competing for contracts, you survive by depending on each other. There's no other way to survive."

It's easy enough to see Josh's appreciation for Superman arising from his father, but Josh seldom discusses the role of Clark Kent. Writers have had a lot to say about Kent (see Andrae 1987, Feiffer 1965), and the comics themselves have gone a long way to justify the presence of a secret identity. In Josh's description of his father, we can find a different interpretation. Kent is a creation of Superman's humility. It's a way to avoid making the people whom he saves uncomfortable by being continually confronted with his presence.

Soon, his father got a job in Kansas, so they moved near Wichita. There, Josh discovered a comic book store. His interest in comics burgeoned along with interests in science, history, and mythology. And around this time he began to question the tenets of religion. "It was a process, probably when I was about seven to ten. Religious icons still hold an emotional value for me, but I know it's because I was raised with them and not because they have any actual power. When I was six, and between four and six was when they taught me to say the rosary, I thought these things had actually power. I thought they meant something beyond the meaning that I applied to me. Because they did for my grandmother."

However, the power of tradition was not enough to keep him in the church. Intellectually, he saw problems. When we spoke about Superman prior to our formal interview, he had explained why he fixed his attention on Superman: "Instead of something they told me, I chose something I liked. If it's all fiction, then we should be able to choose our own sacred stories." He continued that line of thought: "I thought a lot about religion when I was a kid, way more than I should have, because of the convent and the priests. I read Bible stories and I read myth stories, and I remember trying to connect them all in my head, to make them true. I remember thinking about Elijah's glowing chariot and I remember thinking about Helios's flaming chariot and going, 'Well maybe these are the same thing.' I remember trying to connect everything. And then I just got old enough that I thought, 'Well, no, none of it's real. None of it's real. And, well, this is as valid as anything else.' At least [Superman] says things that I like, that I think are right." For Josh, Superman "sort of replaced religion, but it didn't." He then takes a step back, in a self-effacing way, to point out that he knows that the story of Superman wouldn't work for the majority of people the way it works for him. He does see value in religion, but not in his own life.

I comment, "You used it as something to think about until you were ready to embrace atheism."

He agrees, saying that he was ready when he was twenty-four or twenty-five. "Not that I believed in a Christian God before that. It took a long time for me to come to grips with the idea that, you know, in space there is a vacuum, and that just has to be okay." Although he had given up on being a Catholic long before that, he held on to some of the icons of religion. These had a functional value for him; they helped assuage fear: "In first, second, third, fourth grade, I knew vampires didn't exist but they scared the hell out of me. When I was in first and second grade, I slept with a rosary under my pillow. I blessed myself with holy water every night before I went to bed. I prayed hard, I said the rosary. I knew that these things didn't exist, but they still scared me. And I understand now that the fear was emotional. And that for whatever reason I just wasn't ready to let my brain overcome that." He responds to fear by studying the things that frighten him. He returns to the topic of religion: "I know that there was something in it that my brain wasn't strong enough to overcome, or I wasn't ready, or I was just too young. Superman is sort of the same way. I wasn't ready to let go of this idea that something was going to protect us. And then as I got older I wasn't ready to let go of the notion that there is something common about people. That someone, even just a normal human being, was going to protect us because it was right, because these stories tell us that it's right. It doesn't work that way. But I wanted it to.

"When I was really little and I would think about the stories, and I knew that they weren't real, but I thought that everyone was getting the same sort of things out of them that I was. I thought that you did the right thing because that's what Superman would do, and anyone who read these stories (and I thought that everyone did because I was in second grade) would, too. And I just thought it was self-evident that this was the right thing."

For Josh, the primary function of religion is to comfort by providing answers to questions that provoke anxiety. He also sees a moral component to religion, which is conveyed by its mythology. He acknowledges that many good things come from religion, though he also associates these things with his family. He describes his family as inclusive, a feature that he also sees in Superman. They are giving, helping others in need: "My family has done a lot of adopting people from all over the world. For whatever reason, they couldn't live in their own countries, and my family just says OK, you're one of us now. You can show up for holidays, you can come to any of us for help. You've been adopted. Which I really love about them. Based on the say so of one of us, you just accept that person." Recall Mark Waid's reaction to Superman—what he responded to most powerfully was the fact that everyone mattered to Superman, without exception. Recall Josh Elder's notion that if Superman sees someone as special, then that person must be special; most importantly, Superman sees everyone as special.

So, religion can accomplish great things, in Josh's view, but the problems he found with it—such as violence sanctioned in the Bible and observable suffering in the present world—were insurmountable. Particularly troubling for him was the current state of suffering, which led him to several possible conclusions about God: "If he's there and he's watching, he's letting these awful things happen. Or he's not there. Or he wants these awful things to happen." None of these conclusions were acceptable to him, and they all amounted to the same thing: "To believe in a conscious, sentient god," he says, "you'd have to look around and say, 'Well, he's not showing up to work.' This is a god with at best no work ethic. And it's just not one that I would choose to associate myself with. Superman always shows up to work. Someone needs help, he goes to help. It's important. And that one thing speaks to me more than anything. Just having power isn't enough. Just like just having money isn't enough. If you're not going to use it to make the world better for other people, it's useless. And the best Superman stories are the ones that aren't about him fighting crime. The best Superman stories are the ones where Superman makes everyone better." We can see the worldly focus of Josh's philosophy. The otherworldly focus of Christianity doesn't have any affective value to him.

By the time Josh began having these thoughts, he had already ceased to be a Catholic. Superman was merely a focal point for thinking about Catholicism and why it didn't work for him. It's easy to find elements of his morality in Catholicism; after all, he values charity and goodwill. But there's another element explicit in his appreciation for Superman that he does not recognize in religion: restraint. In the same breath as his comments transcribed in the previous paragraph, he says, "And Superman doesn't change the world by going and hitting bad people. He changes the world by going and doing good things, and other people realize that and do the same thing. He changes the world by showing restraint. That's the other side of power. You have to use it, but you have to use it with a lot of restraint. It's the same with money. I mean, that's why these things corrupt. It's because, if you don't have restraint, then it's a big loaded gun that goes off all the time."

He mentions the story *Peace on Earth* (Dini and Ross 1999), discussed in Chapter 5. "Superman doesn't slug anybody in the whole thing," says Josh. "It's about trying to make the world a better place. And if you have that much power, if you're going to imagine that much power, beating up on a giant robot just doesn't do it. You have to figure out a way to change the world so that it stays changed without you."

"He fails in that story," I say.

"That's the best part," Josh says. "Because you can't have that much power and do that. If you have enough power to change the world in that way, it requires you to maintain it." In his view, maintaining a different world is impossible for any one person, even Superman. He brings up real-world political analogues, such as certain Roman emperors and US presidents. These people, he says, had and have tremendous power, but their administrations change, so that others will take the same power. And eventually someone in power will be corrupt. Benign power can be maintained, but not indefinitely.

The solution is the education of the next generation, an issue that Josh—as a father of young children—thinks of frequently. When I interviewed him, he had a young daughter and two teenage stepdaughters.[8] At this point, unsurprisingly, his thoughts turn to his four-year-old daughter: "I'm going to raise Evy and the ideals that I'm going to raise her with are going to be really similar to those I was raised with, which also coincide with what I read in those books. It's not like my dad was a Superman fanatic. He just did the right thing because he was raised to do the right thing. Whether or not I get it from my families or from the stories they're still just the right things to do—helping people, making sure that they're not hurt."

Again and again, he comes back to helping people, which coincides with Scott Bayles's call to service. I ask Josh if he's ever consciously considered Superman when dealing with a moral dilemma. "Yeah," he says, without hesitation. "It comes down to telling the truth when I know that the truth is going to get me into trouble. I have made some serious mistakes in my life. And they're almost always predicated on me trying to cover something up. Telling the truth. But it usually ends up hurting less than what happens later. But telling the truth is important." Still, it's more complex than that, and I hazard a guess that it's largely subconscious, or at least reflexive. He responds: "So there are times when I have based my decisions on the morality that

I have gotten out of these stories and there are times when I wish I would have done the right thing by listening to that the little voice in my head that said this is the wrong thing. It's not like I get this bumper sticker 'What Would Superman Do?' moment out of it, but there is a clear line from the way I think about the way people should treat each other and these stories. It's completely obvious to me." It also helps that his father's morality aligns with Superman's.

Conversations about Superman often turn political. Ours did at this point. Josh offers his perspective on the relationship between the United States, Superman, and the American way. Josh noted that Superman can offer something to people in all sorts of situations, such as the idea of a greater power that protects and cares for you. He brought up some of his friends who, in the process of doing field research in biology, had traveled throughout the world. Knowing that Josh liked Superman, they told him stories of people in areas isolated from the technologies of popular culture nonetheless knowing and asking about Superman. Josh links this to the global image of the US: "And I think that's where part of the American way comes in. A lot of people, at least prior to 9/11 and the Iraqi war, really thought of America as Camelot, even though we never were. And there is this connection between Superman and this idealized America. The America that can do anything and will only do good and is rich and powerful, and if they know about you, will feed you. And for a lot of people, at least during the ten or fifteen years that my friends went all over the world and met people, that's what they thought America was."

"They thought America was like Superman?" I ask.[9]

"They thought of America as the people who were going to protect them. And the reason they weren't being protected is because we didn't know about them."

Here we might consider Levi-Strauss's characterization of totemism as a mode of thought that uses external frames of reference to categorize and exemplify relationships between groups and individuals. Superman isn't America, but he might be the totem of America—a country that, significantly, came to be known as a "superpower" in the latter half of the twentieth century. Josh's analysis of global politics may or may not be correct (it's beyond the scope of this project), but nonetheless he's using the components of the Superman story to understand the relationship between the US and groups of people outside the US. Unstated, though implied, is that the US should help others who need it. It is the natural extension of his own morality, formed on the basis of seeing the similarities between his father's actions and his understanding of Superman. His consideration encompasses the relationship between his father and Superman, in his mind. His father provided a model for action that, as a child, he did not quite comprehend, partly because it was never discussed. Superman stories provide the means to articulate the motives behind his father's actions as well as his morality. They are the way he thinks through the world as he perceives it, enabling a transformation from perception to conception. Thus, the myth of Superman is also the way that Josh projects the personal and local onto a global scale—microcosm becoming macrocosm.

Superman was the mediator between religion and atheism for Josh, who eventually embraced a strictly materialistic worldview. While Josh's emotional attachment to Superman may be mostly in the past, he still keeps up with the comics. He has a metal pin in the shape of the Superman chevron on the collar of his winter coat.[10] He has hung images of Superman on the walls of his home office. He watches the Superman movies and television shows with his kids. Nostalgia plays an important role in his appreciation of Superman, but the stories still interest him intellectually.

THE GOOD

In the introduction to *The Gospel According to Superheroes*, B. J. Oropeza observes that we can interpret superheroes as "a pop-cultural implementation of religious premises . . . their storylines make implicit, and sometimes explicit, points about theology" (2005: 4). Oropeza's reading of superhero stories, including Superman, derives from the idea that they retell or revise biblical messages. He sees superheroes as characters who attempt to either preserve or restore an Edenic status quo, which makes us admire and emulate them (2005: 6).[11] In that same volume, Ken Schenck notes that, though Superman is not Jesus, "some of the same aspects that draw humankind to Jesus have also made Superman an enduring figure in popular culture" (2005: 33). He points out parallels between Superman and Jesus, noting some resonances with American history along the way. Superman stories echo religious stories, but this and other analyses of Superman's similarity to religious tales[12] omit the vital pursuit of how these resonances affect people. Marco Arnaudo offers another reading of the multiple religious valences present in Superman stories and throughout the genre of superhero stories. After reviewing several of the possible religious readings of Superman—notably the resonances of the Moses and Jesus stories—Arnaudo writes, in a footnote, that "the undecidability between different religious perspectives thus makes superhero comics a perfect starting point for dialogue. The shaman, the priest, and the rabbi, based on the above, have to admit that Superman incarnates something that they can all identify with, a meeting point that shows how much they have in common" (Arnaudo 2013: 171).

For Scott Bayles, whose faith in Jesus provided the foundation for a particular affinity to Superman, to contemplate Superman stories is to contemplate morality and goodness, the relationship between himself, his family, and his community. This manifests itself in his costuming as much as in anything else, and costuming has become a tradition in his family. For Josh Walgenbach the Superman story provided an alternate and satisfying way to contemplate the same questions outside a religious context. Both men have tied these questions to their parents and children. Following on Joseph-Witham's comment that costuming enables certain people to find the type of community that often centers on religion, we now see that Superman enables people to approach the same questions often addressed by religion—namely, questions of virtue and morality.[13]

Saunders makes this point when he writes, "The beautiful challenge that Superman sets for his creators—and his audience—is the challenge of imagining what an absolute commitment to virtue might look like, if only it were possible" (2011: 30). The notion of virtue embodied by Superman shifts as cultural values shift, which has informed many of the revisions of the character over the years; as "a moral agent who acts always out of his commitment to 'the good'—a good that for the purposes of the narrative is conceived as absolute, but that is also never more than loosely defined" (Saunders 2011: 31–32), Superman defies attempts to place him within an existing belief system. From this defiance, Saunders derives the notion that "Superman's ethics are theological in form while remaining indeterminate at the level of content" (2011: 32). This content-level indeterminateness enables such apparently divergent strains of thought represented by the stories of Scott Bayles and Josh Walgenbach to employ the same character.

As I watched Scott playing with his children, so thoroughly involved that they forgot that I was there, I noticed that he steered their miniature superhero drama—he as Superman and his daughter as Batgirl fought to subdue his son as Darkseid—toward a cooperative adventure. They rely on each other to get their job done. As I talked to Josh about teaching his children, he told me about watching Superman cartoons and discussing the use of violence to solve problems. Yet when I ask these men direct questions about to the role Superman plays their decisions, answers become vague. That was usually the case with the people I interviewed; only rarely did I find specific examples. Most of the responses resembled Chris Roberson's remark that Superman has saturated his life to the extent that any particular instance would be impossible to pin down. At similar moments in their lives, Scott and Josh both began examining their relationships with Jesus. Here, their stories diverge; Scott embraces his faith to its fullest, while Josh reasons the other way and becomes an atheist. Yet they both want to raise their kids with the same morality: to encourage helping people, to engage with the larger community, and to make the world a better place. They strive to achieve a morality imparted by parents, reinforced by religion, and seen in the bright primary colors of Superman stories.

- 7 -

MYTHOLOGICAL CONSIDERATIONS

TO BRING TOGETHER THE VARIOUS STRANDS OF THE BOOK, I WILL CONCLUDE with an examination of Superman as a mythical character. Approaching Superman from the folkloristic perspective has allowed me to foreground the human beings who use him to make meaning, to see how they communicate this meaning to themselves and to others. This communication flows through genres such as tattoo, personal experience narrative, life story, festival, jokes, and costuming. A Superman tattoo, such as a chevron, signals to others the bearer's affinity to Superman and can spark the discussion of a common interest. The tattoo communicates with the bearer as much as with others, serving as a reminder of hope, strength, and uniqueness. Personal experience narrative and life history show us that Superman stories have become part of how certain people think through their personalities, make moral decisions, and work out their place within a community. The Superman Celebration is one of many events at which a community forms around Superman—others include comic book conventions and regular meetings at comic book stores—and the overt Superman content of that festival emphasizes the community itself. Jokes reveal some of the vectors of possible meanings of Superman in the broader culture, and they comment on Superman and on morality; thus, they have much to say about the human condition. Since costuming is a social activity, it demonstrates another element of community and the meanings made possible by taking on the role of the character. The folkloristic method can, of course, be applied in any number of different ways, and to anyone for whom Superman serves as a meaningful character.

This study has focused on the philosophical idea of "as if"—the acknowledged fiction as a component of logical thought—in order to see how people deal with the fictional status of Superman while nonetheless absorbing his stories and incorporating them into their worldview. Building on the "as if" concept, we saw that the ironic imagination is a useful way of envisioning the world. It is a double-mindedness in which people immerse themselves in a secondary, invented world as a way to understand how to improve the

140

real world. The Superman story resembles a myth, but the ironic imagination makes it a modern myth.

IDEAS OF MYTH

The folkloristic approach to the study of myth requires an examination of context as well as the text itself. Folklorists distinguish myth from other genres, such as folktale or riddle,[1] and the anthropologist William Bascom (1984) demonstrates the ways that context and content differentiate myth, legend, and folktale. Bascom looks across cultures to show that these categories—fundamental truth (myth), recent history (legend), and fiction (folktale)—have currency even when the local terms are vastly different and etymologically unrelated. The folkloristic understanding of what people mean when they use these terms has expanded greatly since Bascom's writing, but his systematic examination provides a good starting point.

Folklorists begin with the idea that a myth is a sacred narrative (Dundes 1984: 1, but Hansen [2002] and others dispute this quality), generally encoding the foundation of worldview and humanity's relationship with divinity and the natural world, thereby fostering community (Glassie 2002). Furthermore, myths dramatize culturally important issues (Toelken 2002). They have their own structural logic (Hansen 2009), and though one way to decode them is to understand them as an expression of the subconscious, myth can be seen as a form of conscious thought akin to philosophy in some ways, particularly in subject matter.[2] In short, folklorists approach myths from a variety of angles, but they stress the human agency behind them. From this perspective, myth, always a tricky term, becomes difficult to pin down; it is simultaneously native and analytic. From the analytic, folkloristic perspective, a myth is a traditional idea—usually though not necessarily encoded in narrative—that ties together a community by providing models both for behavior and for aspiration by referencing the creation of the cosmos or the securing of humanity's place in it; it is ontology given linguistic expression.[3] A mythic story is traditional because of a community's attitude toward it. It comes from the past, and members of the community consider it mythic because of the value placed upon it. This value imparts to the narrative a quality that often, if not always, approaches sacredness. Myth is, like all tradition, an interpretive judgment (Handler and Linnekin 1989). To call something a myth can offend adherents of it because of the negative connotation of myth as misconception. Alternately, calling a story a myth can elevate its status, and this is generally the connotation given to superhero stories, such as those about Superman, when they are labeled myths. *Myth* is indeed a strange term.[4]

I've found Lauri Honko's way of looking at genres, especially myth, through the conceptual lenses of form, function, content, and context to be a useful one, and I'll examine Superman in these terms below. First, it's important to note that the folkloristic perspective isn't the only way to approach the study of myth. In the early years of folklore and anthropology, to study myth was to study *the other*, either the other of the past or the other of a foreign culture. But in the twentieth century the concept of myth changed. The early decades saw the broadening of concepts key to myth (such as Durkheim's declaration that "anything can be sacred" [1915: 37]), a phenomenon that eventually included the concept of myth itself: Roland Barthes, in *Mythologies* (1957), seeks mythic elements in French culture, and he finds them everywhere. He conceptualizes myth as an inclusive term, a semiological construction that doesn't need an element of the sacred for its definition. For Barthes, "everything can be a myth provided it is conveyed by a discourse" (1957: 109). Usage determines myth's status as such.

Barthes's reformulation has had profound ramifications, especially in the study of American culture. Prior to Barthes, American myth meant Native American myth. After *Mythologies*, scholars began to look at mainstream American culture for similar mythical constructions. Myth became cultural myth instead of religious myth.[5] Richard Dorson sums up the situation: "Modern myths resemble tribal myths in concentrating on a special people, in establishing utopian visions of a wondrous life, and in glorifying larger-than-life heroes" (1983: 57). These myths, according to Dorson, are pieced together by social critics from all levels of culture. They carry a solemn force and exert a large influence on society.[6] Today many scholars who address the idea of myth in America mean political myth (Flood 1996). Without sacredness as a criterion for definition, ideology becomes prominent. The difference between myth old and myth new is the difference between tribal and national culture. As communities become "imagined" (Anderson 1991) instead of actual, as religion in America has no grounding in local landscapes, myth—as constructed by scholars—shifts to new subject matter. The specific content of the myth is still relevant, but it is no longer about gods. The new conception of myth doesn't seek to understand what gods are about (having answered this question to their satisfaction; the gods are metaphors: manifestations of ideology and cultural mores, of ontological ideas and history; "extroversive anthropomorphism" [Schrempp 2012: 158]); instead, scholars look for other expressions that dramatize and encode the answers. If ancient gods represent what was unique to those who worshipped them, then new mythologists have to find what expresses the uniqueness to modern culture.

Barthes uses an apt metaphor to characterize his view of myth: "If I am in a car and I look at the scenery through the window, I can at will focus on the scenery or the window-pane. At one moment I grasp the presence of the glass and the distance of the landscape; at another, on the contrary, the transparence of the glass and the depth of the landscape; but the result of the alternation is constant: the glass is at once present and empty to me, and the landscape unreal and full. The same thing occurs in the mythical signifier: its form is empty but present, its meaning absent but full" (1957: 123). The window is the mythical signifier; it is the text of the myth. The landscape beyond is the complex of ideas expressed by the text. For Barthes, the function of the myth is to appear as clear as a window, to show us the ideas in ways that make it seem like there is no glass; he calls this phenomenon the naturalizing function of myth (1972: 129 ff.). Myth is defined by its intention rather than by its content. It is more important that the glass shows us the landscape rather than that we recognize the glass as the barrier between us and the landscape.

Where the older concept of myth focused on genre conventions such as sacredness, gods, and the foundation of the world, the newer concept of myth shifts its focus to underlying meanings, those things laid bare by or latent in the content. Because of this, it doesn't matter where the mythologist looks; myth, as a vehicle for ideology (Flood 1996: 42; Lincoln 1999: 147), is intimately tied to all aspects of culture, especially popular culture.

Mythologists beginning in classical times have often had a negative view of their subject matter, but Barthes inaugurated mythology as a way to see through myth to uncover problems with mainstream culture (Welch 1973: 563–64).[7] Richard Slotkin, whose work on "the frontier myth" follows the contemporary view on myth that I have been outlining, sees in American myth a tendency to "reach out of the past to cripple, incapacitate, or strike down the living" (1973: 5) and blind us to our own needs. His basic formulation of myth, however, is much more objective: "A mythology is a complex of narratives that dramatizes the world vision and historical sense of a people or culture, reducing centuries of experience into a constellation of compelling metaphors" (1973: 6), the function of which "is to reconcile and unite these individuals to a collective identity" (1973: 8). In this I see a reiteration of the tension between the individual and the community that drives much folkloric expression and informs folkloristic analysis. However, Slotkin looks for myth in printed material, a method made necessary by the historical nature of much of his work.[8] What follows now is an examination of Superman as a multifaceted myth, drawing upon the folkloristic approach to myth but supplementing it with ideas taken from structuralism and classical studies.

SUPERMAN AND MYTH

Numerous writers refer to Superman as a myth or describe him using related terminology, recounting his similarities to heroes from myth, legend, and epic—that is, they cast the superhero as a modern version of ancient myth (Eco 1979, Reynolds 1992, Drummond 1996, Somigli 1998, Sherman 1994, Knowles 2007, Beaven 2007, LoCicero 2008, Saunders 2011, Arnaudo 2013). Fred McFadden goes so far as to write, "I wouldn't be surprised one day to pass a church with a stained glass window showing Superman in flight" (1972: 28).[9] I'll now turn to an analysis of Superman using Honko's terms: form, content, context, and function. He describes the form of myth as narrative, a "verbal account of what is known as sacred origins" that includes allusions to other myths and symbols—a background that makes them comprehensible. For Honko, myth can also manifest in other forms, such as ritual drama, song, and visual art. Myth may be "transmitted in speech, thought, dreams, and other modes of behavior: A religious person may in the course of his experience identify himself with a mythical figure" (Honko 1984: 49–50). Myth's content is cosmogonic, which covers more than the birth of the universe; it includes the origin of humanity, the goals that people strive for, and what ought to be considered sacred. Its performance context is ritual, generally sacred ritual, though it is important to attend to other contextual elements, such as the social, economic, and personal mental context of the adherents (see Wilson 1986). Myth's function is more complex since it can vary so widely: "Myths have, of course, numerous functions, but we may generalize and say that they offer both a cognitive basis for and practical models of behavior. From this point of view, myths can be characterized as ontological: they are incorporated and integrated into a coherent view of the world, and they describe very important aspects of life and the universe" (Honko 1984: 51). Myth is the most important contributor to worldview. It is worth exploring how Superman does and doesn't fit the genre conventions delineated by Honko, who intends his scheme to be flexible.

FORM

Honko makes it clear—as do other scholars such as Barthes and Slotkin—
that myth can take nearly any form. He first notes verbal narrative, and the
expressions most commonly called myth do take this form: examples include
the stories in books such as Apollodorus's *Library* and modern handbooks
of mythology. These are often serialized, manifest across a variety of media, which is the form of cycles of trickster myths, Greek hero tales about
Herakles, and—in Terrence R. Wandtke's view—epics (2012: 51 ff.). With
Superman, new media have supplemented, not supplanted, the old. Much of
this book has been devoted to explicating the various forms that Superman
stories take, including jokes, tattoos, festival, and the like. For that reason, I
won't dwell on it here.

CONTENT

According to Honko, myth's content "comprises all those stories that recount
how the world began, how our era started, how the goals that we strive to attain are determined and our most sacred values codified" (1984: 51). Elements
of that last clause, goals and sacred values, are often codified in hero stories
without explicitly cosmogonic content; cosmogony can resonate throughout
other kinds of content. A demonstrative example can be found in stories
of the Scandinavian god Thor, whose primary activity involves slaying the
jotnar—often translated as *giants*, enemies of Thor's race. In John Lindow's
analysis, Thor's slaying of any given *jotun* re-enacts the primordial, cosmogonic drama of his progenitors slaying Ymir, the forefather of the *jotnar*, from
whose body the gods created the cosmos (Lindow 1994: 502).[10] Superman
stories do not often include cosmogonic material; when they do, that material
does not reflect any credible origin of the cosmos. Its purpose is diegetic,
not religious or scientific. Superman stories have instead the same mythical
resonance that we find in myths about Thor. Whenever Superman rescues
a city from a natural disaster or catches a criminal, he reinforces prominent
ideological values held by large numbers of Americans. Superman stories also
dramatize ideas and ideals significant to American culture. To delve into how
Superman stories resonate mythically, I will analyze a generalized version of
the Superman story using a form of structural analysis. Structuralism relies
on finding sets of binary oppositions and analyzing their transformations
in a story or series of stories. Mythologists see in these transformations the

ways in which a culture works to overcome the contradictions they find in their world.[11] A worldview becomes evident, and comprehensible, in the relationships that obtain among elements in the myth (Lévi-Strauss 1955: 86).[12]

The story begins with Superman's biological parents sending him as an infant—known as Kal-El—from the dying planet Krypton to Earth, where he is found and raised by a Midwestern couple.[13] It is a story of the opposition of sky and earth, the very opposition that we find in a great many myths.[14] Growing up, Kal-El creates a dual identity of Superman and Clark Kent as he moves from the Smallville farm to the urban Metropolis. The rural:urban opposition becomes apparent here, as does the occasional clumsy:competent opposition of Kent and Superman (which we might also characterize as mild-mannered:bold). The double identity instigates two different types of stories: Superman rescuing people and Superman maintaining his secret identity as Kent. Kent represents the opposition of romance:occupation, since Superman's devotion to his role as a hero leads him to rebuff the advances of Lois Lane, but as Kent he pursues her. Superman's heroics often take the form of a story about good:evil as he combats criminals such as Lex Luthor, who is sometimes a scientist and sometimes a corporate entrepreneur. The recurrence of characters with the initials "L. L." reveals that these types of stories—stymied romance and crime fighting—are transformations of each other. Superman resists both Lois and Luthor, but if he did not, if either L. L. achieved victory, it would mean the end of Superman as a force for good in the world.[15]

Kent:Superman transforms into other oppositions as well. We see, following Jules Feiffer (1965), that Kent/Lie:Superman/Truth. One might think that Kent's status as a reporter would work to complicate this opposition, but this is not usually the case. Kent is opposed to Lois, as he struggles to hide his secret identity from her efforts to uncover it. Kent/Superman also encodes a false/superficial:real/depth opposition. Recent versions of the character identify Kent as the character's "true" identity. This opposition reveals the dialectical nature of the character, that the story can be used as a way to reflect on the nature of one's true self, the idea of identity as a social construct or as an essence. Superman stories become a discourse on biology as destiny, nature versus nurture.

If the lie:truth opposition essentially arises out of Superman's relationship to Lois Lane, then his relationship to Luthor reveals the complications of the good:evil opposition. Luthor often sees himself as a benevolent force. He has changed from a mad scientist with plans of world domination to an entrepreneur who hates Superman for getting in the way of humanity.

Luthor represents the intellect in a brains:brawn opposition that foregrounds Superman's physical characteristics—his powers of strength and invulnerability—as essential to his nature .[16] Superman thwarts Luthor's efforts at world dominion, and also his efforts to kill Superman. In this sense, Superman represents the regulation of capitalism, which would otherwise allow monopolies, and the preservation of the individual in the face of corporate greed. Luthor's status as a capitalist is tied to technology—he sometimes fights Superman wearing a suit of mechanized armor. Superman thus signifies the triumph of humanity over technology. The opening narration of the *Adventures of Superman* television show gives the most explicit iteration of this triumph: "Faster than a speeding bullet, more powerful than a locomotive, able to leap tall buildings in a single bound . . ." He does not triumph over the natural world so much as render technology obsolete.

The sky:earth opposition that begins the Superman story is thus transformed into a human:technology opposition, which shows humanity triumphing over that which it creates. Paradoxically, this only works if Superman is human, which he is not. Thus, we see what the story is truly about: exogamy. Superman represents *the other*,[17] but nonetheless he marries Lois Lane. Various incarnations of the character have explored this situation, including the comic book version, two television versions, and various "imaginary stories." Larry Niven's essay "Man of Steel, Woman of Kleenex" (1971) explores the ramifications of a human woman bringing a hybrid child to term. Some stories employ cloning technology to explore the possibility of Lois and Superman having children, transforming the human:technology opposition once again. In this case, the opposition is overcome by bio-technology—applying technological craft to the human body—and humanity is thus able to become more like Superman. If I may make a bit of a leap, through stories in which Superman marries Lois Lane and fathers children, we see that Superman does not represent an opposition between humanity and science, but rather between humanity and industrialization. In Superman's early comic book adventures, he fought as a crusader for social justice. Industrialization relies on large-scale use of interchangeable parts, which some people fear leads to the idea that people themselves are interchangeable, precisely the Marxist alienation that Eco (1972) finds at the heart of Superman. The early Superman fought to restore the integrity of the individual suppressed by an industrial, corrupt culture. Biological sciences restore the individual through attention to the idiosyncratic genes of each person. Biology recognizes the differences of the individual within the larger similarities of the species, and, in the science fiction of Superman, it provides the means for unifying the human with *the other*. This difference, in the mechanics of inheritance and mutation, drives the engine of evolution. And Superman, we must not forget, is from a planet whose inhabitants were "millions of years advanced of our own." The earth/human:sky/other opposition transforms in a final iteration into present:future. Superman is a story of human potential. As a myth, it is the story of humanity maturing; it is the story of growing up. Superman tells us that the story of growing up is the story of deciding which parts of your life you wish to emphasize and use as the basis of your decisions. We are not him, but we can become like him. In the words of Josh Elder, "You can all fly with me. One day you will."

We can become like him, but not be the same as him. Perhaps the single interpretation of the content of Superman stories that I can advance as purely my own is that they dramatize the rejection of plastic industry in favor of biological and health science. Superman's story is not one of biology being destiny, but of biological progress leading to utopia. Only when each person is perfect will society be perfect. This is not a terribly felicitous interpretation, and for that reason I look back to the interpretations of those whose association with the character is one of affinity, not scholarly interest. Thus, I turn to Josh Walgenbach's interpretation of the character as a god who shows up to work. I turn to Scott Bayles's idea that we can see a positive strength in Superman. I turn to Brian Morris's expression that he is more than his appearance, and Josh Elder's desire to live life as if the story of Superman is true. I follow Mark Waid's insight that Superman loves everyone, without exception. In the end, their interpretations can temper my own. They are a reminder that biological science is not perfect, that with it must come a perspective that allows for imperfection. What is the truth of Josh Elder's story "Dear Superman"? It is that we are here now, and we should do all we can for each other.

CONTEXT

Honko tells us that the "normal" context for myth is ritual (1984: 51), and I think it's safe to say that ritual includes, implicitly, the social situation, economic concerns, and the mentality of performer and audience. Here, William Bascom's discussion of verbal narrative proves useful. Bascom includes in his analysis a chart for comparing and contrasting important traits of myths, legends, and folktales: belief, setting (including the time and place in which the story events take place), attitude of the audience, types of characters, and function (1984: 9–11). Of these, characters and setting fall under content. A treatment of function will follow, but for the moment let's focus on belief and attitude—the two elements in Bascom's scheme that fit in the category of context. In Chapter 4, I described some ritual contexts of the Superman story cycle. Numerous ritual (or at least ritualesque) activities occur at the Superman Celebration in Illinois and during the repeated, recurrent trip to the comic book store. Mythologically speaking, it's easy enough to describe the Celebration as a ritual performed in honor of a hero figure. It might be interesting to look at it from the perspective of an archaeologist, as if we had only the barest hints of what went on at the Celebration—perhaps some description of events, a few videos of the opening ceremony, and likely the Superman statue itself. What would we conclude? Would we wonder at the people who could believe in such a figure—one who clearly did not exist except in their own minds? Would we write, following Paul Veyne (1988), a book called *Did the Americans Believe in Their Myths?*

We have seen that children under a certain age can believe in Superman without any level of irony. Joseph Torchia (1980) took this idea and developed an epistolary novel from it, the contents of which consist of letters written by the protagonist, Jerry Chariot, to Superman. For Chariot, Superman serves as an outlet for his feelings of isolation and persecution, which, ironically, often stem from his belief in Superman. The relationship between myth and belief has prompted volumes of discourse. Most contemporary work about American popular culture takes it for granted that belief is not a necessary component for myth to operate as myth; its ontological component suffices. And, all rhetoric aside, we really wouldn't say that any adults believe Superman exists. David Bidney's statement that belief "is essential to the acceptance of *myth* and accounts for its effectiveness in a given cultural context" (1953: 294)[18] doesn't carry much weight in the analysis of myth in the United States. The works of writers such as Honko, Barthes, and Slotkin have moved the study of myth beyond belief, which enables us to consider Superman to be mythical even if we don't rely on native classification. Yet the concept of belief encompasses more than just the factual acceptance of the events of a story. Recall, from Chapter 3, Chris Roberson's statement: "I believe in Superman the way some people believe in Jesus."

We must differentiate between two modalities. We can say that "a belief" is a presumption about the way the cosmos works; it is accepted as fact regardless of its empirical status as truth. So the separation of sky and earth as part of cosmogenesis is a belief, as are phlogiston and the first law of motion. Some of these may be demonstrably wrong (such as phlogiston), but someone could still believe them regardless of empirical truth. The second modality, "belief in," is a value judgment. We can believe in the free market because we judge it to be a worthwhile system, just as we can believe in freedom of speech because we deem it a valuable right. These are cultural institutions, choices that belong in a completely different category from the first modality. By differentiating "belief" from "belief in,"[19] we return to the concept of "as if." In the case of Superman, the academic notion of myth as a historical truth recognized by a believer does not apply. Myth refers to something else, some other concept of truth. Superman fans know that he's not real, but that doesn't matter. They believe in make-believe; their belief is ironic. Superman becomes a way to examine the notions of real and make-believe, of truth and fiction. Because he isn't real, people begin to question the criteria, even the necessity, of the real. As Superman writer Grant Morrison states, of his book *Supergods*, "If this book has made any point clear, I hope it's that things don't have to be real to be true. Or vice versa" (2011: 301).

Important for Bidney is that once myth is questioned by its adherents, it ceases to be effective as a guide to conduct and thus becomes myth in their eyes—an obsolete belief. Bidney assumes a monolithic culture. He theorizes that, on the collective level, everyone in a culture adheres to the myths with the same attitude and that they are in the same modality of belief. This is a difficult assumption to agree with. Paul Veyne demonstrates the extent to which certain Greeks were very critical of the myths they still adhered to. His title, *Did the Greeks Believe in Their Myths?* emphasizes the importance of asking fundamental questions, of taking nothing for granted. His solution is to posit multiple modalities of truth. In other words, "'truth' means many things ... and can even encompass fictional literature" (Veyne 1983: 15). He argues that a person effectively believes a novel while reading it; that is part of its power. His line of reasoning leads him to call into question the notion of reality: "The difference between fiction and reality is not objective and does not pertain to the thing itself; it resides in us, according to whether or not we subjectively see in it a fiction" (1983: 21). For Veyne, who makes no reference to Vaihinger, our lives are lived by fictions because the fact of an ultimate truth is in doubt. All we have are the products of our imagination. That is, the imagination is the constitutive unit of our life, and the basis of action.

The congruence of myth and imagination comes up repeatedly. Raffaele Pettazzoni reminds us that myth *is* imagination, not reality. In his view, myth has a truth, but it is of "a religious and more especially magical order" (1984: 103). It is of a modality different than logic. Importantly, however, it is not swept away into the past by the ascendance of logic and science. Because they are of different orders, they can coexist: "Human thought is mythical and logical at the same time" (Pettazzoni 1984: 107). Veyne's modalities of truth allow us to see that thought can be mythical at one moment and logical at another. This is the "double-mindedness" that Michael Saler finds useful in understanding Sherlock Holmes as a cultural phenomenon (2003: 606). An additional example of double-mindedness, drawn from ethnographic field-work, comes in Barre Toelken's "Native American Reassessment and Reinter-pretation of Myth." Toelken notes that there is "a venerable and continuing Native oral tradition of discussion, critique, reassessment, and reinterpreta-tion" of myths that continues to this day (2002: 90). His primary examples are Navajo creation stories that include animals such as sheep, which, the Navajo are fully aware, were brought to the Americas by Europeans and could not possibly have been present in primordial times. The Navajo have modified their stories to "narratively claim the world into which they moved, and to adjust that claim as the world has subsequently moved in on them" (Toelken 2002: 92). They are aware of their myths as myths, and they adjust them to fit their experience. This willingness to alter the story, regardless of its sanctity, reveals its fictive quality.

Vaihinger's "as if" mode provides a way to understand the uses to which certain people put fictions in their thought processes. In the end, philoso-phers remove the fictional component of their logistic so that they can fully confront reality. They acknowledge the fiction and jettison it. The classical case is Plato, whose narrative of the cave in the *Republic* was a useful fiction, acknowledged as such. Its very purpose was to allow those who heard it to transcend it and to realize the need for transcendence. Its truth is merely educational. In this light, Superman differs, and I propose that the difference gets to the heart of myth in America. Myth is the fiction that its adherents acknowledge as such but choose not to jettison, because it is recurrently ap-plicable. With Superman, people see him as fiction, but declare his fictiveness relevant.

Bidney, though primarily concerned with the notion that a myth must be believed, nonetheless acknowledges that there can be myths that are not believed, and he refers to Vaihinger's "as if" philosophy in explanation (1953: 299). In this case, adherents seek a truth that is not verifiable by sci-ence. These "people of truth" (Schrempp 2002) may acknowledge the value of science while simultaneously finding value in other philosophical endeavors, such as theology. Schrempp characterizes Bidney's people of truth as those "who espouse empirical investigation and critical thought to guide the design of human life, and who refuse to be cowed by unexamined orthodoxies"

(2002: 54). This seems awfully close to Brian Morris describing Superman fans as people who like to take the watch apart to see how it works. Superman invites a critical approach because of his unreality, a fact that Brian appreciates. Superman cannot be interpreted literally, so he must be interpreted hermeneutically. An extensive hermeneutic interpretation provided the impetus behind Steven Seagle's *It's a Bird* . . . (2004); Seagle, when offered the chance write stories for Superman at DC Comics, took a critical look at Superman and found him symbolically viable. He says, in an interview on NPR, "And I thought, 'That's a pretty strong character, you know. If I can really deconstruct him and still find him to be a powerful figure iconically, then maybe I should try to take him on.'"[20]

A society's most vital concerns will show up in their mythology (Slotkin 1985: 23). Superman mythologizes many things. We have seen the extent to which he permeates popular culture and has entered folklore, and in the process discovered how people use him to work through the relationship of humanity and divinity (Chapter 6) and the role of the individual within the community (Chapter 4). We have seen how people use him to address issues of personal significance, such as loneliness, occupational choices, and physical hardship (Chapter 2). And in the above discussion of content we have now seen how Superman is the mythologization of power relations among humanity and technology, individual and corporate interests. He is a potent way to dramatize ideal morality. He has ultimate power, but he does not abuse it. He uses it in service of others, and this has remained constant in every era. Through his restraint, he becomes a public servant, not unlike a president of the United States.

I offer the presidential comparison not merely because of the images of President Obama as Superman. Consider the limits placed on the presidency. The US is not alone among nations that require leaders to step down from office on a predetermined timeline, but it is certainly an integral component of the national character. It was a precedent set by George Washington, who was offered kingship but declined. He then stepped down, and every president in history, with one exception, followed his lead of two terms. The exception, Franklin Roosevelt, chose not to maintain his power by fiat, but to run for re-election. He kept power, but not without going through the popular channels. His violation was of tradition, not of law. Every president, no matter how much power accrues while in office, must be willing to give it up. They show restraint, if only in this one way.

Superman, analyzed through the lens of mythological context, critiques the common maxim that power corrupts. He is the example of absolute power without corruption, and he avoids corruption because he had a traditional American upbringing that combined urban ambition with the grounding of a rural ethic. He follows in the tradition of George Washington, the farmer who rose to immense power and yet transcended corruption by limiting that power. It is power used for service, not for personal gain. People consider the defining characteristic of Superman to be moral and emotional, not physical. He can do anything he wants, and he chooses to be a hero. This is the very aspect of his morality that is critiqued by the jokes examined in Chapter 5, in which Superman does abuse his powers. It is inherent in the discussions with Brian, Sean, and Cookie in Chapter 4, which is summed up nicely by Brian: "He doesn't win because he is stronger, or faster, or does things we can't do, but because he is morally right." When Josh Elder refers to Alan Moore's formulation of Superman as a man who came to Earth to do only good, his moral power is foregrounded. And Josh Walgenbach puts it into perspective when he says of Superman, "He changes the world by showing restraint."

FUNCTION

The functional approach to myth has evolved quite a bit since Bronislaw Malinowski initiated it early in the twentieth century. It would be a stretch to call it a formal theory as practiced today, but the original thought was that all aspects of a culture worked together to keep that culture in equilibrium. Function has been disregarded to the extent that Robert Segal, in his summary of theoretical approaches to myth (2004), doesn't even include function as a separate category (though he mentions Malinowski in his discussions of myth's relation to science and psychology). Nonetheless, a perspective that begins with function can be insightful. The notion of function rests upon understanding what people do with myths, so I would be remiss if I didn't point out that many studies of superheroes as mythology often make some effort to take into account what fans and readers do when they encounter the stories. Richard Reynolds and Terrence Wandtke both bring up what readers are doing with the stories; however, their focus is on analyzing texts in relation to other texts. They write of a theorized, invented audience, for whom myth exists only in imaginary space; superheroes are "the protagonists of a myth which is constructed as an intertextual reading of their careers" (Reynolds 1992: 52). Myth does exist in the minds of readers, but that is not the myth he is examining, only the myth he theorizes.

My analysis through this book has, of course, relied on the creation of other texts: tattoos, jokes, costumes, festival dramas—and these are the sorts of texts on which the study of folklore thrives. The advantage here is that looking at these texts does not require a theorized reader. I have drawn meaning—and myth is supremely a meaning-making endeavor—from interviews, stories, and conversation, even when a text is available. Each story presented in this book demonstrates that Superman provides a cognitive basis for, and a model of, behavior. Josh Walgenbach describes Superman's honesty as the foundation for his own, and Superman serves as a way to understand and apply the nebulous and implicit morality of his father. J. Michael Straczynski, Mark Waid, and Josh Elder all tell stories about moral decisions they have made using Superman as a cognitive tool and call to action. Adherents to the Superman myth think of him when considering courses of conduct.

In his characterization of the function of myth as cognitive, as providing the basis and models for behavior, Honko follows Malinowski's *Myth in Primitive Psychology* (1926). Malinowski's title gives away his subject matter. Does this function apply to twenty-first-century America? My data, derived from fieldwork, indicate that it does. To further articulate the function of myth, I turn to Walter Burkert, a classicist. Burkert, in *Structure and History in Greek Mythology and Ritual,* describes myth as "a traditional tale with secondary, partial reference to something of collective importance. Myth is a traditional tale applied; and its relevance and seriousness stem largely from this application" (1979: 23). He contrasts myth to fables, whose meaning is often stated explicitly. Myth, in contrast, can only be interpreted as it is applied; that is, in context. Because myth is multivalent, or plastic (Firth 1984), the application need not be dictated by the content, merely by the adherent's interpretation of that content. Mythical thinking has direct reference to real, relevant, and important aspects of life, but there is not an explicit moral attached to myth; the reference is partial, Burkert asserts, and because it is partial, because it does not map onto reality in an allegorical way, it is widely applicable.[21] The reference directs it toward one aspect of life, but does not limit it. If the reference is removed, as often happens with Greek myths in the modern US, myth becomes folktale.

In Burkert's view, myth's performance context may still be that of ritual, but the application context could be any given moment when decisions of conduct are required. This is its cognitive aspect. Myth is the narrative mode of philosophy,[22] ontological in its orientation. As Barthes and others have demonstrated, any story can be a myth, either for a group of people or for a single person. The key is to see that the native classification of myth is important. Examining what people label as myth leads us to see the story as the dramatization of the important things in their lives, and thus as a clue to their worldview and the thrust of their culture. As Burkert and Honko note, the subject matter can be quite diverse, ranging from cosmogony and anthropogony to the foundation of social institutions, to subsistence and personal relationships.

In folkloristics we look at variation, but we also look at what is fixed, because that is the foundation of meaning. I asked everyone I interviewed what aspects of Superman shouldn't change, and everyone responded similarly: the values he holds, his morality. All else can vary, but he must not lie except to protect his secret identity, he must not kill, he must use violence only when there is no other recourse. He must inspire us to be better people, to treat each other with respect, and to help each other when we need it. But I cannot ignore other aspects of the character, and the one that came up again and again in interviews is the fact that Superman changes. He exhibits the same variation that we find in oral tradition, and that he does so is another piece of evidence pointing to his mythic stature. Burkert writes, "If we are to understand any given myth in all its details, we have to face the fact that it bears the marks of its history, of multiple levels of application and crystallization" (1979: 23). Variation is written into myth because of its application. The world changes, and the myth changes to meet the needs of those who tell it.

Because of the relative permanence of Superman stories—we can get a copy of virtually any Superman story ever told at this moment through reprints and online resources—people are aware of the changes.[23] Whereas in oral tradition a story could change without leaving any physical evidence of that change, in popular culture change is recorded in media. People can become Superman historians, and new Superman stories have the option of commenting directly on what has come before Superman with the knowledge that audience members are or can be intimately familiar with these earlier versions. Superman is a myth of change (see Karp 2009, Saunders 2011, and Darowski 2012). It has become common for Superman fans to point out that Superman in different eras—the Depression, World War II, the '60s, the '70s—reflects the zeitgeist of those eras. Thus, Superman dramatizes American history as well as morality.

As Burkert notes, myths do not force a single interpretation. The polysemy of myth requires audience members to come to their own interpretations. Reynolds, writing about superheroes, cites Claude Lévi-Strauss on this point: "Myth and music thus appear as conductors of an orchestra of which the listeners are the silent performers" (Reynolds 1992: 45; Lévi-Strauss 1968: 25–26). Edmund Leach, in his book-length study of Lévi-Strauss, explicates that statement as follows: "[W]hat the individual listener understands when he hears a myth or a piece of music is in many ways personal to himself; it is the receiver who decides what the message is" (1974: 129–30). With the similarity of music and myth in mind, consider the description of cartooning offered by comic book creator Scott McCloud in *Understanding Comics*. For McCloud, cartooning—the process of drawing comics—is a process of abstraction. Cartooning reduces the contours and texture of reality to a simplified image. Eventually, through this process aligned with the natural human inclination toward closure (to fill in gaps and infer completion), a pair of dots and a line can refer to any human face; in contrast, a detailed drawing or photograph can be only an individual face. The simplified cartoon image requires the viewer to engage in an interpretive act to make sense of it (1993: 59).[24] There's a parallel here with mythology. In archaic myth, characters are broadly and simply portrayed. Complex motivation does not exist. Even the most complex characters, such as tricksters whose motivations vary wildly throughout a cycle of stories, are not complex within a given story. This is part of the appeal for scholars. How to fit together the characterization of Loki in the *Thrymksveda* and the *Lokasenna*? It's a puzzle with many pieces missing. It demands interpretation, which is similar to the manner in which McCloud characterizes the appeal of the cartoon image. Mythology, like cartooning and superheroes, works through iconography, symbols, and narrative. The tattoo of Superman's chevron alone can invoke every Superman story. This simplicity provides for a broad range of interpretation, and thus for a multitude of applications.

I ASKED BRIAN AND COOKIE MORRIS WHAT A MYTH IS. COOKIE SAID, "I TEND to think of myths as the stories from ancient times. That they have lasted this long. Not just thirty, forty, seventy years. They've lasted hundreds of years. Basically if it can stand the test of time, then it's a myth." Danny Fingeroth writes that the stories mean a lot because they don't change too much over time, which is valuable in an uncertain world. The world of superheroes, for Fingeroth, is immune from aging and death, which "may be their greatest power and the one that ultimately means the most to us . . . the lives of the costumed adventurers will transcend that of any actor or writer or artist—or audience member. . . . We achieve immortality through the superheroes" (2004: 37). Two of the most famous writers of Superman share a similar sentiment: Alan Moore writes, "All myths are true. . . . Given that they last

longer, they're even truer than the so-called 'real world'" (2002: 20). Grant
Morrison notes that superheroes will be here longer than any of us—that is,
he believes the superhero stories will be in publication long after anybody
currently living has died—and so they are more real than we are (2011: 220).

Brian added, "And I would say that Superman would certainly be a modern myth, a very contemporary one, because I look at myths as having a
certain amount of recognition factor, even if you don't recognize specifics
about a character, like Hercules. Everybody knows who Hercules is, but they
may not know the whole story about sweeping out the Augean stables. They
don't need to [know] in order to understand the essence of a super powerful character who fought for good. And I think Superman is the same way."
Their answers reveal a contemplation of myth, and of Superman's role as a
myth. They reveal something else as well: cultural saturation is an important
factor in myth. Myths, as Veyne writes, are "the stories that everyone knows,
or should know" (1983: 45), but every culture produces people who know
the stories better than others. And in the US, this level of expertise is spread
across a great many stories; there are fans of nearly everything. So we can
look at the personal level and see that any story might be a myth for someone.
I related my encounter with a Spider-Man fan at the beginning of this book,
and for her Spider-Man had more resonance—and, I must assume, more ap-
plicability—than Superman does. I would not deny that Spider-Man can be
called mythic, but I would need more evidence. The personal becomes mythic
when it resonates with the larger culture. We can speak of mythology, and
of personal mythology. The qualifier *personal* becomes necessary because,
though the basic concept of myth adheres on the larger level, it grows out
of the individual—recall the folkloristic interest in the tension between the
individual and the collective. Certainly most people in this country have
heard of Spider-Man, but he lacks the cultural resonance of Superman.

Since any story could become a myth, at least theoretically, the term
must have limits or it becomes meaningless. A story becomes a myth when
people use it as a foundation for personal contemplation and action; this idea
flows throughout the works of many mythologists, from classical theories
to folkloristics to Barthes and Slotkin. Adherents to myth apply what they
have learned in contemplation of it to their conduct. If a myth is a tale applied, then why do people apply it? The stories we call myths are multivalent
enough to be of many uses, polysemous enough to be malleable, and, most
importantly, resonant with the individual and collective experience. This
resonance comes from several possible sources. It can arise from belief, but
it can come from other sources, such as association with a sacred ritual. With

Superman, resonance arises from similarities to fathers or father figures, from a story structure similar to extant religious traditions, and from associations with fond memories of childhood.

Superman fans know that he is fictional, and in fact that makes his myth altogether more potent. It cannot be demythologized; it cannot be debunked; it cannot be exposed as fraudulent history. Albert Friedman argues that Americans do indeed have myths in the unselfconscious sense, but they are covert, only expressed in "a shadow world of ideality" (1971: 43). He's thinking of Bidney, and of Barthes. Barthes conceptualizes myth as a window (1957: 123), which serves to convey that which lies beyond. Myth is a rhetorical tool. Where Barthes and Slotkin study myth as a means to point out its flaws, my own goal, grounded in performance and folkloristics, is to find benevolent myth, which led me to Superman. Furthermore, where American scholars such as Slotkin take as their subject matter the overarching culture of the US, I have examined the more personal connections developed by people with affinities for Superman stories to show how they find in the myth of Superman strategies for coping with difficulties and for plotting the course of their lives in terms of morality and virtue. Barthes's window pane can divide the viewer from the outside world, but it can just as easily protect the viewer from inclement weather and allow a vision of the paths opening up before them. Perhaps we might say that, for Americans, the window of myth is tinted.

NOTES

CHAPTER 1

1. The anthropologist William Bascom discusses the notion of literature entering oral tradition, a process he calls "folklorization" (1955: 249). Although the idea of referring to a folklorized Superman is enticing, I have opted not to use Bascom's term. See also McDowell 2010 for alternative uses of the term, which are sometimes opposite to Bascom.

2. A. David Lewis refers to Superman as a "collective," which at first seems to mean that he is made up of the many versions of his story. But there's some ambiguity to this appellation. Lewis is referring to Superman's role in his fictional universe, and he follows his use of collective with an explanation: "Said another way, Superman is less a character than a container" (2010: 179). That is, Superman's story encompasses those of the other characters in the DC Comics' universe. Yet Lewis's analysis also acknowledges Superman's impact on the real world, as will be explored in this book.

3. See Coogan 2006 for a discussion of the superhero genre in general, and of Superman in particular.

4. A variety of encyclopedias list these details. Michael Fleisher's (1978), while dated, is perhaps the most thorough.

5. He's referring to *Adventures of Superman*, which was the title of a radio program in the 1940s and a television show in the 1950s. See Hayde 2009 for a book-length study of these programs and a thorough discussion of the material quoted here.

6. Communicated in a personal e-mail message on August 30, 2010.

7. It's worth noting that everything considered essential in DeHaven's description, with the sole exception of flight, is present in Superman's first appearance in *Action Comics* 1. Both Nicolas Michaud (2013) and Dennis Knepp (2013) explore the continuity of Superman's identity, from several philosophical viewpoints.

8. For descriptions of some genres important to fan cultures that aren't folkloric in nature (such as fan fiction and videos), see Jenkins 1992, Bacon-Smith 1992, and Lancaster 2001.

9. In fact, several early definitions of folklore consisted of lists of genres; see Dundes 1985 and 1999.

10. See Bauman 1972 for a discussion of the definition of performance; Sawin 2002 provides an insightful response.

11. See Wandtke 2012 for a discussion of variation and oral tradition as it relates to superhero comics, especially Superman comics. Wandtke analyzes the ways superhero stories
vary over time as ongoing series revisit old plots and themes. Wandtke calls this variation,
producing variants, though folklorists would call this the production of different versions,
since the stories themselves are available in the same form, fixed in media. For example,
Superman's origin is told in *Action Comics,* vol. 1, no. 1; *Superman,* vol. 1, no. 1; *Man of Steel;*
and *Secret Origin.* Each of these stories revisits the same plot, but with different details.
None of them contain variation that is the result of live performance, and so wouldn't be
considered a variant in the folkloristic sense.

12. Henry Glassie (1982) integrates the study of live performance of verbal art with
music and material culture. Barre Toelken's studies of Navaho coyote tales (1969, 1987,
1998, 2002, 2004; Toelken and Scott 1981) focus on how a story can encode multiple meanings depending on context and the questions a scholar chooses to ask. John McDowell
(1994) also integrates fieldwork with the study of texts as he examines myths of the Kamsá
people in Columbia. William Hansen (2009) points to the narrative components of myth
as important in understanding the mode of thought behind the genre. Yet Hansen is also
interested in the persistence of mythical narratives in the modern world, finding that tales
from the *Odyssey* remain in oral tradition (Hansen 1983, 1990).

13. The anthropologist Edmund R. Leach (1967) puts forward a different idea. He claims
that the variation in sacred texts such as the Bible arises from the need for people to find a
reinforcing redundancy in their sacred tales.

14. There are other tensions relevant to the study of folklore, particularly nature/culture
and insider/outsider, which don't directly apply to this study.

15. For some other perspectives on the interplay of comics and folklore that do not
specifically influence this study, see Brewster 1950, Smith 1952, and Wooley 1974.

16. Grant Morrison, also a writer of Superman comics, likens the creation of superhero
comics to renewing "aboriginal" paintings on cave walls (2011: 118, 408–409). There's something to this idea, as superhero comics seldom remain in the hands of their creators. It
didn't take long for Jerry Siegel and Joe Shuster to lose creative control of Superman. Once
subsequent writers and editors took over, the stories became something different.

17. Wandtke's focus on the mentality and psychology of comic book artists, editors, and
readers begs for ethnographic testing. His book was published after I had completed my
research, and thus I am not able to provide a full discussion in light of his ideas.

18. A. David Lewis (2002) discusses the similarities of midrash to the comic book retcon
(retroactive continuity changes), in which current writers add to, explore, or change events
from previously published stories.

19. Following up on Walter Benjamin's ideas in "The Work of Art in the Age of
Mechanical Reproduction," Johnson communicated these ideas to me in personal conversation, and he taught them in his introductory folklore course at Indiana University.
Similar ideas can be found in discussions of the relationship between folklore and popular
culture. Martin Laba describes a related distinction when he writes of popular culture as "a
matrix of symbolic forms established and situated through technological means" (1986: 9).
Laba, however, is focused on the folkloristic attention to context, rather than to text, while

prescribing for scholars to look to the social context of consumption and interpretation that people make of popular culture. He wants to shift the focus from the popular culture material to the "human communicative acts in everyday life" that accompany it (1986: 13), which is essentially what I'm trying to do with this project. Laba, while emphasizing social context, de-emphasizes folkloric genres, which is one reason his analytical perspective has not played a larger role in this opening chapter. I'm being a bit more old-fashioned in my attention to specific genres, but I think it's appropriate to the material I've found through fieldwork. For an earlier formulation of this dichotomy, with special attention to the persistence of folklore forms, see Jakobson and Bogatyrev 1980.

20. Lawrence W. Levine makes the same point: "[W]hile culture may not be seamless, it is connected; it does not exist—at least not outside the academic world—in neatly separate boxes waiting for the scholar's labels" (1992: 1372).

21. This has been done to some extent (see Coogan 2006: 116–25).

22. See Darowski 2012, for example.

23. The term *folklore* was originally coined (with a hyphen) as part of an ongoing discussion in England about what to call the things that a number of ambitious amateurs were interested in collecting, which were generally survivals from cultures of the past as they persisted into the mid-nineteenth century; it was essentially an analytical term (Dundes 1999a: 9–14). The term *folklore* was picked up in general use and came to have the connotations it has today of something dated, traditional, false, and, well, folksy. It refers to old wives' tales and superstitions.

24. See Fulk 2002 for the early English-language uses of the term *myth*.

25. There is precedent for this sort of conflation; see Rosenberg 1991: 22 ff.

26. For the inverse perspective (a folkloristic approach to the Bible itself), see Dundes 1999b.

27. Interestingly, Friedman reports that poets such as Dante saw the presence of their writing in folklore—sung by gondoliers, in this case—as an undesirable development, at least initially (1967: 55).

28. There are examples of Superman folklore that provide economic benefits, notably the Superman Celebration explored in Chapter 4.

CHAPTER 2

1. I choose the term *life story* carefully here, and follow Jeff Todd Titon's (1980) use, which emphasizes the story as a meaningful rather than a documentary construction. I give several cases here, beginning in Chapter 2 and continuing in Chapters 3, 4, and 6. Although I do not doubt the factuality of what people have told me regarding their lives, my goal as a folklorist is to ascertain what Superman means to them rather than what they were doing at any given moment. Again and again in interviews, the past came up and could not be ignored. I call the results of these interviews life stories because of their resemblance to this sort of ethnographic category, instead of, say, calling them personal experience narratives. Titon points out the ongoing methodological problem of the life story/life history genre,

but it is not my intention to get involved in this discussion. Therefore, I aspire to transparency with regard to how I got information from those with whom I talked. When I omit things, it is because I have other goals than to fully represent my conversations. Yet I cannot claim full exoneration from my role as the recorder of life stories. When I began to notice the pattern of responses to my inquiries about Superman tended to look like life stories, I started pursuing this. I brought it up in recorded conversations, and I looked for aspects of each interview that lined up with what I had noticed in others. See also Oring 1987b and Kirshenblatt-Gimblett 1989.

2. See Coogan 2006: 33, 254, n. 10.

3. http://www.iwilldare.com.

4. For one example, see http://metropolisplus.com/superman.

5. It is important to note that a great many fans, both casual and devoted, wear Superman T-shirts, which we might see as existing on the same spectrum of fan devotion as the tattoo, though the impermanence of clothing (of which the T-shirt is but one of the many varieties) does not mark the wearer in the same way that a tattoo does. Because of the folkloristic focus of this study, I will not be discussing T-shirts and other mass-produced commodities that, while important to fans, are not, strictly speaking, folklore. See Chapter 6 for a discussion of the related genre of costuming. Brown (2012) provides an ethnographically oriented study of fans and superhero T-shirts, with particular attention to the group affiliation and subcultures as fans. He points out that fans who wear superhero T-shirts do so to declare themselves to be serious fans or experts: "In other words, the shirts indicate a possession of subcultural capital of a higher level than that obtained by more casual fans" (2012: 286). If we apply the same thinking to tattoos, we see that a permanent modification of the body, at greater expense than an article of clothing, marks the wearer with perhaps a greater amount cultural capital. Brown even includes some discussion of fans who make their own clothing in a manner that is different from costuming (2012: 286–87). These examples demonstrate the permeable boundary between folklore and popular culture. He also discusses some of the difficulties in conducting fieldwork with contemporary comic book fans. See also Brian Swafford's chapter, "Critical Ethnography" (2012: 291–302), in the same volume.

6. As the time of this writing, Superman's morality—specifically whether or not he should kill criminals—is the center of many conversations due to the 2013 film *Man of Steel*, in which the character does kill a villain. Since this book is not intended as an examination of Superman's morality, I won't engage in that conversation. Some people like it, others don't. The one point that seems relevant has to do with medium: In Marco Arnaudo's view, the frequency with which superheroes kill or allow villains to die in cinema, which is much higher than in comics, has to do with the fact that the cinematic superhero conforms to the conventions of the action movie genre. In action movies, audiences readily accept the slaying of the villain at the end, whereas the conventional comic book superhero makes every effort not to kill (Arnaudo 2013: 91–92).

7. The monologue in this film, written by Quentin Tarantino, is likely inspired by a passage in Jules Feiffer's book *The Great Comic Book Heroes* (1965). The primary similarity between them is the idea that Superman is the real identity while Clark Kent is the mask

(a notion that was important in the comics in 1986, when John Byrne's mini-series *Man of Steel* made it a key point in Superman's concept of himself primarily as Clark Kent). This difference is that Tarantino turns the Kent identity into a critique on humanity, rather than a comment on male and female relationships.

8. I've noticed some angst in versions of the story that dramatize Clark Kent's teenage years. That's to be expected, I suppose, but I've also noticed that this angst vanishes when Clark discovers that he can fly. This occurs in several versions: *Superman: The Animated Series* (2005) shows us this in its origin episodes; a children's book *The True Story of Superman* (Simonson 1995) tells us that Clark's powers "scared him," right up to the moment he learns he can fly; the television show *Smallville* takes ten years for him to learn to fly, which is when he accepts his position as a public hero and puts on his suit.

9. When transcribing interviews such as this one, I have used an ellipsis to mark a pause, not to indicate that I have omitted anything the speaker has said.

10. During the years that have passed since I interviewed Jeff, I have regrettably lost contact with him and cannot say for sure how things have changed.

11. This runs counter to the Sanders's finding that women tend to get tattoos in places where they are easily covered (2008: 49–50).

12. http://superfriends.spruz.com/ (accessed 10/10/2015).

13. Terrence R. Wandtke discusses this phenomenon in relation to superheroes in general as part of the "rebirth of orality (or traditionalism)" in comic books and popular culture in general (Wandtke 2012: 9ff.).

14. I want to point out that Sanders doesn't ignore the intrapersonal discourse of tattoos; he does include a brief discussion of it, but it is not his focus. When quoting one of the tattoo artists whom he interviewed as saying, "It's almost like a tattoo pulls you back into a certain kind of reality about who you are as an individual" (2008: 44), Sanders relates this statement to the act of separating the self from a group or from other individuals.

15. We will see this theme again in Chapter 5 as we examine Superman humor.

CHAPTER 3

1. Vaihinger's reception among literary critics has been, to say the least, complicated (see Stampfl 1998), but this discussion will largely avoid that subject. My concern here is the use to which Elder puts the "as if" mode.

2. Ritual, to some extent, operates this way as well; see Turner 1988 and Handleman 1977.

3. This point is made early on in the documentary *The Science of Superman* (2006).

4. This sentiment echoes the film *The Iron Giant* (Bird 1998), in which a boy presents Superman comics to a powerful alien robot to use as a model for morality; see Hopkins 2005 for a discussion of that film and its use of Superman.

5. http://www.statesman.com/life/books/how-one-austinite-became-supermans-brain-1163690.html (accessed 03/11/2011). This page has since been removed, but Roberson mentions it on his blog: Roberson 2011, http://www.chrisroberson.net/2011/01/12/truth-justice-and-the-american-way/ (accessed 11/10/2016).

6. It's tempting to see a similarity to the concept of ostension, as defined by folklorists (see Dégh and Vázsonyi 1983).

7. For a discussion of the way writers, artists, and editors of Superman stories have the character respond to real-world wars and conflict, see Gordon 2015.

8. This was part of a podcast available at http://www.the-isb.com/?cat=200&paged=4 (accessed 06/15/2013).

9. Joseph Darowski (2012) analyzes Roberson's 2011 run on the *Superman* comic book.

10. There are exceptions. When children would approached Jerry Siegel's house to ask if Superman really lived there, Siegel would reply that he did, but he was out saving the world. As proof, he would show them one of the hero's spare costumes (Kobler, 1941). Additionally, the official Superman at the Metropolis Celebration (see Chapter 4 below) never breaks character while he is in public.

11. Museum of Comic and Cartoon Art.

12. "Dear Superman" was published digitally in November of 2013 (and is still available at the DC Comics website: http://www.readdcentertainment.com/). A print version (Elder et al 2014) came out in February of 2014.

13. This is part of the opening caption to Moore's story "Whatever Happened to the Man of Tomorrow?" (Moore et al 1985).

14. The story as published differs from the version he told me during our interview. He had to trim a large amount of material to fit the eight pages he was allotted. The printed version begins with Connie's trip to Metropolis in the hopes of seeing Superman. She sees him fight Metallo, and writes him a letter about the experience. This prompts Superman to visit her, and we learn that she is in the hospital receiving treatment for cancer. As he uses his heat vision and cold breath to make her a glass chevron to hold together her makeshift cape, he says, "You kids may not know it, but you have someone very special in your midst here today. Now she's not faster than a speeding bullet, and she's not able to leap tall buildings in a single bound. Yet no matter what burdens the world puts on her shoulders, she still finds the strength to carry on. She still finds the courage to hope. Her name is Connie, and she's my superhero" (Elder et al 2014).

15. Although he does warn that this has happened in the past; he calls it "metaphorical contamination" (1967: 115). There are shades of Max Muller's "disease of language" here.

CHAPTER 4

1. See *The Myth and Ritual Theory: An Anthology* (Segal 1998) for a history of scholarship concerning the relationship between these two genres.

2. Three versions demonstrate the range of tellings: a children's book by Mark Tyler Nobleman called *Boys of Steel* (2008); Gerard Jones's *Men of Tomorrow* (2005), an historical account woven into the history of comic books in general; and Brad Meltzer's novel *The Book of Lies* (2008), in which the story of Jerry Siegel forms part of the backstory and mystery that unfold. The first is a typical children's picture book, with illustrations; the

second approaches the early days of comics through investigative journalism; and the third is a thriller that ties the story into the story of Cain and Abel.

3. Brian Swafford sees a similar attitude toward the comic book stores he visited for his research, and he uses the concept of the clubhouse to describe that environment. His discussion emphasizes some examples of the folk speech of the fan community that separates members from those outside their community (2012: 296–98).

4. The statue, erected in 1993, is but one part of the town's ongoing effort to bring in tourists by playing upon its shared name with the fictional city where Superman lives. In 1972, the town was officially declared "Superman's Hometown" (http://www.metropolistourism.com/).

5. During my interviews, I never encountered the term *cosplayer*. Everyone I talked to used *costumer* though it is the less common term in media. Some drew a distinction between a cosplayer, who makes every attempt to portray a character in public, and a costumer, who merely wears the costume of the character and maintains his or her own personality.

6. Meeting people at the Superman Celebration was tough, but once I was able to do so it wasn't difficult to get them to talk about themselves. Lisa Gabbert writes that her family's presence in the town of McCall, where she conducted a study of a winter festival, aided in her ability to interview people because the residents were able to immediately assign her to a familiar social status (Gabbert 2011: 11). I think that the ecumenical and open nature of the Superman Celebration worked in my favor; since so many of the attendees are already from out of town, my presence wasn't seen as unusual.

7. Jim Hambrick told me he moved to Metropolis because it was the ideal place to make a permanent home for the Super Museum, the contents of which had previously been a mobile exhibit. I did not meet Catherine Busbee—who has since moved out of Metropolis but keeps a house there and has attended the Celebration regularly—but found an interview with her conducted by Ronda Kelly for the Superman Homepage: http://www.supermanhomepage.com/news.php?readmore=9969 (accessed 06/29/2011).

8. "I am a fan of Superman," Michelle told me, "but I'm not fanatical (there's probably a better word) in that I can't rattle off dates of major events in the comics, I don't collect action figures or movie props, and the Metropolis Superman Celebration is usually the only comic 'convention' that I attend each year. But I am a fan of the character and what he represents."

9. Brian wrote to me, "I recall in 2002, David Olsen—then one of the organizers of the Saturday Night Auction—put on a play with volunteers holding their scripts and emoting (that's when I met Steve Kirk as I volunteered to help with the writing at that time.) I believe this happened in 2003 and not long afterwards, Scott Cranford took it upon himself to write, direct, and perform a short play to add value to attending the opening ceremony."

10. I focus on Brian for several reasons, not the least of which is that he is easy to talk to and keeps up with correspondence. He has stressed again and again the fact that the opening ceremony, and all the events that form the Celebration, are collectively organized. I have talked to all of the people involved in the skit to some extent, but I have chosen to

engage in a deeper discussion with one of them, Brian, instead of giving a more superficial but inclusive analysis.

11. There are numerous studies of the secret identity motif in superhero comics: see Andrae 1987, Wandtke 2012 (56–57), Russell 2009, and, from a perspective outside academia, Fingeroth 2007.

12. Karla Ogle told me that, to win the role of the official Superman, a contestant must be able to fit the size twelve boots.

13. Stoeltje includes "drama and contest" as a separate structure; it is uncommon to incorporate drama into the opening ceremony in this fashion.

14. Roger Abrahams points out that the important communicative energies of the folk drama are directed toward the audience members, not the other players on the stage (1972: 359).

15. And of folk groups, see Alan Dundes's essay "Who Are the Folk?" (1980).

16. B. J. Oropeza (2006) discusses the maintenance of a status quo as the defining trait of the superhero narrative.

17. The joining of a fan community is often an initiation process, a sort of rite of passage; see Bacon-Smith 1992.

18. See Smith 1972 for a discussion of the need to attend to the entire festival instead of separating elements and decontextualizing them.

19. Throughout this discussion, I knowingly conflate the verb *to play* with the noun *play*, as in a stage play.

20. See Connors 1988 for a look at the Freudian interpretation of dreams of flying as it applies to Superman.

21. Brian Morris told me that it never occurred to them to dramatize the origin story, in part because they figured that everyone already knew it; "I'd rather amuse them by introducing the audience to someone possibly unfamiliar like Darkseid, Bibbo Bibowski, General Zod, and even Mind-Grabber Kid. Besides, it's hard to get laughs by the horrific deaths of several billion Kryptonians."

22. The DC liaison to the Celebration has requested that only DC characters be represented in the skit. The Red Mullett has since appeared in other contexts, particularly fan films.

23. See Harrison 2010 for a reading of Superman's origin story as a sacrifice on the part of his parents.

24. Marco Arnaudo sees the entire genre of comic book superheroes as one that foregrounds inclusivity, multiplicity, coexistence (Arnaudo 2013: 60–61, 153).

25. See Lloyd 2006 for a discussion of Superman's evolving morality.

26. "Event analysis," writes Paul Jordan Smith, "based only on division of an event into component parts is inadequate" (1999: 48). See also Georges 1969.

CHAPTER 5

1. Superman's status as an immigrant also comes up a lot in the literature, but there is more support that this is a key element of the figure, a reason he resonates with people. In

the documentary *Look, Up in the Sky! The Amazing Story of Superman* (2006), musician Gene Simmons, himself an immigrant from Israel, says that this aspect of Superman was meaningful to him.

2. See Oring 2003 (129–40) for a discussion of humor on the internet.

3. This joke with this precise wording is on far too many websites to count, and I was unable to locate a source (this is from http://www.commonsenseevaluation.com/tag/snow -white/#sthash.jy4xK2Hv.dpbs [accessed 01/10/2010]). It is often told about Nancy Pelosi, a prominent member of the United States House of Representatives at the time of this writing who was in the news because of evidence that she had lied about knowing about state-endorsed torture of prisoners to obtain information. The joke was also told with President Barack Obama as the punch line, but the reference was less obvious. At the end of March 2011, it was also told with Australian Prime Minister Julia Gillard as the punch line. The earliest version I found is from November 8, 2008, and is about Obama, but the interesting thing is that it was posted before his inauguration. The highest number of jokes comes from the period between April and August of 2009.

4. This joke, insofar as I can tell, exists only online. No one I interviewed has heard it, and my requests for interviews among the six people who have posted it online have turned up no relevant information as to the joke's origin. It is, I should note, posted verbatim on all six websites. Literary details such as Ray's "voice hushed with conspiracy" and the use of the past tense make the joke feel like it is written (Elliott Oring [1989: 350] notes that jokes tend to be narrated in the present tense). The joke can be found at these addresses:

http://www.extremelyfunny.co.uk/index.php?action=dispsjoke&jid=12870&type=jks (accessed 10/10/2010),

http://www.misscellania.com/miss-cellania/2010/4/11/growing-up-superman.html (accessed 10/10/2010).

5. I interviewed John and his brother Alex at the 2009 Superman Celebration in Metropolis, Illinois.

6. http://www.bluetights.net/theplanet/showthread.php?t=4574&page=2 (accessed 10/11/2010).

7. http://www.bluetights.net/theplanet/showthread.php?t=4574.

8. He's referring to a bit on Cosby's comedy album *Bill Cosby Is a Very Funny Fellow Right!* (Warner Brothers: 1965/1995).

9. D'Orazio rejects this notion of sacredness.

10. Citing newspaper and internet cartoons is a troublesome task. I found many of them posted in discussion forums and on websites that have nothing to do with their creators. I have made every effort to contact those who posted them to find out where they found them, with no success. I have done my best to give credit to the cartoonists and artists, where possible. Many of these images come from a pair of online galleries posted on the Superman Homepage.com (http://www.supermanhomepage.com/images/gallery/gallery .php?topic=comedy (accessed 10/15/2016), http://www.supermanhomepage.com/images/ gallery/gallery.php?topic=comedy2 (accessed 10/16/2016).

11. Dennis has portrayed Superman to pose for photographs with tourists outside Mann's Chinese Theater in Hollywood. The documentary profiles several of the men and women who perform as superheroes in this way.

12. Found on http://www.supermanhomepage.com/images/gallery/gallery.php?topic=comedy (accessed 10/16/2016). The image there was cropped so that no title or cartoonist's name could be seen.

13. January 21, 2002: http://www.offthemark.com/cartoons/superman/pg/2 (accessed 10/16/2016).

14. Published August 31, 2006: http://www.grimmy.com/search-grimmy-archive-results.php (accessed 10/16/2016).

15. A similar thematic recurrence shows Superman commiserating at a bar with someone else.

16. This theme is common in analyses of the character. Michael Fleisher's Superman encyclopedia (1978) includes a lengthy discussion of Superman's psyche; Peter Coogan's *Superhero* (2006) looks at the Oedipal nature of his character.

17. I found this at the website http://www.citizenmom.net/2008/12/lois-i-dropped-my-pencil-.html (accessed 10/16/2016). The blogger cites the cartoon as the work of Rob Tornoe for the website Politicker.com, but I was unable to locate the image there.

18. http://www.supermanhomepage.com/images/gallery/gallery.php?topic=comedy. The cartoon itself includes Jeff Stahler's signature, and that it was printed in the *Columbus Dispatch* in 2009. I could not find it on that newspaper's website.

19. *Speed Bump*, March 18, 2009: http://www.speedbump.com and http://www.cartoonistgroup.com/store/add.php?iid=58568 (accessed 10/19/2014).

20. December 30, 2009: http://www.grimmy.com/search-grimmy-archive-results.php?page=2 (accessed 10/16/2016).

21. October 1, 2008: http://www.grimmy.com/search-grimmy-archive-results.php?page=2 (accessed 10/16/2016).

22. *Bizarro*, February 8, 2004: http://www.supermanhomepage.com/images/comedy/sup-lois-15yrs-tb.html (accessed 10/16/2016).

23. *Pardon My Planet*, September 2: http://www.supermanhomepage.com/images/comedy/pardonmyplanet-tb.html (accessed 10/16/2016).

24. Bizarro.com, May 9, 2003 (accessed 10/16/2016).

25. http://www.supermanhomepage.com/images/comedy/oldsupes-farside-tb.html (accessed 10/16/2016).

26. http://www.supermanhomepage.com/images/comedy/costume-22jun06-tb.html (accessed 10/16/2016).

27. This resembles a theme in *Watchmen* (Moore et al. 1986), a comic book series that deconstructed the superhero genre. Among its many themes, it explores the idea that anyone who dresses up in skintight outfits to fight crime could be a sexual deviant.

28. From *The Simpsons* episode, "Lost Our Lisa" (1998), written by Brian Scully, directed by Pete Michels.

29. May 12, 2009: http://www.supermanhomepage.com/images/comedy/SpeedBump051209-tb.html (accessed 10/16/2016).

30. August 25, 2009: http://www.supermanhomepage.com/images/comedy/strangebrew082509-tb.htm (accessed 10/16/2016).

31. http://www.cartoonistgroup.com/store/add.php?iid=31454 (accessed 10/16/2016).

32. January 23, 2009: http://www.theeditorialcartoons.com/subject/The-Superman
-Editorial-Cartoons-by-Mike+Luckovich%27s+Editorial+Cartoons.php (accessed 10/16/
2016).

33. http://dailycaller.com/2011/01/23/colin-powell-on-obama-we-didnt-elect-superman
-we-elected-a-human-being/#ixzz1KBBh2TYb (accessed 10/16/2016).

34. http://www.youtube.com/watch?v=jach29wcM-Q (accessed 10/16/2016).

35. February 22, 2009: http://nickandzuzu.com/; http://www.supermanhomepage.com/
images/comedy/helpyourself-tb.html (accessed 10/16/2016).

36. "The Stock Tip," 1990, written by Larry David and Jerry Seinfeld, directed by Tom
Cherones.

CHAPTER 6

1. Many costumers engage in exercise regimens designed to increase their resemblance
to the characters they portray.

2. "In fact," writes Gary Engle, "one is hard pressed to find any precedent in popular
culture for the kind of cape Superman wears. It emerges in a seamless line from either side
of the front yoke of his tunic. It is a veritable growth from behind his pectorals and hangs,
when he stands at ease, in a line that doesn't so much drape his shoulders as stand apart
from them and echo their curve, like an angel's wings" (Engle 1987: 86). For another reading
of Superman as an angel, see Lewis 2010: 180.

3. In this balance of fidelity and personal taste, I'm reminded of how Pravina Shukla
describes tradition in costuming as a "balance of preservation and innovation" (2015: 112).

4. McLeod 2008.

5. Scott tells the story of his entry into costuming in the introduction to his own book
on superheroes and Christianity (Bayles 2016: XIII–XVI).

6. Darowski (2012: 166–76) sees this storyline and those that follow it as representative
of American identity concerns after the end of the cold war and the revolution in technology that was happening at the time.

7. Scott writes about the religious aspects of Superman in his book: Bayles 2016: 8–10.
See also Garrett 2005, Brewer 2004, and Skelton 2006.

8. At the time of this writing, he also has a son.

9. Susan Faludi (2007) uses Superman to discuss the perception of the United States
after the terrorist attacks on September 11, 2011.

10. Upon showing it to me, Josh said that for some fifteen years it was the closest thing
he had to a religious symbol, though he no longer thinks of it in that way.

11. Arnaudo disagrees with the notion of the Edenic status quo; for him, superheroes
fight not for the status quo, "but rather the conditions of freedom that allow citizens to
decide for themselves whether to maintain the status quo or whether and in what way to
change it" (2013: 111).

12. Describing the similarities and differences between Superman and Jesus has almost
become a literary subgenre; see Galloway 1972, White 1978, Kozloff 1981, Koslovic 2002,

Garrett 2005, Brewer 2005, Skelton 2006, and Herrick 2008. Saunders argues that "such arguments reveal more about the interpretive desire to claim Superman for this or that tradition (whether Jewish, Christian, or Pagan) than they do about Superman himself" (2011: 17).

13. Ian Gordon calls Superman "a product by which we consume virtue" (2001: 180).

CHAPTER 7

1. But an important facet of folklore is that genres are interdependent; see Honko 1984.

2. Schrempp (1992) begins his analysis of Greek and Maori myth with the notion of myth as the opposite of logos. Both present lessons—myth does so narratively, but logos employs logical argument. Myth is thus a framework for understanding, especially for understanding the cosmos and the situation of humanity within it.

3. For Dundes, only stories that describe the origin of the cosmos, gods, and people qualify as myths (see Segal 2004), but the general folkloristic perspective on myth is more nuanced than this.

4. Within the United States today, *myth* has two valences, both of which date to antiquity and come to us through Romanticism (Von Hendy 2002). The first is a foundational and ontological story. The second is myth as a tenacious misconception, which, despite its lack of veracity, may be a formative component of ideology (Hughes 2004; Raphael 2006). From the folkloristic perspective, these could be studied independently. Folklorists favor the fundamental story over the misconception, possibly because the misconception tends to be less developed as a narrative.

5. The shift in conception wasn't instant, of course. Richard Dorson writes, "The rise of the monotheistic religions, Judaism, Christianity, and Islam, displaced the older mythologies and relegated them to children's stories about gods and heroes. In this sense we cannot refer to American mythology" (1983: 57). What he means is that the United States has no unique and indigenous system of stories about gods that describes its origins. Nonetheless, the American people have made religious narratives their own, to the extent that Francis Lee Utley (1945), as discussed in Chapter 1, writes about "the Bible of the Folk."

6. Dorson can be read as lamenting the lack of precision in the current usage of the term, which he calls "metaphorical" (1983: 57).

7. Barthes's analysis is flavored with Marxism, and many of the myths he examines are of the bourgeois type.

8. Slotkin has written three books about the American frontier myth (1973, 1985, 1998), which he traces back to the seventeenth century. There remains little recorded oral tradition of the nascent American colonies, and what little was being attended to regarding the native population wasn't recorded with scholarly rigor. Still, Slotkin contrasts mythologies of preliterate and literate societies, stating that those arising in preliterate eras are "'artless' in their portrayal of the world and the gods, appealing to the emotions rather than the intelligence" (1973: 6). On this point, I disagree, but his use of "artless" is hard to parse. He doesn't seem to mean that there was a lack of artistic skill or sensibility, but the notion that

preliterate mythology appeals to the emotion and excludes the intellect has been refuted by Claude Levi-Strauss (1963, 1968). Slotkin's most cogent statement on myth can be found in *The Fatal Environment* (1985: 13–32).

9. Discussing various aspects of American hero stories as compared to European counterparts, McFadden makes the intriguing point that the United States is "too knowledgeable of its origins, whereas Europe was able, like all other world cultures, outside the U.S., to create a mythology where origins simply faded into an obscure past" (1972: 33). Other scholars of myth in America would no doubt disagree. Slotkin, for one, sees the construction of the American myth of the frontier as having proceeded as a mixture of conscious and unconscious mythologizing.

10. In "Poverty of Cause in Mythological Narrative" (2010), William Hansen's attention to the mechanics of storytelling allows scholars to look at myths with the idea that sometimes a narrator includes an element that seems mythological just because it works on a narrative level.

11. Peter Coogan (2012: 203–220) applies structural analysis to *All-Star Superman*, looking at both the plot and images, as well as the story's place in the larger context of the evolution of the superhero genre.

12. Lévi-Strauss, inaugurator of the structural study of myth (in Lévi-Strauss 1955), insists that all variants of a myth must be taken into account when conducting a structural study. He demonstrated this method in a four-volume study of South American mythology, but there is precedent for the more limited analysis I've engaged in here; see Köngäs-Maranda 1973 and Schrempp 2014.

13. The two sets of parents echo the story pattern described by Otto Rank in *The Myth of the Birth of the Hero* (2004).

14. Reynolds notes the prominence of the image of Superman's spaceship having dug a deep trench in the earth, writing that "Superman is born from a marriage of Uranus (Heaven) and Gaia (earth)" (1992: 13).

15. The primary support for this is the plot of the film *Superman II*, in which Superman gives up his powers to consummate his love for Lois. The comic books from approximately 1996 to 2011, in which Superman marries Lois, refute this viewpoint.

16. *All-Star Superman* includes an exploration of this opposition, showing that Superman can exploit Luthor's ego to defeat him. The climactic panel of the Superman/Luthor battle shows Superman punching Luthor into submission while saying, "Brains beats brawn every time."

17. Superman is not often analyzed as an alien contact science fiction story, most likely because he looks human. But this aspect does play into many versions, often in Luthor's opposition to him as *the other* (see Peretti 2010).

18. I want to include the rest of Bidney's sentence: " . . . but the very fact of belief implies that subjectively, that is, for the believer, the object of the myth is not mythological."

19. There is a third modality: that of confidence, which is related to the second modality. We find this modality in such statements as "I believe in you." Interestingly, it has one of its most common applications in elections, during which people are constantly affirming

belief in particular candidates. This is related to what may constitute a fourth modality, that of accepting what a person says as factual, which brings us back to the first modality.

20. http://www.npr.org/templates/story/story.php?storyId=1950633 (accessed 10/11/2011).

21. Bidney also tackles the ideas of myth and allegory, emphasizing this very difference (1953: 302–304).

22. Schrempp writes that the contrast between mythos and logos comes down to the recurrence of several basic themes, one of which is, "roughly speaking, between the presentation of a lesson in a traditional story, on the one hand [myth], and presentation in a logical or mathematical argument, on the other" (1992: 10–11).

23. Wandtke attributes the very survival of the superhero genre to the public's willingness to embrace the changing nature of the stories as they develop (2007: 5–6).

24. For a critique of McCloud, see Wandtke 2012: 86–91.

BIBLIOGRAPHY

Abrahams, Roger D. 1972. "Folk Drama." In *Folklore and Folklife: An Introduction*. Edited by Richard M. Dorson. Chicago and London: University of Chicago Press.

Abrahams, Roger D. 1987. "An American Vocabulary of Celebrations." In *Time out of Time: Essays on the Festival*. Edited by Alessandro Falassi, 175–82. Albuquerque: University of New Mexico Press.

Aichele, George. 1997. "Rewriting Superman." In *The Monstrous and the Unspeakable: The Bible as Fantastic Literature*. Edited by Aichele and Tina Pippins. England: Sheffield Academic Press.

Andrae, Thomas. 1980. "From Menace to Messiah: The History and Historicity of Superman." Originally published in *Discourse*, no. 2 (Summer), an excerpted version appears in 1987. *American Media and Mass Culture: Left Perspectives*. Edited by Donald Lazere. Berkeley, Los Angeles, and London: University of California Press.

Arnaudo, Marco. 2013. *The Myth of the Superhero*. Translated by Jamie Richards. Baltimore: Johns Hopkins University Press.

Bacon-Smith, Camille. 1992. *Enterprising Women: Television Fandom and the Creation of Popular Myth*. Philadelphia: University of Pennsylvania Press.

Baker, Ron. 1975. "Folklore Motifs in Comic Books of Superheroes." *Tennessee Folklore Society Bulletin*, vol. 41, no. 4: 170–74.

Bakhtin, Mikhail. 1968. *Rabelais and his World*. Translated by Helene Iswolsky. Cambridge: MIT Press.

Barthes, Roland. 1957/1988. *Mythologies*. Translated by Annette Lavers. New York: Noonday Press.

Bascom, William. 1955. "Verbal Art." *Journal of American Folklore*, vol. 68: 245–52.

Bascom, William. 1984. "The Forms of Folklore: Prose Narratives." In *Sacred Narrative: Readings in the Theory of Myth*. Edited by Alan Dundes, 5–29. Berkeley, Los Angeles, and London: University of California Press.

Basso, Keith. 1996. *Wisdom Sits in Place: Landscape and Language among the Western Apache*. Albuquerque: University of New Mexico Press.

Bauman, Richard. 1972. *Verbal Art as Performance*. Bloomington: Indiana University Press.

Bayles, Scott. 2016. *Holy Heroes: The Gospel According to DC & Marvel*. Valley Forge, PA: Judson Press.

Beaudrillard, Jean. 1991. "Simulacra and Science Fiction." Translated by Arthur B. Evans. In *Science Fiction Studies*, vol 18, no. 3, *Science Fiction and Postmodernism* (Nov. 1991): 309–313.

Beaven, Lisa. 2007. "Someone to Watch over Me: The Guardian Angel as Superhero in Seicento Rome." In 2007. *Super/Heroes: From Hercules to Superman.* Edited by Wendy Haslem, Angela Ndalianis, and Chris Mackie. Washington, DC: New Academia Publishing.

Ben-Amos, Dan. 1976. *Folklore Genres.* Austin: University of Texas Press.

Benjamin, Walter. 1968. *Illuminations.* New York: Schocken Books.

Bidney, David. 1953. *Theoretical Anthropology.* New York: Schocken Books.

Bidney, David. 1955. "Myth, Symbolism, and Truth." In *Myth: A Symposium.* Edited by Thomas Sebeok. Bloomington: Indiana University Press.

Bolton, Andrew. 2008. *Superheroes: Fashion and Fantasy.* New York: Metropolitan Museum of Art.

Brednich, Rolf Wilhelm. 1976. "Comic Strips as a Subject of Folk Narrative Research." Translated by Susanne Siegert and Agnes Hostettler. In *Folklore Today: A Festschrift for Richard M. Dorson.* Edited by Linda Dégh, Henry Glassie, and Felix J. Oinas, 45–55. Bloomington: Indiana University Press.

Brewer, H. Michael. 2004. *Who Needs a Superhero?: Finding Virtue, Vice and What's Holy in the Comics.* Grand Rapids, MI: Baker Books.

Brewster, Paul G. 1950. "Folklore Invades the Comic Strips." *Southern Folklore Quarterly,* vol. XIV: 97–102.

Brown, Jeffrey A. 1997. "Comic Book Fandom and Cultural Capital." *Journal of Popular Culture,* vol. 30, no. 4: 13–31.

Brown, Jeffrey A. 2012. "Ethnography: Wearing One's Fandom." In *Critical Approaches to Comics: Theories and Methods.* Edited by Matthew J. Smith and Randy Duncan. New York and London: Routledge.

Bukatman, Scott. 2003. *Matters of Gravity: Special Effects and Supermen in the 20th Century.* Durham and London: Duke University Press.

Burkert, Walter. 1979. *Structure and History in Greek Mythology and Ritual.* Berkeley, Los Angeles, and London: University of California Press.

Campbell, Joseph. 1959. *The Masks of God: Primitive Mythology.* New York: Viking Press.

Castle, Alice W. 2016. "How Superman Saved my Life." *Book Riot.* http://panels.net/2016/07/05/superman-saved-life/ (accessed 10/11/2016).

Chabon, Michael. 2008. "Secret Skin: An Essay in Unitard Theory." In *Superheroes: Fashion and Fantasy.* New Haven and London: Yale University Press.

Chapman, Anthony, and Hugh C. Foot. 1977. *It's a Funny Thing, Humor.* Oxford and New York: Pergamon Press.

Chromey, Jodi. 2008. "I Think This Means I Win." *I Will Dare.* http://www.iwilldare.com/2008/10/29/i-think-this-means-i-win (accessed 11/15/2016).

Chromey, Jodi. 2009a. "It's Not Easy Being Blue." *MN Reads.* www.minnesotareads.com/2009/04/its-not-easy-being-blue/ (accessed 11/14/2016).

Chromey, Jodi. 2009b. "Superman Comics Make Me Cry." *I Will Dare.* http://www.iwilldare.com/2009/04/08/superman-comics-make-me-cry/ (accessed 11/15/2016).

Connors, Joanne. 1987. "Female Meets Supermale." In *Superman at 50: The Persistence of a Legend.* Edited by Denis Dooley and Gary Engle. Cleveland: Octavia.

Coogan, Peter. 2006. *Superheroes: The Secret Origin of a Genre*. Austin, TX: Monkey Brain Books.

Coogan, Peter. 2012. "Genre: Reconstructing the Superhero in *All-Star Superman*." In *Critical Approaches to Comics: Theories and Methods*. Edited by Matthew J. Smith and Randy Duncan. New York and London: Routledge.

Darowski, Joseph J. 2012. *The Ages of Superman: Essays on the Man of Steel in Changing Times*. Jefferson, NC, and London: McFarland.

De Caro, Frank, and Rosan Augusta Jordan. 2004. *Re-Situating Folklore: Folk Contexts and Twentieth-Century Literature and Art*. Knoxville: University of Tennessee Press.

De Caro, Frank. 2013. *Folklore Recycled: Old Traditions in New Contexts*. Jackson: University Press of Mississippi.

Dégh, Linda, and Andrew Vázsonyi. 1983. "Does the Word 'Dog' Bite? Ostensive Action: A Means of Legend-Telling." In *Journal of Folklore Research*, vol. 20, no. 1 (May): 5–34.

DeHaven, Tom. 2010. *Our Hero: Superman on Earth*. New Haven and London: Yale University Press.

DeScioli, Peter, and Robert Korzban. 2008. "Cracking the Superhero's Moral Code." In *The Psychology of Superheroes: An Unauthorized Exploration*. Edited by Robin S. Rosenberg, 245–59. Dallas: Benbella Books.

Dini, Paul, and Alex Ross. 1998. *Superman: Peace on Earth*. New York: DC Comics.

Dolby, Sandra K. 1996. "Essential Contributions of a Folkloristic Perspective to American Studies." In *Journal of Folklore Research*, vol. 33, no. 1 (Jan.–April): 58–64.

Donner, Richard. 1978. *Superman: The Motion Picture*.

Dooley, Dennis, and Gary Engle, eds. 1987. *Superman at Fifty: The Persistence of a Legend*. Cleveland: Octavia.

D'Orazio, Valerie. 2008. "Dopey Is Sacred Here." *Memoirs of an Occasional Superheroine*. http://occasionalsuperheroine.blogspot.com/2008/08/dopey-is-sacred-here.html (accessed 08/17/2009).

Dorson, Richard. 1945. "Print and American Folk Tales." *California Folklore Quarterly*, vol. 4, no. 3 (July): 207–215.

Dorson, Richard. 1959. "Theories of Myth and the Folklorist." In *Daedalus*, vol. 88, no. 2: 280–90.

Drummond, Lee. 1996. *American Dreamtime: A Cultural Analysis of Popular Movies and their Implications for a Science of Humanity*, Lanham, MD: Littlefield Adams Books.

Dundes, Alan. 1962. "From Etic to Emic Units in the Study of Folklore." *Journal of American Folklore*, no. 75: 95–105.

Dundes, Alan. 1965. "The Study of Folklore in Literature and Culture: Identification and Interpretation." *Journal of American Folklore*, vol. 78, no. 308 (April): 136–42.

Dundes, Alan. 1966. "Metafolklore and Oral Literary Criticism." *Monist*, no. 50: 505–516.

Dundes, Alan. 1969. "Folklore as a Mirror of Culture." *Elementary English*, no. 46: 471–82.

Dundes, Alan. 1972. "Folk Ideas as Units of Worldview." In *Toward New Perspectives in Folklore*. Edited by Richard Bauman and America Paredes. Bloomington: Indiana University Press.

Dundes, Alan. 1976. *The Hero Pattern and the Life of Jesus*. Berkeley, CA: Center for Hermeneutical Studies.

Dundes, Alan. 1980. "Who Are the Folk?" In *Interpreting Folklore*. Bloomington: Indiana University Press, 1–19.

Dundes, Alan. 1999a. *International Folkloristics: Classic Contributions from the Founders of Folklore*. New York: Rowman & Littlefield.

Dundes, Alan. 1999b. *Holy Writ as Oral Lit: The Bible as Folklore*. Lanham, MD: Rowman & Littlefield.

Dundes, Alan. 2002. "The Psychoanalytic Study of Religious Custom and Belief: Ritual Fasting, Self-Mutilation, and the *Deus Otiosus*." In *Bloody Mary in the Mirror: Essays in Psychoanalytic Folkloristics*, 3–15. Jackson: University Press of Mississippi.

Dundes, Alan, ed. 1984. *Sacred Narrative: Readings in the Theory of Myth*. Berkeley and Los Angeles: University of California Press.

Eberhard, Wolfram. 1970. "Notes on Chinese Storytellers." *Fabula*, no. 11: 1–31.

Eco, Umberto. 1979. "The Myth of Superman." In *The Role of the Reader: Explorations in the Semiotics of Texts*. Bloomington and London: Indiana University Press.

Elder, Josh. 2013. Untitled Facebook post. https://www.facebook.com/Josh.elder1/posts/10152757956440360?stream_ref=10 (accessed 06/10.2013).

Elder, Josh, et al. 2008. "A Tale of Two Cities." *The Batman Strikes*, no. 44. New York: DC Comics.

Elder, Josh, et al. 2014. "Dear Superman." *Adventures of Superman*, no. 10. New York: DC Comics.

Ellis, Havelock. 1923. *The Dance of Life*. Boston, New York: Houghton Mifflin.

El-Shamy, Hasan. 1980. *Folktales of Egypt*. Chicago: University of Chicago Press.

Engle, Gary. 1987. "What Makes Superman So Darned American?" In *Superman at Fifty: The Persistence of a Legend*. Edited by Dennis Dooley and Gary Engle. Cleveland: Octavia.

Falassi, Alessandro. 1980. *Folklore by the Fireside: Text and Context of the Tuscan Veglia*. London: Scolar Press: 1980.

Falassi, Alessandro. 1987. "Festival: Definition and Morphology." In *Time out of Time: Essays on the Festival*, 1–10. Albuquerque: University of New Mexico Press.

Faludi, Susan. 2007. *The Terror Dream: Fear and Fantasy in Post-9/11 America*. New York: Metropolitan Books, Henry Holt and Co.

Featherstone, Michael. 2002. *Body Modification*. London: Sage Publishing.

Fedorenko, Janet S., Susan C. Sherlock, and Patricia L. Stuhr. 1999. "A Body of Work: A Case Study of Tattoo Culture." *Visual Arts Research*, vol. 25, no. 1: 105–114.

Feiffer, Jules. 1965. *The Great Comic Book Heroes*. New York: Bonanza Books.

Fingeroth, Danny. 2004. *Superman on the Couch: What Superheroes Really Tell Us about Ourselves and our Society*. New York: Continuum.

Fingeroth, Danny. 2007. *Disguised as Clark Kent: Jews, Comics, and the creation of the Superhero*. New York, London: Continuum.

Firth, Raymond. 1984. "The Plasticity of Myth: Cases from Tikopia." In *Sacred Narrative*. Edited by Alan Dundes, 207–216. Berkeley: University of California Press.

Fleisher, Michael L. 1978. *The Original Encyclopedia of Comic Book Heroes, Volume Three: Superman*. New York: DC Comics.

Flood, Christopher G. 1996. *Political Myth: A Theoretical Introduction*. New York and London: Garland Publishing.

Fontenrose, Joseph. 1966. *The Ritual Theory of Myth*. Berkeley: University of California Press.

Frank, Lawrence K. 1976. "The Validity of Play." In *The Therapeutic Use of Children's Play*. Edited by Charles Schaefer. New York: Jason Aronson.

Freud, Sigmund. 1989. *The Future of an Illusion*. Translated by James St. Rachey. New York and London: W. W. Norton and Company.

Friedman, Albert B. 1967. "Tasso among the Gondoliers." In *Folklore International: Essays in Traditional Literature, Belief, and Custom in Honor of Wayland Debs Hand*. Edited by D. K. Wilgus, 55–66. Hatboro: PA: Folklore Associates.

Friedman, Albert B. 1971. "The Usable Myth: The Legends of Modern Mythmakers." In *American Folk Legend: A Symposium*. Edited by Wayland Hand, 37–46. Berkeley: UCLA Press.

Fuller, Lon L. 1967. *Legal Fictions*. Stanford: Stanford University Press.

Gabbert, Lisa. 2011. *Winter Carnival in a Western Town: Identity, Change, and the Good of the Community*. Logan: Utah State University Press.

Galloway, Jr., John T. 1973. *The Gospel According to Superman*. Philadelphia and New York: A. J. Holman.

Garrett, Greg. 2005. *Holy Superheroes! Exploring Faith and Spirituality in Comic Books*. Colorado Springs: Piñon Press.

Georges, Robert. 1969. "Toward an Understanding of Storytelling Events." *Journal of American Folklore*, no. 82: 313–29.

Glassie, Henry. 1982. *Passing the Time in Ballymenone*. Bloomington: Indiana University Press.

Glassie, Henry. 1995. "Tradition." *Journal of American Folklore*, vol. 108, no. 430 (Autumn): 395–412.

Glassie, Henry. 2002. "Mud and Mythic Vision: Hindu Sculpture in Bangladesh." In *Myth: A New Symposium*. Edited by Gregory Schrempp and William Hansen, 203–222. Bloomington: Indiana University Press.

Glassie, Henry. 2006. *The Stars of Ballymenone*. Bloomington: Indiana University Press.

Glassie, Henry. 2010. *Prince Twins Seven Seven*. Bloomington: Indiana University Press.

Gordon, Ian. 2001. "Nostalgia, Myth, and Ideology: Visions of Superman at the End of the 'American Century.'" In *Comics & Ideology*. Edited by Matthew P. McAllister, Edward H. Sewell, Jr., and Ian Gordon. New York, Washington, DC, and Baltimore: Peter Lang.

Gordon, Ian. 2012. "Culture of Consumption: Commodification through *Superman: Return to Krypton*." In *Critical Approaches to Comics: Theories and Methods*. Edited by Matthew J. Smith and Randy Duncan. New York and London: Routledge.

Gordon, Ian. 2015. "The Moral World of Superman and the American War in Vietnam." *Journal of Graphic Novels and Comics*, vol. 6, no. 2: 172–81.

Gresh, Lois, and Robert Weinberg. 2002. *The Science of Superheroes*. Hoboken, NJ: John Wiley and Sons.

Grider, Sylvia. 1981. "The Media Narraform: Symbiosis of Mass Media and Oral Tradition." *Arv*, no. 37: 125–31.

Grossman, Lev. 2004. "The Problem with Superman." *Time*, May 17, 2004: 70–72.

Handleman, Don. 1977. "Play and Ritual." In *It's a Funny Thing, Humor*. Edited by Anthony Chapman and Hugh C. Foot. Oxford and New York: Pergamon Press.

Handler, Richard, and Jocelyn Linnekin. 1989. "Tradition, Genuine or Spurious." In *Folk Groups and Folklore Genres: A Reader*. Edited by Elliott Oring. Logan: Utah State University Press.

Hansen, William. 1983. "Greek Mythology and the Study of the Ancient Greek Oral Story." *Journal of Folklore Research*, vol. 20, no. 2/3 (June–Dec. 1983): 101–112

Hansen, William. 1990. "Odysseus and the Oar: A Folkloric Approach." In *Approaches to Greek Myth*. Edited by Lowell Edmunds, 241–72. Baltimore: Johns Hopkins University Press.

Hansen, William. 2002. "Meanings and Boundaries: Reflections on Thompson's 'Myth and Folktales.'" In *Myth: A New Symposium*. Edited by Gregory Schrempp and William Hansen, 19–28. Bloomington: Indiana University Press.

Hansen, William. 2009. "Poverty of Cause in Mythological Narrative." *Folklore*, no. 120: 241–52.

Harrison, Richard. 2010. "The Dark Knight Origin of the Man of Steel." In *Secret Identity Reader: Essays on Sex, Death, and the Superhero*. Edited by Lee Easton. Hamilton, ON: Wolsak and Wynn.

Haslem, Wendy, Angela Ndalianis, and Chris Mackie, eds. 2007. *Super/Heroes: From Hercules to Superman*. Washington, DC: New Academia Publishing.

Hayde, Michael J. 2009. *Flights of Fantasy: The Unauthorized but True Story of Radio and TV's Adventures of Superman*. Duncan, OK: Bear Manor Media

Herrick, James A. 2008. *Scientific Mythologies: How Science and Science Fiction Forge New Religious Beliefs*. Downers Grove, IL: InterVarsity Press.

Hoffman, Daniel G. 1961. *Form and Fable in American Fiction*. New York: Oxford University Press.

Holbek, Bengt. 1987. *The Interpretation of Fairy Tales: Danish Folklore in a European Perspective*. Helsinki: Suomalainen Tiedeakatemia.

Honko, Lauri. 1984. "The Problem of Defining Myth." In *Sacred Narrative*. Edited by Alan Dundes, 41–52. Berkeley: University of California Press.

Hornby, James. 1984. "Rumors of Maggie: Outlaw News in Folklore." In *Media Sense: The Folklore-Popular Culture Continuum*. Edited by Peter Narváez and Martin Laba, 99–112. Bowling Green, OH: Bowling Green State University Popular Press.

Hughes, Richard T. 2004. *Myths America Lives By*. Chicago: University of Illinois Press.

Inge, M. Thomas. 1990. *Comics as Culture*. Jackson and London: University Press of Mississippi.

Jakobson, Roman, and Petr Bogatyrev. 1980. "Folklore as a Special Form of Creation." Translated by John M. O'Hara. *Folklore Forum*, vol. 13, no. 1: 3–21.

Jenkins, Henry. 1992. *Textual Poachers: Television Fans and Participatory Culture*. New York: Routledge.

Jenkins, Henry. 2006. "Why the World Doesn't Need Superman." *Confessions of an Aca-Fan*. http://henryjenkins.org/2006/07/why_the_world_doesnt_need_supe.html (accessed 11/19/2011).

Jones, Gerard. 2002. *Killing Monsters: Why Children Need Fantasy, Super Heroes, and Make-Believe Violence*. New York: Basic Books.

Jones, Gerard. 2006. *Men of Tomorrow: Geeks, Gangsters, and the Birth of the Comic Book*. New York: Perseus Books.

Jones, Gerard, and Will Jacobs. 1997. *The Comic Book Heroes*. Rocklin, CA: Prima Publishers.

Jones, Michael Owen. 1989. *Craftsman of the Cumberlands*. Lexington: University Press of Kentucky.

Jones, Steven Swan. 1985. "Joking Transformations of Popular Fairy Tales: A Comparative Analysis of Five Jokes and their Fairy Tale Sources." *Western Folklore*, vol. 44, no. 2 (April): 97–114.

Joseph-Witham, Heather R. 1996. *Star Trek Fans and Costume Art*. Jackson: University Press of Mississippi.

Kakalios, James. 2009. *The Physics of Superheroes: Spectacular Second Edition*. New York: Gotham Books.

Karp, Lauren N. 2008. "Truth Justice, and the American Way: What Superman Teaches us about the American Dream and Changing Values within the United States." Master's thesis.

Khouri, Andy. 2012. "Remembering *All-Star Superman* on World Suicide Prevention Day." *Comics Alliance*. http://www.comicsalliance.com/2012/09/10/all-star-superman-world-suicide-prevention-day/ (accessed 10/10/2012).

Kirshenblatt-Gimblett, Barbara. 1989. "Authoring Lives." *Journal of Folklore Research*, vol. 26, no. 2 (May–Aug.): 123–49.

Kleefeld, Sean. 2009. *Comic Book Fanthropology*. Hamilton, OH: Eight Twenty Press.

Knepp, Dennis. 2013. "Superman Family Resemblance." In *Superman and Philosophy: What Would the Man of Steel Do?* Edited by Mark D. White, 217–24. Oxford: Wiley-Blackwell.

Knowles, Christopher. 2007. *Our Gods Wear Spandex: The Secret History of Comic Book Heroes*. San Francisco and Newberry Port, MA: Weiser Books.

Kobler, John. 1941. "Up, Up and Awa-a-a-y! The Rise of Superman, Inc." *Saturday Evening Post*, June 21: 14–15, 70–78.

Köngäs-Maranda, Elli. 1973. "Five Interpretations of a Melanesian Myth." *Journal of American Folklore*, vol. 86, no. 339 (Jan.-March): 3–13.

Koslovic, Anton Karl. 2002. "Superman as Christ-figure: The American Pop Culture Movie Messiah." *Journal of Religion*, vol. 6, no. 1.

Kosut, Mary. 2000. "Tattoo Narratives: The Intersection of the Body, Self-Identity and Society." *Visual Sociology*, vol. 15, no. 1: 79–100.

Koven, Mikel. 2007. *Film, Folklore, and Urban Legends*. Lanham, MD: Scarecrow Press.

Kozloff, S. R. 1981. "Superman as Saviour: Christian Allegory in the Superman Movies." *Journal of Popular Film and Television*, vol. 9, no. 2: 78–82.

Kuwahara, Makiko. 2005. *Tattoo: An Anthropology*. Oxford and New York: Berg.

Laba, Martin. 1986. "Popular Culture and Folklore: The Social Dimension." In *Media Sense: The Folklore-Popular Culture Continuum*. Edited by Peter Narváez and Martin Laba, 9–18. Bowling Green, OH: Bowling Green State University Popular Press.

Lancaster, Kurt. 2001. *Interacting with Babylon 5: Fan Performances in Media*. Austin: University of Texas Press.

Leach, Edmund. *Claude Lévi-Strauss*. 1974. New York: Viking Press.

Levine, Lawrence W. 1992. "The Folklore of Industrial Society: Popular Culture and Its Audiences." *American Historical Review*, vol. 97, no. 5 (December): 1369–99.

Lévi-Strauss, Claude. 1955. "The Structural Study of Myth." In *Myth: A Symposium*. Edited by Thomas Sebeok. Bloomington: Indiana University Press.

Lévi-Strauss, Claude. 1963. *Totemism*. Boston: Beacon Press.

Lévi-Strauss, Claude. 1966. *The Savage Mind*. Chicago: University of Chicago Press.

Lévi-Strauss, Claude. 1992. *The Raw and the Cooked: Mythologiques Vol. 1*. New York: Penguin Books.

Lewis, A. David. 2002. "The Secret, Untold Relationship of Biblical Midrash and Comic Book Retcon." *International Journal of Comic Art*, vol. 4, no. 2: 261–75.

Lewis, A. David. 2010. "Superman Graveside: Superhero Salvation Beyond Jesus." In *Graven Images: Religion in Comic Books and Graphic Novels*. New York and London: Continuum.

Lincoln, Bruce. 1999. *Theorizing Myth*. Chicago: University of Chicago Press.

Lindow, John. 1994. "Thor's 'Hamarr.'" *Journal of English and Germanic Philology*, vol. 93, no. 4 (Oct.): 485–503.

Lloyd, Peter B. 2006. "The Moral Evolution of Superman." In *The Man from Krypton: A Closer Look at Superman*. Edited by Glenn Yeffeth. Dallas: Benbella Books.

LoCicero, Don. 2008. *Superheroes and Gods: A Comparative Study from Babylonia to Batman*. Jefferson, NC, and London: McFarland.

Maggin, Elliot S., and Curt Swan. 1972. "Must There Be a Superman?" *Superman*, vol. 1, no. 247. New York: DC Comics.

Malinowski, Bronislaw. 1922. *Argonauts of the Western Pacific*. New York: E. P. Dutton.

Malinowski, Bronislaw. 1926. *Myth in Primitive Psychology*. New York: W. W. Norton and Co.

Manning, Frank E. 1983. *The Celebration of Society: Perspectives on Contemporary Cultural Performance*. Bowling Green, OH: Bowling Green University Popular Press.

McCloud, Scott. 1993. *Understanding Comics: The Invisible Art*. New York: HarperCollins.

McDowell, John. 1994. *So Wise Were Our Elders: Mythic Narratives from the Kamsá*. Lexington: University Press of Kentucky.

McDowell, John. 2010. "Rethinking Folklorization in Ecuador: Multivocality in the Expressive Contact Zone." *Western Folklore*, vol. 69, no. 2 (Spring 2010): 181–209.

McFadden, Fred. 1972. "The Pop Pantheon." In *Heroes of Popular Culture*. Edited by Ray B. Browne, Marshall Fishwick, and Michael T. Marsden. Bowling Green, OH: Bowling Green State University Press.

McLeod, Bob. 2008. *Superhero ABC*. New York: HarperCollins Publishers.

McMillan, Graeme. 2013. "Orson Scott Card's Controversial Superman Story Put on Hold." *Wired* (accessed 11/10/16).

Meltzer, Brad. 2008. *The Book of Lies*. New York: Grand Central Publishing.

Michaud, Nicolas. 2013. "'It's a Bird, It's a Plane, It's . . . Clark Kent?': Superman and the Problem of Identity." In *Superman and Philosophy: What Would the Man of Steel Do?* Edited by Mark D. White, 207–216. Oxford: Wiley-Blackwell.

Millar, Mark. 2008. Foreword. In *Superman vs. Hollywood: How Fiendish Producers, Devious Directors, and Warring Writers Grounded an American Icon*. By Jake Rossen. Chicago: University of Chicago Press.

Moore, Alan, and Curt Swan. 1986. *Whatever Happened to the Man of Tomorrow?* New York: DC Comics.

Moore, Alan, and Dave Gibbons. 1986b. *Superman: For the Man Who Has Everything*. New York: DC Comics.

Moore, Alan, and J. H. Williams III. 2003. *Promethea* Book 2. New York: Wildstorm.

Morris, Tom, and Matt Morris, eds. 2005. *Superheroes and Philosophy: Truth, Justice, and the Socratic Way*. Chicago and LaSalle, IL: Open Court Press.

Morrison, Grant, Frank Quitely, and Jamie Grant. 2011. *All-Star Superman*. New York: DC Comics.

Morrison, Grant. 2011. *Supergods: What Masked Vigilantes, Miraculous Mutants, and a Sun God from Smallville can Teach Us about Being Human*. New York: Spiegel and Grau.

Mesnil, Marianne. 1987. "Place and Time in the Carnivalesque Festival." In *Time out of Time: Essays on the Festival*. Edited by Alessandro Falassi, 184–96. Albuquerque: University of New Mexico Press.

Narayan, Kirin. 1995. "The Practice of Oral Literary Criticism: Women's Songs in Kangra, India." *Journal of American Folklore*, vol. 108, no. 429 (Summer 1995): 243–64.

Narváez, Peter, and Martin Laba, eds. 1984. *Media Sense: The Folklore-Popular Culture Continuum*. Bowling Green, OH: Bowling Green State University Popular Press.

Niven, Larry. 1971. "Man of Steel, Woman of Kleenex." In *All the Myriad Ways*. New York: Ballantine Books.

O'Neil, Dennis. 1987. "The Man of Steel and Me." In *Superman at Fifty: The Persistence of a Legend*. Edited by Dennis Dooley and Gary Engle. Cleveland: Octavia.

Oring, Elliott. 1987a. "Jokes and the Discourse on Disaster." In *Jokes and their Relations*. Lexington, KY: University Press of Kentucky.

Oring, Elliott. 1987b. "Generating Lives: The Construction of an Autobiography." *Journal of Folklore Research*, vol. 24, no. 3 (Sept.–Dec. 1987): 241–62.

Oring, Elliott. 2003. *Engaging Humor*. Urbana and Chicago: University of Illinois Press.

Oropeza, B. J. 2005. "Superhero Myth and the Restoration of Paradise." In *The Gospel According to Superheroes: Religion and Popular Culture*. Edited by B. J. Oropeza, 1–24. New York: Peter Lang.

Oropeza, B. J., ed. 2005. *The Gospel According to Superheroes: Religion and Popular Culture*. New York: Peter Lang.

Peretti, Daniel. 2010. "Superman as Science Fiction." *Strange Horizons*. March 15. http://www.strangehorizons.com/2010/20100315/peretti-a.shtml.

Peretti, Daniel. 2015. "Comics as Folklore." In *The Folkloresque: Reframing Folklore in a Popular Culture*. Edited by Michael Dylan Foster and Jeffrey A. Tolbert. Boulder, CO: Utah State University Press.

Peretti, Daniel. forthcoming. "Whatever Happened to the American Way?" In *Global Mythologies and World Cinema*. Edited by Mikel Koven. Salt Lake City: University of Utah Press.

Pocius, Gerard L. 1984. "Holy Pictures in Newfoundland Houses: Visual Codes for Secular and Supernatural Relationships." In *Media Sense: The Folklore-Popular Culture Continuum*. Edited by Peter Narváez and Martin Laba, 124–48. Bowling Green, OH: Bowling Green State University Popular Press.

Pound. Louise. "'Monk' Lewis in Nebraska." *Southern Folklore Quarterly*, no. 9: 107–110.

Pustz, Matthew J. 1999. *Comic Book Culture: Fanboys and True Believers*. Jackson: University Press of Mississippi, 2000

Rank, Otto. 2004. *The Myth of the Birth of the Hero: A Psychological Exploration of Myth*. Expanded and updated edition. Translated by Gregory C. Richter and E. James Liberman. Baltimore and London: Johns Hopkins University Press.

Raphael, Ray. 2004. *Founding Myths: Stories that Hide Our Patriotic Past*. New York: New Press.

Reeve, Christopher. 1998. *Still Me*. New York: Random House.

Reynolds, Richard. 1992. *Super Heroes: A Modern Mythology*. London: BT Batsford.

Rhoads, Ellen. 1973. "Little Orphan Annie and Lévi Strauss." *Journal of American Folklore*, vol. 86, no. 342.

Roberson, Chris. 2011. "Truth, Justice, and the American Way." *The Myriad Worlds of Chris Roberson*. http://www.chrisroberson.net/2011/01/12/truth-justice-and-the-american -way/ (accessed 11/10/2016).

Roberson, Chris, et al. 2011. "Grounded." *Superman*, vol 1, nos. 711–714. New York: DC Comics.

Rosenberg, Robin S. 2008. "Superman's Personality." In *The Psychology of Superheroes*. Edited by Robin S. Rosenberg, 29–49. Dallas: Benbella Books.

Rosenberg, Robin S., ed. 2008. *The Psychology of Superheroes: An Unauthorized Exploration*. Dallas: Benbella Books.

Rossen, Jake. 2008. *Superman vs. Hollywood: How Fiendish Producers, Devious Directors, and Warring Writers Grounded an American Icon*. Chicago: Chicago Review Press.

Russell, Vanessa. 2009. "The Mild-Mannered Reporter: How Clark Kent Surpassed Superman." In *The Contemporary Comic Book Superhero*. Edited by Angela Ndalianis. London and New York: Routledge.

Saler, Michael. 2003. "Clap if You Believe in Sherlock Holmes: Mass Culture and the Re-Enchantment of Modernity, c. 1890–1940." *Historical Journal*, vol. 46, no. 3 (Sept. 2003): 599–622.

Saler, Michael. 2012. *As If: Modern Enchantment and the Literary History of Virtual Reality*. Oxford: Oxford University Press.

Sandeen, Autumn. 2013. "Would Superman Support Marriage Equality?" *San Diego LGBT Weekly*. February 21.

Sanders, Clinton R., and D. Angus Vail. 2008. *Customizing the Body*. Philadelphia: Templeton University Press.

Santino, Jack. 2011. "The Carnivalesque and the Ritualesque." *Journal of American Folklore* vol. 124, no. 491 (January): 61–73.

Saunders, Ben. 2011. *Do the Gods Wear Capes?: Spirituality, Fantasy, and Superheroes*. New York and London: Continuum.

Sawin, Patricia E. "Performance at the Nexus of Gender, Power, and Desire: Reconsidering Bauman's Verbal Art from the Perspective of Gendered Subjectivity as Performance." *Journal of American Folklore*, vol. 115, no. 455: 28–61.

Schelly, Bill. 1995. *The Golden Age of Comic Fandom*. Seattle: Hamster Press.

Schrempp, Gregory. 1992. *Magical Arrows: The Maori, the Greeks, and the Folklore of the Universe*. Madison: University of Wisconsin Press.

Schrempp, Gregory. 2002. "David Bidney and the People of Truth." In *Myth: A New Symposium*. Edited by Gregory Schrempp and William Hansen. Bloomington: Indiana University Press.

Schrempp, Gregory. 2012. *The Ancient Mythology of Modern Science*. Montreal: McGill-Queen's University Press.

Schrempp, Gregory. 2014. *Science, Bread, and Circuses: Folkloristic Essays on Science for the Masses*. Logan: Utah State University Press.

Schrempp, Gregory, and William Hansen. 2002. *Myth: A New Symposium*. Bloomington: Indiana University Press.

Schwartz, Howard. 1998. *Reimagining the Bible*. New York and Oxford: Oxford University Press.

Scobie, Alex. 1980. "Comics and Folkliterature." *Fabula*, vol. 21, no. 1: 70–81.

Seagle, Steven, et al. 2004. *It's a Bird. . . .* New York: DC Comics.

Segal, Robert A., ed. 1998. *The Myth and Ritual Theory: An Anthology*. Malden, MA: Blackwell Publishers.

Segal, Robert. 2004. *Myth: A Very Short Introduction*. Oxford: Oxford University Press.

Shooter, Jim, et al. 1966. "The Four Elemental Enemies." *Superman*, vol. 1, no. 190. New York: DC Comics.

Shukla, Pravina. 2010. *The Grace of Four Moons*. Bloomington: Indiana University Press.

Shukla, Pravina. 2015. *Costume: Performing Identities through Dress*. Bloomington: Indiana University Press.

Simonson, Louise, et al. 1995. *The True Story of Superman*. New York: Golden Books.

Singh, Arune. 2003. "Gonna Party Like it's Yer Birfright (Part 1): Mark Waid Talks *Superman: Birthright*." *Comic Book Resources*. http://www.comicbookresources .com/?page=article&id=2595 (Accessed 11/22/2016)

Skelton, Stephen. 2006. *The Gospel According to the World's Greatest Superhero*. Eugene, OR: Harvest House.

Slotkin, Richard. 1973. *Regeneration through Violence: The Mythology of the American Frontier, 1600–1860*. Middletown, CT: Wesleyan University Press.

Slotkin, Richard. 1985. *The Fatal Environment: The Myth of the Frontier in the Age of Industrialization, 1800–1890*. Norman: University of Oklahoma Press.

Slotkin, Richard. 1998. *Gunfighter Nation: The Myth of the Frontier in Twentieth-Century America*. Norman: University of Oklahoma Press.

Smith, Grace Partridge. 1952. "The Plight of the Folktale the Comics." *Southern Folklore Quarterly,* vol. XVI: 124–27.

Smith, Paul Jordan. 1999. "Folk Event Analysis." *Folklore Forum,* vol. 30, no. 1/2: 45–54.

Smith, Robert J. 1972. "Festivals and Celebration." In *Folklore and Folklife: An Introduction.* Edited by Richard M. Dorson, 159–72. Chicago: University of Chicago Press.

Somigli, Luca. 1998. "The Superhero with a Thousand Faces: Visual Narratives on Film and Paper." In *Play it Again, Sam: Retakes on Remakes.* Edited by Andrew Horton and Stuart Y. McDougal, 279–94. Berkeley, Los Angeles, and London: University of California Press.

Stampfl, Barry. 1998. "Hans Vaihinger's Ghostly Presence in Contemporary Literary Studies." *Criticism,* vol. 40, no. 3 (Summer): 437–54.

Stern, Roger, et al (uncredited). 1984. "The Kid Who Collected Spider-Man." *The Amazing Spider-Man,* vol. 1, no. 248. New York: Marvel Comics.

Stoeltje, Beverly. 1983. "Festival in America." In *Handbook of American Folklore.* Edited by Richard M. Dorson, 239–46. Bloomington: Indiana University Press.

Tarantino, Quentin. 2004. *Kill Bill, Vol. 2.*

Taylor, Aaron. 2007. "He's Gotta Be Strong, and he's Gotta Be Fast, and He's Gotta Be Larger than Life: Investigating the Engendered Superhero Body." *Journal of Popular Culture,* vol. 40, no. 2.

Taylor, Robert. 2008. "Reflections: J. Michael Straczynski, Part II." *Comic Book Resources.* http://www.comicbookresources.com/?page=article&id=17059 (accessed 10/10/2011).

Titon, Jeff Todd. 1980. "The Life Story." *Journal of American Folklore,* vol. 93, no. 369 (July–Sept.): 276–92.

Toelken, Barre. 1969. "The 'Pretty Languages' of Yellowman: Genre, Mode, and Texture in Navaho Coyote Narratives." *Genre,* no. 2: 211–35.

Toelken, Barre. 1987. "Life and Death in the Navajo Coyote Tales." In *Recovering the Word: Essays on Native American Literature.* Edited by Arnold Krupat and Brian Swann, 388–401. Berkeley: University of California Press.

Toelken, Barre. 1990. "Folklore and Reality in the American West." In *Senses of Place: American Regional Culture.* Edited by Barbara Allen and Thomas J. Schlereth. Lexington: University Press of Kentucky.

Toelken, Barre. 1998. "The Yellowman Tapes, 1966–1997." *Journal of American Folklore,* vol. 111, no. 442: 381–91.

Toelken, Barre. 2002. "Native American Reassessment and Reinterpretation of Myths." In *Myth: A New Symposium.* Edited by Gregory Schrempp and William Hansen. Bloomington: Indiana University Press.

Toelken, Barre. 2004. "Beauty Behind Me, Beauty Before." *Journal of American Folklore,* vol. 117, no. 466: 441–45.

Toelken, Barre, and Tacheeni Scott. 1981. "Poetic Retranslation and the 'Pretty Languages' of Yellowman." In *Traditional Literatures of the American Indian.* Edited by Karl Kroeber, 65–116. Lincoln: University of Nebraska Press.

Torchia, Joseph. 1980. *The Kryptonite Kid.* New York: Henry Holt & Co.

Turner, Victor. 1988. *The Anthropology of Performance.* New York: PAJ Publications.

Turner, Victor, ed. 1982. *Celebration: Studies in Festivity and Ritual*. Washington, DC: Smithsonian Institute Press.

Utley, Francis Lee. 1945. "The Bible of the Folk." *California Folklore Quarterly*, vol. 4, no. 1 (Jan. 1945): 1–17.

Vaihinger, H. 1924. *The Philosophy of "As If": A System of Theoretical, Practical and Religious Fictions of Mankind*. Translated by C. K. Ogden. New York: Harcourt, Brace, and Co.

Von Hendy, Andrew. 2002. *The Modern Construction of Myth*. Bloomington: Indiana University Press.

Waid, Mark. 1993. *The Golden Age of Superman: The Greatest Covers of Action Comics form the '30s to the '50s*. New York, London, and Paris: Artabras.

Waid, Mark. 2005. "The Real Truth about Superman: And the Rest of Us, Too." In *Superheroes and Philosophy: Truth, Justice, and the Socratic Way*. Edited by Tom Morris and Matt Morris, 3–10. Chicago and LaSalle, IL: Open Court Books.

Waid, Mark. 2009. "I Believed a Man Could Fly." http://markwaid.com/howigothere/i-believed-a-man-could-fly/.

Wandtke, Terrence R. 2007. *The Amazing Transforming Superhero! Essays on the Revision of Characters in Comic Books, Film, and Television*. Jefferson, NC: McFarland.

Wandtke, Terrence R. 2012. *The Meaning of Superhero Comic Books*. Jefferson, NC: McFarland.

Watt-Evans, Lawrence. 2005. "Previous Issues." In *The Man From Krypton: A Closer Look at Superman*. Edited by Glenn Yeffeth, 1–7. Dallas: Benbella Books.

Welch, Liliane. 1973. Review of *Mythologies*. *Journal of Aesthetics and Art Criticism*, vol. 31, no. 4 (Summer): 563–64.

White, John Wesley. 1978. *The Man from Krypton: The Gospel According to Superman*. Minneapolis: Bethany Fellowship.

White, Mark D., ed. 2013. *Superman and Philosophy: What Would the Man of Steel Do?* Oxford: Wiley-Blackwell.

Wilson, William A. 1986. "Documenting Folklore." In *Folk Groups and Folklore Genres: An Introduction*. Edited by Elliott Oring, 225–34. Logan: Utah State University Press

Wooley, Charles. 1974. "An American Mythology." *Harvard Journal of Pictorial Fiction* (Spring): 24–30.

Wolverton, Mark. 2002. *The Science of Superman: The Official Guide to the Science of the Last Son of Krypton*. New York: iBooks.

Yeffeth, Glenn, ed. 2006. *The Man from Krypton: A Closer Look at Superman*. Dallas: Benbella Books.

Yockey, Matt. 2008. "Somewhere in Time: Utopia and the Return of Superman." *Velvet Light Trap*, no. 61: 26–37.

INDEX

29, 52–53, 127; as immigrant, 166n1; as inspiration, 38, 43, 48, 53, 90, 108, 118, 128, 155; as old-fashioned, 114; origin, 4, 20, 39, 48, 62, 84–86, 89, 129, 160n11, 163n8, 165n2, 166n21, 166n23; as orphan, 98; as Prince Charming, 3, 52; restraint, 25, 108, 134–35, 152; sacred quality of, 107, 118, 132, 141, 143, 145, 151, 157, 167n9; as savior, 56, 115–19; and technology, 9, 147, 152

Superman: The Movie, 28, 30–31, 36, 47

Superman Celebration, XI, XIII, 19, 27, 33–34, 36, 42, 51, 58, 63–89, 93–97, 121, 124, 126–27, 140, 149, 161n28, 164n10, 165n6, 165nn8–10, 166n22, 167n5; aural aspects, 69–70; gustatory aspects, 70; olfactory aspects, 70; opening ceremony, 64–66, 69–70, 74–87, 93, 96–97, 126, 149, 165n9, 166nn13–14, 166n21; tactile aspects, 70; types of attendees, 71–72, 96; visual aspects, 66–69

Superman II, 28, 79

Superman Statue, 66–71, 74, 80, 95, 149, 165n4

tall tales, 3, 10

tattooes, 3, 19–26, 32–39, 49, 67, 75–76, 99, 140, 145, 154, 156, 162n5, 163n11, 163n14

tension: corporate/local, 65, 83, 152; folkloric, 8, 143, 160n14; and humor, 109; individual/collective, 7, 8, 143, 160n14; insider/outsider, 64–65, 160n14; local/fan, 81–83, 96–97; new/old, 8; and tattoo display, 24, 163n14

Toelken, Barre, 98, 141, 151, 160n12

Truth, Justice, and the American Way, 5, 30, 66, 79, 93, 95, 136

Turner, Victor, 84, 96, 163n2

Utley, Francis Lee, 14, 31, 170n5

Vaihinger, Hans, 41–43, 60, 150–51, 163n1

variations, 7–8, 10–11, 23, 84, 93, 105–7, 155, 160n11, 160n13, 170n12

Veyne, Paul, 149–51, 157

Waid, Mark, 20, 26, 30, 45, 47–49, 61, 134, 148, 154

Walgenbach, Josh, 120, 130–39, 147, 153, 154, 169n10

Wandtke, Terrence R., 10–11, 145, 153, 160n11, 160n17, 163n13, 166n11, 172nn23–24

Washington, George, 95, 152, 153

"What Would Superman Do?," 45–46, 136

Wonder Woman, 25, 104–6, 116

writers, 11, 30, 32, 44–50, 52, 60–61, 85–86, 89, 98, 103, 115, 117–18, 160n16, 164n7

X-ray vision, 109, 113

"You're much stronger than you think you are," 50, 54, 56

www.ingramcontent.com/pod-product-compliance
Lightning Source LLC
Chambersburg PA
CBHW030650270326
41929CB00007B/295